THE GUNFIGHTERS

PROCLAMATION

OF THE

GOVERNOR OF MISSOURI!

REWARDS

FOR THE ARREST OF

Express and Train Robbers.

STATE OF MISSOURI, }
EXECUTIVE DEPARTMENT.

WHEREAS, It has been made known to me, as the Governor of the State of Missouri, that certain parties, whose names are to me unknown, have confederated and banded themselves together for the purpose of committing robberies and other depredations within this State; and

WHEREAS, Said parties did, on or about the Eighth day of October, 1879, stop a train near Glendale, in the county of Jackson, in said State, and, with force and violence, take, steal and carry away the money and other express matter being carried thereon: and

WHEREAS, On the fifteenth day of July 1881, said parties and their confederates did stop a train upon the line of the Chicago, Rock Island and Pacific Railroad, near Winston, in the County of Daviess, in said State, and, with force and violence, take, steal, and carry away the money and other express matter being carried thereon; and, in perpetration of the robbery last aforesaid, the parties engaged therein did kill and murder one WILLIAM WESTFALL, the conductor of the train, together with one JOHN McCULLOCH, who was at the time in the employ of said company, then on said train; and

WHEREAS, FRANK JAMES and JESSE W. JAMES stand indicted in the Circuit Court of said Daviess County, for the murder of JOHN W. SHEETS, and the parties engaged in the robberies and murders aforesaid have fled from justice and have absconded and secreted themselves:

NOW, THEREFORE, in consideration of the premises, and in lieu of all other rewards heretofore offered for the arrest or conviction of the parties aforesaid, or either of them, by any person or corporation, I, THOMAS T. CRITTENDEN, Governor of the State of Missouri, do hereby offer a reward of five thousand dollars ($5,000.00) for the arrest and conviction of each person participating in either of the robberies or murders aforesaid, excepting the said FRANK JAMES and JESSE W. JAMES; and for the arrest and delivery of said

FRANK JAMES and JESSE W. JAMES,

and each or either of them, to the sheriff of said Daviess County, I hereby offer a reward of five thousand dollars, ($5,000.00,) and for the conviction of either of the parties last aforesaid of participation in either of the murders or robberies above mentioned, I hereby offer a further reward of five thousand dollars, ($5,000.00.)

IN TESTIMONY WHEREOF, I have hereunto set my hand and caused to be affixed the Great Seal of the State of Missouri. Done

[SEAL.]   at the City of Jefferson on this 28th day of July, A. D. 1881.

THOS. T. CRITTENDEN.

By the Governor:

MICH'L K. McGRATH, Sec'y of State.

BURCH & FERGUSON, STATE PRINTERS, JEFFERSON CITY, MO.

THE GUNFIGHTERS

By the Editors of

TIME-LIFE BOOKS

with text by

Paul Trachtman

TIME-LIFE BOOKS / ALEXANDRIA, VIRGINIA

Time-Life Books Inc.
is a wholly owned subsidiary of
TIME INCORPORATED

Founder: Henry R. Luce 1898-1967

Editor-in-Chief: Henry Anatole Grunwald
President: J. Richard Munro
Chairman of the Board: Ralph P. Davidson
Corporate Editor: Ray Cave
Group Vice President, Books: Reginald K. Brack Jr.
Vice President, Books: George Artandi

TIME-LIFE BOOKS INC.

Editor: George Constable
Executive Editor: George Daniels
Editorial General Manager: Neal Goff
Director of Design: Louis Klein
Director of Editorial Resources: Phyllis K. Wise
Editorial Board: Dale M. Brown, Roberta Conlan,
Ellen Phillips, Donia Ann Steele, Rosalind Stubenberg,
Kit van Tulleken, Henry Woodhead
Director of Research and Photography:
John Conrad Weiser

President: Reginald K. Brack Jr.
Executive Vice Presidents: John M. Fahey Jr.,
Christopher T. Linen
Senior Vice President: James L. Mercer
Vice Presidents: Stephen L. Bair, Edward Brash,
Ralph J. Cuomo, Juanita T. James, Wilhelm R. Saake,
Robert H. Smith, Paul R. Stewart, Leopoldo Toralballa

THE OLD WEST

EDITORIAL STAFF FOR "THE GUNFIGHTERS"
Editor: George Constable
Assistant Editor: Joan Mebane
Picture Editor: Myra Mangan
Text Editor: William Frankel
Designer: Herbert H. Quarmby
Assistant Designer: James Eisenman
Staff Writers: Marilyn Daley, Lee Greene, Alice Kantor,
David Lawton, James Randall, Gerald Simons,
Jill Spiller
Researchers: Loretta Britten, Jane Coughran,
Lea G. Gordon, Nancy Miller, Mary Kay Moran,
Ann Morrison, Jane Sugden
Copy Coordinator: Barbara H. Fuller
Picture Coordinator: Barbara S. Simon

EDITORIAL OPERATIONS
Copy Chief: Diane Ullius
Editorial Operations: Caroline A. Boubin (manager)
Production: Celia Beattie
Quality Control: James J. Cox (director)
Library: Louise D. Forstall

COVER DESIGN
Renée Boudreau

THE AUTHOR: Paul Trachtman contributed as both writer and editor to volumes in the LIFE Science Library and the LIFE History of the United States. He later served as an associate editor of LIFE and a senior editor of the magazine's international editions. He has written articles for a number of national periodicals. To gather research for *The Gunfighters,* Trachtman crisscrossed the Western states, combing local court records and newspaper files in towns from Dodge City to Tombstone.

THE COVER: The sheriff's star worn by the weather-beaten rider in E. F. Ward's painting stamps him as a gunfighter recruited to preserve law and order in a frontier county. The outlaw, at the opposite pole of the same gunfighting breed, is represented by the frontispiece: an 1881 bounty poster for gang leaders Frank and Jesse James, whose raids on trains and banks for 15 years made them the scourge, and wonder, of the border state.

CORRESPONDENTS: Elisabeth Kraemer-Singh (Bonn); Dorothy Bacon, Lesley Coleman (London); Susan Jonas, Lucy T. Voulgaris (New York); Maria Vincenza Aloisi, Josephine du Brusle (Paris); Ann Natanson (Rome). Valuable assistance was also provided by: Judy Aspinall, Karin B. Pearce (London); Carolyn T. Chubet, Miriam Hsia, Christina Lieberman (New York); Mimi Murphy (Rome); Martha Green (San Francisco); Craig Van Hote (Washington).

Library of Congress Cataloguing in Publication Data
Time-Life Books
    The gunfighters. By the editors of Time-Life Books, with text
by Paul Trachtman. New York, Time-Life Books [1974]
    238 p. illus. 29 cm. (The Old West)
    Bibliography: p. 234-235.
    Includes index.
    1. Crime and criminals — The West.   2. The West — History — 1848-1950.   I. Trachtman, Paul.   II. Title.   III. Series:
The Old West (Alexandria, Va.)
F594.T57   364'.978   74-80284
ISBN 0-8094-1481-3
ISBN 0-8094-1480-5 (lib. bdg.)
ISBN 0-8094-1479-1 (retail ed.)

Other Publications:

HEALTHY HOME COOKING
UNDERSTANDING COMPUTERS
YOUR HOME
THE ENCHANTED WORLD
THE KODAK LIBRARY OF
    CREATIVE PHOTOGRAPHY
GREAT MEALS IN MINUTES
THE CIVIL WAR
PLANET EARTH
COLLECTOR'S LIBRARY OF THE
    CIVIL WAR
THE EPIC OF FLIGHT
THE GOOD COOK
WORLD WAR II
HOME REPAIR AND IMPROVEMENT

For information on and a full description
of any of the Time-Life Books series
listed above, please write:
Reader Information
Time-Life Books
541 North Fairbanks Court
Chicago, Illinois 60611

*This volume is one of a series that
chronicles the history of the American West
from the early 16th Century to the end of
the 19th Century.*

CONTENTS

1 | The deadly brotherhood of the gun
7

2 | Buccaneers of the border states
52

3 | The man with the badge
95

4 | A slow triumph for the gavel
136

5 | Sinister masters of murder
166

6 | Frontier justice, vigilante style
194

Credits 232   Acknowledgments 234   Bibliography 234   Index 236

When Guns Speak, Death Settles Disputes was Russell's epigrammatic title for this rendition of a frontier clash.

1 | The deadly brotherhood of the gun

Caught in the blaze of a midnight shootout, the men in this scene are instantly recognizable as specimens of the Old West's most flamboyant breed—the gunfighters. Whether they were lawmen, bandits or wanton killers, all of them shared a deadly purposefulness. Bat Masterson, a renowned peace officer among the breed, recalled that when it came to settling a dispute, any one of the numerous gunfighters he had known "would not have hesitated a moment to put up his life as the stake to be played for."

Here and in the following paintings, artist Charles Russell records the sudden violence that made these men legends in their own day—and thereafter.

7

In the wake of a card-game quarrel, a vengeful cowhand dispatches one player and mortally wounds another in *Death of a Gambler*.

9

His mount down, a horse thief blasts away at a posse as his partner starts to make a run for it in *When Horseflesh Comes High*.

In *Smoke of a .45*, a fusillade of gunfire claims two victims as cowboys race out of town at the convulsive end of a drinking spree.

THE PALACE FEED STABLE

LICENSED
GAMBLING

$1000
REWARD

An epic showdown at the O.K. Corral

On a blustery day toward the end of October, 1881, the town of Tombstone, Arizona, witnessed the most notorious shoot-out in the history of the West. In a vacant lot at the rear of the O.K. Corral, City Marshal Virgil Earp and his brothers Wyatt and Morgan, joined by a gambler friend, Doc Holliday, exchanged gunfire with four local cowboys, the Clanton and McLaury brothers. "Three Men Hurled into Eternity in the Duration of a Moment," blared the headline over the first report of the affair in *The Tombstone Epitaph.* The duration, in fact, was slightly more than half a minute, although a deadly staccato of vengeful gunfire echoed for months afterward.

The clash was not unique. Possession of firearms was far more commonplace on the frontier than back East, and newspapers across the West carried accounts of gunfights of every variety—saloon brawls, outlaw raids, vigilante wars and even an occasional face-off in the style of European duels. But the shoot-out at the O.K. Corral was better documented than most, and its fame as a classic confrontation of gunfighters was well deserved, for it embodied some basic frontier animosities —lawman against outlaw, cardsharp against cowboy, citified carpetbagger against weather-beaten settler.

Yet these divisions were far from clear-cut, as the shoot-out also made plain. Though some Western gunfight participants represented the law, the line between bad men and good was, at best, blurred. The facing foes usually had more in common than they cared to admit. Most were men of bristling spirit and minimal compassion or scruple. When they had scores to settle, it hardly mattered which side of the law they were on;

their law was the gun, their reflex response the stance of the gunfighter. In Tombstone, as everywhere in the West, the label of gunfighter applied to sheriffs and horse thieves alike, to men respected in the community as well as to those who were despised. Their motives differed, but their basic objective was always the same. Wyatt Earp summed it up succinctly after the shoot-out. "I did not intend," he said, "that any of the band should get the drop on me if I could help it."

Even his most disapproving listeners could appreciate this candor. The 19th Century was by then in its final quarter, yet law and order had simply not kept pace with the waves of settlement in the West. While most citizens of the region were sober and upstanding, frontier society also included large numbers of floaters, as reckless as they were rootless: itinerant cowboys and prospectors and railroad men; brash youths from the East bent on enjoying a few years of deviltry before settling down; fugitives on the run from the law; and easy-money artists of every kind.

Their natural habitat was the frontier town. Whether cattle town, railroad town or mining town, it was not much to look at. It had its wide, unpaved main street, sun-baked in summer, rock-hard in winter, lined by tents or flimsy wooden shacks. Dispersed among these jerry-built structures was the roistering nether world of the saloon, the dance hall and the brothel. The saloon might be a mere tent, with a bar consisting of a plank laid across two beer kegs, or it might be a permanent establishment resplendent with mirrors, chandeliers, paintings of enticing nudes and a great carved mahogany bar brought all the way from St. Louis. The brothel might be a small shack or a large dance hall with a couple of rooms in the rear. The decor, or lack of it, made no difference; to a miner after hours or a cowboy in from the range, they were all oases of pleasure where sex and drinks and money flowed freely. When gunfighters

Three cattle rustlers who roved New Mexico in the 1870s indulge in a ritual favored by many gunfighters — sitting for a formal studio portrait with weapons in open view.

A dapper but deadly trio, the Earp brothers tangled with some of Tombstone's toughest cowboys at the O.K. Corral. Though officers of the law, the Earps tended to overlook its fine points in matters of self-interest.

WYATT EARP

MORGAN EARP

VIRGIL EARP

clashed, one or another of these elements was almost always a contributing cause.

From the outset Tombstone promised to be as lusty a town as any in the West. When Wyatt Earp and his brothers first set eyes on it in December of 1879, it was 10 months old, a dust-blown collection of tents and shanties perched on a high plateau between the Dragoon and Whetstone mountains. But wealth was pouring from the silver mines in the nearby San Pedro Hills, and the population would soar from zero to 5,600 in two years. On the day the Earps hit town, the main street swarmed with prospectors buying tools, merchants setting up new shops, and carpenters erecting storefronts, complete with board sidewalks in front of each entrance. Confidence men loitered about, waiting to tempt strangers with offers of town lots that had no legal title or of shares in mines that had no ore. No doubt they viewed the three long-legged, mustachioed Earps with expectation. Dressed in black frock coats and stiff-brimmed hats, politely helping their wives down from the trail-worn wagons, the brothers looked as respectable as deacons.

They had come a long way: Wyatt and James 750 miles from Dodge City, Kansas, detouring to Prescott, Arizona, to pick up Virgil, who had been prospecting there. What brought them to Tombstone was the lure

that had drawn most others: the sweet scent of opportunity. James, at 38 the oldest of the three, hoped to elevate himself from his former trade of bartending to saloonkeeping. Virgil, a stolid man of 36 who had been a stage driver in Iowa and Kansas, planned to prospect for silver, or at least to find claims that the Earps could sell at a quick profit. Recently, however, he had acquired a sideline. At Prescott he had served as a part-time deputy sheriff, and en route to Tombstone he had been sworn in as a deputy U.S. marshal by the federal officer for the Arizona Territory.

Wyatt Earp, 31, had plans of his own, based on experiences so varied as to suggest a distinct ambivalence toward the law. Eight years earlier, he and a friend had been charged with stealing some horses near Fort Gibson in what is now Oklahoma; they were indicted by a grand jury, but Wyatt fled before the case came to trial. His next contacts with the law were on the other side. He worked as a policeman in Wichita, Kansas, where the town fathers had to warn him that if the fines he collected were not turned in to the city treasurer, he would get no pay. Wyatt then moved on to Dodge City, where he became assistant marshal. At the town's leading saloon, the Long Branch, he more than doubled his peace officer's pay by moonlighting as a dealer of faro and monte, the card games most popular with frontier gamblers. As a dealer, Wyatt took a percentage of the house winnings; as an officer of the law, he saw to it that sullen losers made orderly departures from the premises. In Tombstone he proposed to work out a similar division of his energies.

At the time of the Earps' appearance there, they were not widely known as gunfighters. James would not have merited the reputation in any case. Wounded in the Civil War, he had a game arm and a passive nature, and he was to play no part in the shoot-out at the O.K. Corral. Virgil and Wyatt were cut from a different cloth. Both had considerable expertise with firearms and few qualms about using them. Wyatt in particular had earned local fame in Kansas as a formidable foe in a fight—imperturbable and fearless.

That the need for gunfighting skills would arise in Tombstone was evident not long after the Earps settled in. James removed himself from possible trouble by devoting his time to the business end of saloonkeeping. But Virgil and Wyatt were plunged almost at once into the thick of things. Virgil had to drop his idea of using law enforcement as just a sideline when a cattle rustler, in town for a night of carousing, casually shot and killed the city marshal. Virgil was asked to occupy this full-time post temporarily, and later his appointment was renewed. Wyatt's original plans were undeflected. He bought into the gambling concession at the fanciest and most profitable establishment in town, the Oriental Saloon, and he also ran a nightly faro game at a saloon across the street, the Eagle Brewery. In addition to his gambling activities, he plied the peace officer's trade, first as a deputy sheriff, and later, when Virgil became city marshal, as an assistant to his brother.

The three Earps were joined in Tombstone early in 1880 by a fourth brother, Morgan, a 28-year-old hothead whose only known prior occupations were those of laborer and occasional policeman. Wyatt introduced him to the local Wells, Fargo agent, who hired him to ride shotgun on the 11-hour stagecoach run to Tucson. Like Wyatt, Morgan found periodic added employment on the city police force.

The tightly knit Earp clan soon had a cohort in a friend of Wyatt's from Dodge City days, John Holliday, an ardent gambler and sometime dentist who had once opened an office with the dubiously reassuring announcement that "where satisfaction is not given,

money will be refunded." He came to Tombstone not long after the Earps, having been slightly delayed in Prescott by a run of luck at faro. Alcoholic and tubercular at 28, he was a walking cadaver, with a flash temper and a cold-blooded readiness to kill.

With each passing month Tombstone gave signs of acquiring a civilized gloss. So, at least, thought Wells Spicer, a serious young attorney with a penchant for statistics. In a letter in early 1880 he reported that Tombstone had two dance halls, a dozen gambling places and more than 20 saloons. "Still," he wrote, "there is hope, for I know of two Bibles in town." In the months to come, such toney haunts as Julius Caesar's New York Coffee House and the Cosmopolitan Hotel's Maison Dorée would open for business, featuring brisket of beef *à la flamande* and ham in champagne sauce. The Bird Cage Theatre would stage *Pinafore* along with less refined entertainments *(page 23)*, and after the performance ladies and their escorts had a choice of two ice cream parlors to patronize, while young blades strolled the street singing snatches from the operetta. An era of propriety appeared to be on the way.

But for the moment Tombstone remained basically a rowdy, rambunctious place, taking its seamier elements in stride. The editor of the Tombstone *Nugget* began to feel that things were getting out of hand only when, one Sunday night, a bunch of "lewd women" and their men friends held an impromptu street celebration with blazing six-shooters. "We live mostly in canvas houses up here," the editor fumed, "and when lunatics like those who fired so promiscuously the other night are on the rampage, it ain't safe, anyhow!"

Clearly, control of the town lay either in vigorously enforcing the law or in wielding influence over the fractious world of Tombstone after dark. More by happenstance than by design, Virgil and Wyatt Earp found themselves holding the reins of power in both spheres. This unexpectedly neat arrangement gave the brothers advantages that they were entirely willing to exploit —and to preserve, if necessary, at the point of a gun.

Predictably, the Earps soon had enemies, and none more prickly than the ranchers, cowboys and rustlers who lived outside of Tombstone. The hostility was based in part on the antipathy that festered between many town and country people. To the ranchers and their friends, some of whom were second-generation in-

A fledgling boomtown in 1879, Tombstone sprawls across a treeless plateau in southeastern Arizona, thriving on silver in the surrounding hills. Within five years, mines like the one at far right would yield ore that was worth more than $25 million—enticing adventurers of every stripe.

19

habitants of the area, the residents of Tombstone were rank newcomers, even interlopers; and the town itself represented a blot on what had been limitless landscape. To Tombstone's citizens, on the other hand, the men who periodically rode into town were just plain hell-raisers, grown wild on the range, ready to take umbrage at any attempts to constrain them. They were, moreover, much too free with their guns, especially after a night in the saloons, even—as *The Tombstone Epitaph* complained—"firing at the moon and stars." Wyatt Earp detested the breed. Cowboys had been the bane of his life as a peace officer in the cattle towns of Kansas, and they spelled nothing but trouble here.

The most troublesome, as it turned out, were two sets of brothers, the Clantons and the McLaurys. They had been friends since the early 1870s, raising cattle along the San Pedro River west of Tombstone before the town was born. Originally, they had sold their livestock to the U.S. government to feed Apaches on the San Carlos preserve; now Tombstone was a big customer for their beef, and when they rode into town it was usually to settle accounts or close a new deal at one of the meat markets. But it wasn't all their own beef the brothers were selling. A lot of the cattle grazing along the San Pedro had been rustled in Mexico.

Of the three Clanton boys—Ike, Phineas and Billy—Ike was the most boisterous, and the most devoted to the high life of Tombstone. Whenever he showed up there, he liked to introduce himself as a successful stock dealer and sport. The Earps quickly learned what kind of sports the Clantons were. Ike had acquired some fast horses in Texas and he was always ready to race them. Wyatt Earp owned a mount he considered as fast as any in those parts, but he was in no position to prove it, for someone had stolen the horse. When Wyatt found it months later, Billy Clanton was in the saddle.

That situation was written off as a misunderstanding —perhaps because, in the matter of horse theft, Wyatt had reason to be charitable. But a more serious problem arose with the Clantons' allies, the McLaurys, when six mules disappeared from a nearby Army post. Virgil Earp, acting in his capacity as a deputy U.S. marshal with authority to recover stolen federal property, went out in search of the mules with Wyatt, Morgan and a detail of soldiers led by an Army lieutenant. They found the animals on the McLaury ranch, just as the brothers

A cockfight held in a roped-off arena on the outskirts of
Tombstone in the 1880s draws a crowd eager to see the
feathers—and blood—fly. The popularity of this gory sport,
a favored diversion among the ranchers of the area, reflected
the raw and often violent tenor of life in frontier Arizona.

A doctor's note cites the reason for a prostitute's involuntary retirement. What he delicately referred to as an "avocation," Tombstone regarded as a profession, charging a license fee of seven dollars a month.

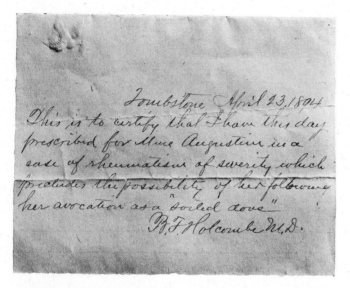

Tombstone April 23, 1804
This is to certify that I have this day prescribed for Mme Augustine in a case of rheumatism of severity which precludes the possibility of her following her avocation as a "soiled dove"
B.F. Holcombe M.D.

had begun to alter the "U.S." brand. On receiving the McLaurys' promise to yield the mules to the lieutenant, the Earps left—only to learn later that the brothers had somehow found it impossible to stop some rustler friends from making off with the prize, thus removing both the evidence and the hope of prosecution.

One reason the Clantons and McLaurys were able to continue their dubious livestock dealings was that they soon gained a well-placed sympathizer—John Behan, the sheriff of newly formed Cochise County, of which Tombstone was county seat. Appointed in February 1881 by Arizona's territorial governor, the explorer John C. Frémont, Behan was required by law to run for election when his current term expired. He was keenly aware that his chances of staying in office depended on winning a majority of the cowboys' vote. Consequently, he remained solicitous of their interests, legal and otherwise.

As the cowboys' benefactor, Behan enjoyed little respect from the Earps, and he returned the feeling. Virgil Earp was a natural rival, since as city marshal of Tombstone it was he—not Behan—who headed the forces of law in the town itself. Wyatt, too, was a Behan rival. He coveted the sheriff's own job and planned to run against Behan in the election; furthermore, he had started squiring a pretty young actress from the cast of *Pinafore* who had been living with Behan, and had completely captured her affections.

The antagonism between the Earp and cowboy factions gradually hardened into hatred. In July 1881

Behan arrested the Earps' crony, Doc Holliday, on suspicion of killing a stage driver during an attempted holdup some miles outside of town. Though the charge was dismissed for lack of evidence, Holliday was not a man to forgive and forget. Nor were the Earps deaf to rumors—source uncertain—that they had masterminded the robbery attempt, using Morgan's inside knowledge as a Wells, Fargo messenger. These whispers the brothers could shrug off, but—according to their later court testimony about the feud—they also heard reports that the Clantons and McLaurys felt Tombstone would be a better place if the Earps were done away with.

In September 1881 the Earps scored a double hit on the cowboys and Behan when Virgil, in his capacity as a deputy U.S. marshal, ordered the arrest of one of Behan's deputies, Frank Stilwell, and a friend of the Clantons, Pete Spence, for holding up a stage. Ike Clanton appeared in court and posted bail for the prisoners. Hearing of the arrest, Frank McLaury also came into town: any friends of the Clantons were friends of his. By chance, he met Morgan Earp on the sidewalk and angrily invited him to step into the middle of the street, where Ike Clanton and a few companions had collected. As they stood silent, Frank told Morgan, "If you ever come after me, you'll never take me."

Now a challenge had been publicly flung and a bloody denouement was all but inevitable. Apparently the cowboys believed that it would come at a time and place of their own choosing—an advantage the Earps were hardly disposed to give them.

On October 25—the day before the fatal encounter—Ike Clanton and Tom McLaury arrived in Tombstone in a wagon, left it and their team at a corral owned by Sheriff Behan, and put up at separate hotels. Billy Clanton and Frank McLaury were due in town the next day. The McLaury brothers planned to collect a payment from Bauer's Union Market on a sale of some of their cattle. Billy Clanton may have had no other errand than a morning-after mission to collect Ike. Billy was the younger but more mature of the two, tending to keep a kind of paternal eye on his brother; and Ike's stated purpose on this visit to Tombstone was pleasure—a long, sodden night in its saloons.

Ike began making the rounds early in the evening of the 25th, downing shot after shot of whiskey until past midnight. At 1 o'clock in the morning he walked into

Tombstone after dark: a combustible mix of women and whiskey

One of Tombstone's most raucous and combustible night spots was the Bird Cage Theatre, which offered a smorgasbord of delights ranging from imported vaudeville acts to prostitution. The smoke-filled establishment was named, with heavy frontier humor, for the 12 tiny balcony boxes where soiled doves plied their trade behind curtains. When uncaged, the painted ladies pursued less profitable sidelines such as shilling drinks and dancing with drunken cowboys, hardhanded miners, and nimble-fingered gamblers and gunmen.

The theater's owners, Billy and Lottie Hutchinson, prudently requested that incoming patrons check their hardware. Observance of the rule was uneven at best: before long, more than 100 bullet holes dappled the theater's ceiling, walls, and even the huge painting at right, hung in tribute to a popular performer named Fatima.

The casualties in all this gunplay were never totted up, though one visitor claimed to have witnessed a single shoot-in that left 12 men dead. Whatever the true tally, performers and patrons alike had good reason to fear for their safety. Once, a secondrate magician named Charles Andress told his audience that he would catch bullets in his teeth; as an assistant fired blank cartridges, he spit out slugs he had concealed in his mouth. Suddenly a besotted customer drew his six-gun and shouted, "Catch this one, Professor!" A quick-thinking spectator jogged the man's arm and the shot went astray, leaving the quaking target to make his exit with a minimum of dignity and a maximum of haste.

A portrait of Fatima, who belly-danced to acclaim at the Bird Cage in 1882, decorated the bar.

Sheriff John Behan of Tombstone, attended here by his wife, Victoria, was the principal lawman of the county and an archfoe of Wyatt Earp. After he left office, Behan was indicted for collecting taxes after his term expired, but he was never prosecuted.

the Alhambra Saloon, sat down at a table in the lunchroom at the back and ordered something to eat. He did not notice Wyatt Earp, who was sitting at the lunch counter, or Morgan Earp, who was standing at the bar beyond it. Then Doc Holliday walked in. Instantly inflamed at the sight of the enemy, Doc tried to provoke a showdown then and there. He strode to Clanton's table and snarled, "You son-of-a-bitch of a cowboy, get out your gun and get to work."

"I don't have any gun," Ike replied. As the men exchanged words, Wyatt called to his brother at the bar. Morgan was serving one of his stints as a policeman, and Wyatt suggested he separate the quarreling pair. Morgan swung his long legs over the lunch counter, took Holliday's arm and pulled him out into the street. Ike rose and followed them. Wyatt, as usual, was more deliberate; he finished his meal, then stepped outside.

Doc Holliday was still fuming on the sidewalk. "You ain't heeled, go heel yourself," he told Ike. Morgan added fuel to the fire. "You can have all the fight you want, now," he offered. Ike, being handicapped by the lack of a six-shooter, declined and walked off. But he did not go to bed; an all-night poker game in another saloon engaged his attention—a fateful diversion, for by sunup he was blurry and belligerent.

At 11:30 that morning Wyatt Earp was awakened by Ned Boyle, the bartender at the Oriental Saloon, who had just met Ike Clanton on the street. Ike had told Boyle, "As soon as those damned Earps make their appearance on the street today, the ball will open." Wyatt hurried to the saloon, learned that Ike was now armed with a rifle and a six-shooter, and went in search of Virgil. Together they went looking for Ike. The prelude to the shoot-out had begun.

Virgil spotted Ike in an alley, approached him from behind, and grabbed his rifle with one hand. Ike tried to draw his six-shooter but Virgil hit him over the head with a revolver, knocking him to his knees.

"You been hunting for me?" Virgil asked gently.

"If I'd seen you a second sooner I'd of killed you," Ike said. Virgil promptly arrested him for carrying firearms within the city limits. Morgan Earp arrived at this moment, and the two brothers marched him to Justice of the Peace A. O. Wallace's court.

Hearing of the encounter, Wyatt went to the courtroom. There, he found Ike sitting outside the railing,

An ominous report on Cochise County

In September 1881, just a month before the shoot-out at the O.K. Corral, the lawless conditions that led to that paroxysm of gunplay were lengthily reported to the U.S. Secretary of State by John Gosper, acting as governor of the Arizona Territory in the absence of John C. Frémont. Gosper had found that cowboys were running rampant in Cochise County—robbing stages, rustling cattle, and rarely getting caught. His outraged account of the situation, excerpted below, was based on personal interviews; it laid the blame on the suspicious inactivity of local peace officers.

The cow-boy element at times very fully predominates, and the officers of the law are either unable or unwilling to control this class of out-laws, sometimes being governed by fear, at other times by a hope of reward. At Tombstone, the county seat of Cochise County, I conferred with the Sheriff upon the subject of breaking up these bands of out-laws, and I am sorry to say he gave me but little hope of being able in his department to cope with the power of the cow-boys. He represented to me that the Deputy U.S. Marshal, resident of Tombstone, and the city Marshal for the same, seemed unwilling to heartily cooperate with him in capturing and bringing to justice these out-laws.

In conversation with the Deputy U.S. Marshal, Mr. Earp, I found precisely the same spirit of complaint existing against Mr. Behan (the Sheriff) and his deputies. Many of the very best law-abiding and peace-loving citizens have no confidence in the willingness of the civil officers to pursue and bring to justice that element of out-lawry so largely disturbing the sense of security, and so often committing highway robbery and smaller thefts. The opinion in Tombstone and elsewhere in that part of the Territory is quite prevalent that the civil officers are quite largely in league with the leaders of this disturbing and dangerous element.

Something must be done, and that right early, or very grave results will follow. It is an open disgrace to American liberty and the peace and security of her citizens, that such a state of affairs should exist.

Overoptimistic about his success as Tombstone's top peace officer, Virgil Earp called for a reduction in his police force from six to two. Only a few weeks later, the shootout at the O.K. Corral cost him his job.

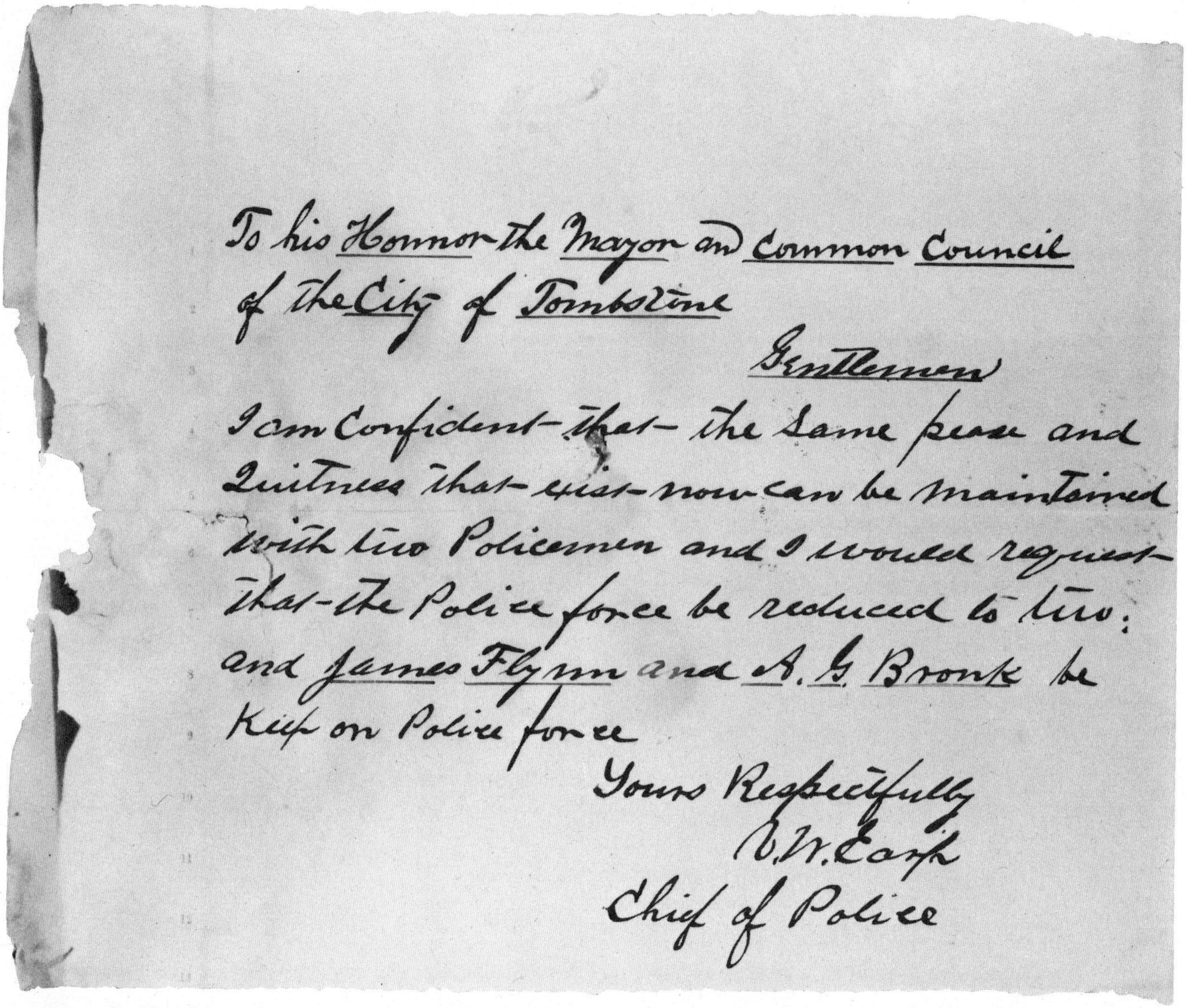

To his Honnor the Mayor and Common Council of the City of Tombstone

Gentlemen

I am Confident that the Same peace and Quitness that exist now can be maintained with two Policemen and I would request that the Police force be reduced to two; and James Flynn and A. G. Bronk be Kept on Police force

Yours Respectfully
V. W. Earp
Chief of Police

wiping the blood from the side of his head with a handkerchief. Wyatt went past him, sat down on a bench inside the railing to await the judge, then looked back at Ike and said: "You've threatened my life two or three times. I want this thing stopped." Ike muttered a few words. "You damn dirty cow thief," Wyatt went on, "if you're anxious to fight, I'll meet you."

"I'll see you after I get through here," Ike answered. "All I want is four feet of ground."

At that point Morgan Earp took charge of Ike's rifle and six-shooter, which had been brought in as evidence. Holding the Winchester with its butt to the floor, Morgan tauntingly offered to pay Ike's fine if Ike would fight him. "I'll fight you anywhere, or any way," Ike replied.

Without waiting to testify, Wyatt now left the courtroom and came face to face with Tom McLaury, who was about to step inside to check on Ike. A brief, angry exchange ensued. McLaury said, "If you want to make a fight, I'll make a fight with you anywhere." Drawing his revolver, Wyatt answered, "All right, make a fight right here" — then slapped McLaury in the face with his left hand and with his right brought his pistol barrel across the side of McLaury's head. McLaury sprawled in the street, glassy-eyed, and Wyatt walked on.

A gangling young wagon driver named Billy Claibourne, a friend of the Clantons and McLaurys, hap-

26

John "Doc" Holliday, dentist by trade and gambler by choice, fought beside the Earps in Tombstone. A fellow gunfighter noted that he had "an ungovernable temper and was given to both drinking and quarreling."

pened to be in Tombstone that day. Learning of Ike's arrest, he hurried to the courtroom. Ike had paid his fine; now his head wound needed dressing. Claibourne took him to Doctor Gillingham's office and left him there. A few minutes later he ran into Billy Clanton and Frank McLaury, newly arrived in town, and told them the news. Billy Clanton was plainly agitated over his brother's latest fix. "I want Ike to go home," he said. "I didn't come here to fight anyone, and no one wants to fight me." In a few more minutes Ike came along, his head bandaged. "Get your horse and go home," Billy Clanton demanded.

"I'm going directly," Ike reassured him. Together the men headed for Bauer's market on Fremont Street.

At that moment Sheriff Behan was getting a shave in a barber shop on Allen Street near Fourth. From where he sat he could see a crowd collecting at the corner. Wyatt and Morgan Earp were standing with Doc Holliday; Virgil lingered nearby, holding a shotgun at his side. The barber remarked that it looked like trouble for sure between the Earps and the cowboys. This was the first Behan had heard of the day's developments. He hurried outside and told Virgil he intended to disarm the cowboys if the Earps would give him a few minutes alone with them. The Earps remained where they were, but shortly after Behan left, someone reported that the cowboys were still on Fremont Street and still armed. The Earps started off, announcing that they were going to arrest the Clantons and McLaurys.

In their black Stetsons and greatcoats, string ties dangling down their white shirt fronts, the Earps moved slowly and deliberately, almost as if with measured tread. In their wake trailed Doc Holliday, wearing a long, gray coat and carrying a cane.

"Doc, this is our fight," Wyatt said over his shoulder. "There's no call for you to mix in."

"That's a hell of a thing for you to say to me," Doc replied. He was offended; Wyatt was the best friend he had in the world. Virgil paused, then deputized Doc on the spot. He took Doc's cane and gave him his own

shotgun, telling him to carry it under his coat, and the four men resumed their march.

At the corner of Fourth Street, looking down Fremont, they saw the Clantons and McLaurys—Frank McLaury with his horse's bridle in hand—on the sidewalk near the far side of Camillus Fly's place, a combination photography gallery and lodginghouse. Sheriff Behan was trying to persuade them to surrender their guns. Ike Clanton insisted he wasn't armed, a fact Behan confirmed by feeling around Ike's waist. Tom McLaury threw open his vest, to show that he, too, was unarmed. But Billy Clanton and Frank McLaury were wearing six-shooters, and a rifle hung in a scabbard on Frank's horse. "Boys, you must give me your arms," Behan told them. "Not unless you disarm the Earps," Frank said.

"Stay here," Behan ordered, and headed toward the approaching Earps. He met them under the awning of Bauer's meat market. "Earp, for God's sake, don't go down there," he said to Virgil.

"I'm going to disarm them," Virgil snapped.

The Earps and Doc Holliday brushed past Behan. "Go back! I am sheriff of this county!" he shouted, and hurried after them.

As the Earps and Doc Holliday reached Fly's place, the Clantons and McLaurys backed into a vacant lot next to it. Bordering the lot on the other side was a smaller private house, owned by a William Harwood. The Clantons and McLaurys lined up with their backs to it, Frank McLaury's horse beside him. The Earps moved a few steps forward. Virgil, holding Doc's cane in his right hand, stood in front. Behind him were Wyatt and Morgan, and behind them Doc, the shotgun Virgil had given him clearly visible as his coat flapped open in the breeze. As the two groups eyed each other across a distance of no more than six feet, Sheriff Behan slipped off to the side of Fly's house, where he was hastily joined by the cowboys' friend, Billy Claibourne.

The Clantons and McLaurys, without realizing it, had boxed themselves in. The Earps blocked the front

Tombstone's Allen Street, a commercial center by day, gives no hint of the bedlam it will become after dark. Scores of saloons were tucked between the shops and they spawned brawls that furnished the town, according to its own indelicate boast, with "a dead man for breakfast every morning."

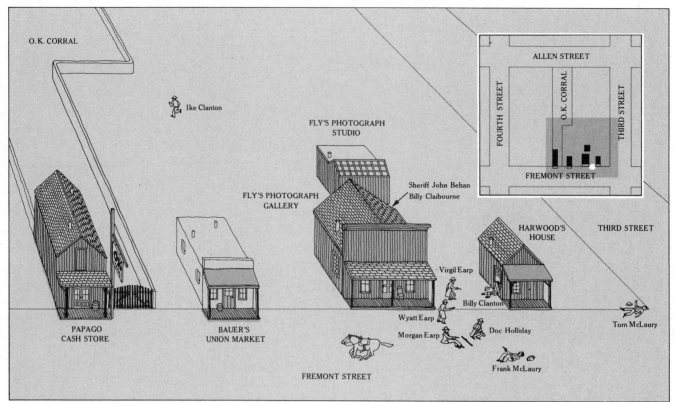

O.K. CORRAL

Ike Clanton

FLY'S PHOTOGRAPH
STUDIO

FLY'S PHOTOGRAPH
GALLERY

Sheriff John Behan
Billy Claibourne

HARWOOD'S
HOUSE

THIRD STREET

Virgil Earp

Billy Clanton

Wyatt Earp

Doc Holliday

Morgan Earp

Tom McLaury

Frank McLaury

PAPAGO
CASH STORE

BAUER'S
UNION MARKET

FREMONT STREET

ALLEN STREET

FOURTH STREET

O.K. CORRAL

THIRD STREET

FREMONT STREET

THE BLOODY CLIMAX OF THE SHOOT-OUT staged on Tombstone's Fremont Street near the O.K. Corral (*overview, inset*) is reconstructed in the diagram above. Frank McLaury, shot by both Wyatt and Morgan Earp, sprawls dying in the street, having just wounded Doc Holliday. Tom McLaury, blasted by Holliday's shotgun, lies at the corner of Fremont and Third. Billy Clanton, suffering two hits from Morgan Earp, slumps against a wall of the Harwood house; still shooting, he manages to wing both Morgan and Virgil Earp. Wyatt Earp stands unscathed. Ike Clanton, unarmed, sprints toward safety. Frank McLaury's spooked horse also flees. Sheriff John Behan and Billy Claibourne cringe under cover in Fly's photo gallery, powerless to aid their cowboy friends.

of the lot; the Fly and Harwood houses blocked its sides. Only the back of the lot offered room for maneuver; behind it lay more vacant property and the open stalls of the O.K. Corral. Within the lot itself—a strip of scrubby, empty land about 20 feet wide—there could be no evasive tactics, no place to hide.

But if the cowboys felt trapped, they did not show it. Chance, in the form of the random encounters of the past few hours, had brought them past the point of no return, to a place of final showdown more to the Earps' benefit than theirs. Still, though ill-prepared, the cowboys now took the initiative. In the silence, a click, click could be heard as Billy Clanton and Frank McLaury cocked their holstered six-shooters. "Hold! I want your guns," Virgil Earp called out. Then someone shouted, "Son-of-a-bitch"—and the next words

were lost in the first exchange of shots. Eyewitnesses later testified to the swirling, deadly melee.

Billy Clanton leveled his pistol at Wyatt Earp, holding it at arm's length. Wyatt, ignoring him, whipped a six-shooter out of his coat pocket and fired at Frank McLaury, known to be the best marksman of the four cowboys. Billy missed; Wyatt did not. Shot in the stomach, Frank McLaury staggered toward the street. Seeing his brother hit, Tom McLaury threw open his vest, shouting, "I have nothing." He had reached in vain for the rifle in the scabbard on Frank's horse, and now he took cover behind the animal.

Billy Clanton was the next to be hit, the target of Morgan Earp's six-shooter. One bullet went through Billy's right wrist; another struck him in the chest. Reeling, he fell back against a window of the Harwood

DAILY EPITAPH

Thursday Morning ..... Oct. 27, 1881

LOCAL SPLINTERS

KNIGHTS OF PYTHIAS meet to-night at the court room at 7.30, for regular drill.

THE CITY COUNCIL will meet to-day as a Board of Equalization from 10 a. m. to 3 p. m. All persons wishing to correct their assessment for city taxes will please call on the Board. The Board will sit only until Nov. 1st.

WE call attention to Charles Glover & Co's advertisement, in another column, which is only surpassed by their sign upon the reservoir on Comstock Hill. All that is promised in this their latest proclamation, will be fully sustained upon investigation at their store.

THE Tombstone W. M. & L. Co's reservoir on the summit of Comstock Hill is a conspicuous landmark for miles around. It can be seen from the mesa back of Contention. What makes it more conspicuous is the big sign of Charles Glover & Co, in letters of white upon the red back-ground of the tank, of a size that enables one to read it from Third street. This is what we call mammoth advertising. Glover & Co. do not propose to be outdone, either in the line of business or way of advertising.

Reported Sale.

It is reported that the property known as Smith's ranch, at the mouth of Carper Canyon, near the south end of the Huachuca mountains, has been sold for $5000...

Growth of the City.

Nothing gives a more definite idea of the growth of a place than the Assessor's roll...

Meeting of School Trustees

The School Trustees met at 1 o'clock. Present, J. L. Flood, J. P. Clum and T. J. Drum.

Commissioner's Court.

BEFORE T. J. DRUM.

In the matter of the application of Emma Parker to be discharged on writ of habeas corpus, after hearing the proofs and argument of counsel, the defendant was remanded into custody and the writ dismissed...

Hotel Arrivals Yesterday.

AT THE GRAND.

S Evers, U S A, Benicia, E Olcott, Los Delicias, Sonora; Wm Moore, Tucson.

AT THE COSMOPOLITAN.

J B Kilffer, Chicago; J H Hakie, C L Herman, Sonora; E Alden, Huachuca.

Passenger Departures.

BY SANDY BOB'S STAGE.

John Cremer, Mrs Smith, Mrs Jones, H J McKasick and wife, W B Benson, J Haynes and wife, E Shipman, J Gabell, S Mel, H Seamans, W George, A Cowen, 1 Chinaman.

BY KINNEAR'S LINE.

Chas Shibell, Frank Renshaw

Cochise County Records.

The following instruments were filed for record in the County Recorder's office yesterday:

YESTERDAY'S TRAGEDY.

Three Men Hurled into Eternity in the Duration of a Moment.

The Causes that Led to the Sad Affair.

Stormy as were the early days of Tombstone, nothing ever occurred equal to the event of yesterday. Since the retirement of Ben Sippy as marshal and the appointment of V. W. Earp to fill the vacancy, the town has been noted for its quietness and good order. The fractions and formerly much dreaded cow-boys when they came to town upon their good behavior, and so unseemly brawls were indulged in, and it was hoped by our citizens that no more such deeds would occur as led to the killing of Marshal White, one year ago. It seems that this quiet state of affairs was but the calm that precedes the storm that burst in all its fury yesterday, with this difference in results, that the lightning's bolt struck in a different quarter than the one that fell one year ago...

THE PROXIMATE CAUSE.

Since the arrest of Stilwell and Spence, for the robbery of the Bisbee stage, there have been oft repeated threats conveyed to the Earp brothers—Virgil, Morgan and Wyatt—that the friends of the accused, or in other words, the cow-boys, would get even with them for the part they had taken in the pursuit and arrest of Stilwell and Spence...

THE ALARM GIVEN.

The moment the word of the shooting reached the Vizina and Tough Nut mines the whistles blew a shrill signal, and the volunteer fire company was brought to the front...

THE EARP BROTHERS JUSTIFIED.

The feeling among the best class of our citizens is that the Marshal was entirely justifiable in his efforts to disarm these men, and that being fired upon they had to defend themselves...

The Unreliability of Street Rumors

As a striking instance of the unreliability of street reports and rumors in general, but more particularly in times of public excitement, we publish the following story...

THE AFTER-OCCURRENCE.

Close upon the heels of this came the finale, which is best told in the words of R. F. Coleman, who was an eye-witness from the beginning to the end. Mr. Coleman says: I was in the O. K. Corral at 2:30 p. m., when I saw the two Clanton's (Ike and Bill), and the two McLowry boys (Frank and Tom), in earnest conversation across the street, in Dunbar's corral...

The Dcu I Love.

Tbe latest news at Glover's.

TUCSON SHALL TALK.

Mr. George A. Clum has gone on a brief trip to Altar, Sonora.

Clay W. Taylor, one of California's ablest citizens, is the new M. W. Grand Master of the Masonic Grand Lodge of Arizona and California.

James Hervey, of the sheriff's office, returned from Greaterville yesterday...

CITY ITEMS

The very lowest prices at Glover's.

Attention, Hooks!

There will be a meeting of the members of Rescue Hook & Ladder Company, at Judge Wallace's court room, this evening at 7 o'clock. A full attendance is desired, as business of importance will be transacted.
W. E. LUDLOW, Secretary.

See the news from Glover's in to-day's EPITAPH.

Election of Officers.

Siedpath Branch of the Irish National Land League will hold its regular meeting at Turn-Verein Hall on Wednesday evening October 26, at which time an election of officers will take place. A full attendance is requested. By order of the Board.
N. KENEALY, Prest.
JOSEPH POYNTON, Sect.

The latest style overcoats at Glover's.

Notice to Tax Payers

The members of the Board of Common Council will sit as a Board of Equalization on the 27th, 28th, 29th and 31st days of October, 1881...
S. B. CHAPIN, Clerk.

WINTER underwear, of every conceivable kind, at Glover's.

Attention, Ladies

Go to the Boot and Shoe Store, 505 Allen street, between Fifth and Sixth, for your shoes, as it is the only place to get a good fit at a reasonable price.

Woodland & Gay's Cash Store. Some of the finest Humboldt and Jersey Blue Potatoes ever brought to Tombstone; Eggs and Butter by the box; Fresh Grapes and Apples, Barley, Flour, Beans, Lard, Etc. We will sell to dealers or those requiring large amounts at a very close margin.
P. N. WOLCOTT, Manager
Third Door from Brown's Hotel, on Fourth Street.

Occidental Chop House.

From this date onward, to the advent of the western again, the proprietor of the Occidental Chop House will keep a supply of fresh California Salmon and Eastern Oysters, which, in addition to the other elaborate bill of fare, will be served in the best style and the lowest price possible...
A. PETTON, Proprietor.

EVERYBODY'S goods at everybody's prices, at Glover's.

Delmonico Lodging House.

Mrs. T. J. Cunningham, a sister of Miss Nellie Cashman, has rented the Vickers' building on Fremont street, between Fourth and Fifth, and has repainted and fitted up the rooms for a lodging house. The beds and furniture are all new and will be kept cleanly and in the best of style. This is one of the most pleasant and desirable houses in the city and we bespeak for the lady a liberal patronage.

THEY are always selling out, but not for cost, at Glover's.

MACDONALD goes to Los Angeles will find the Cosmopolitan the only first-class hotel, and headquarters for Arizona people. Hammel & Denker, Proprietors.

The largest variety of infants' and children's clothes can be found at the Boot and Shoe Store, 505 Allen street, between Fifth and Sixth.

MEN'S nailed mining shoes at $2, at the Boot and Shoe Store, 505 Allen street, between Fifth and Sixth.

ALL kinds of repairing in gents' and ladies' boots and shoes neatly and cheaply done at the Boot and Shoe Store, 505 Allen street, between Fifth and Sixth.

Carpets! Carpets!

J. Lenoir has received from New York a large invoice of Brussels, tapestry, three-ply and ingrain carpets of the latest patterns, all of which he desires parties desiring carpets to call and examine before purchasing elsewhere.

Wall Paper.

Those intending to rehabilitate their houses by supplying fresh wall paper will do well to call and examine the huge stock just received from New York by J. Lenoir. It is of the latest patterns and exquisite coloring.

P. W. Smith is sole agent for the celebrated Anason Whisky and St. Louis Rohnbeck Beer.

MEN'S heavy brogans at $1.75 per pair at the Boot and Shoe Store, 505 Allen street between Fifth and Sixth.

SHERMAN, CLAY & Co., manufacturers of church organs, keep the celebrated Mason organs, Weber and Haines Bros. Pianos. Instruments sold on instalments. For everything in the music line address Glover's.

FOR a neat, comfortable bed go to the Empire Fremont street, near Fifth. Lodgings, 50 cents.

LADIES' Fall Dress Goods, Broadcloth Silks, Satins, all shades, best Dress Trimmings, and Silk Cord and Tassels, at Hamburg's.

The shoot-out at the O.K. Corral fills two columns on page three of the next day's local paper but fails to crowd out social notes or ads.

The casualties of the shoot-out, Tom and Frank McLaury and Billy Clanton, repose in silver-trimmed caskets supplied by kinfolk. The bodies were displayed in a hardware store that boasted a large window.

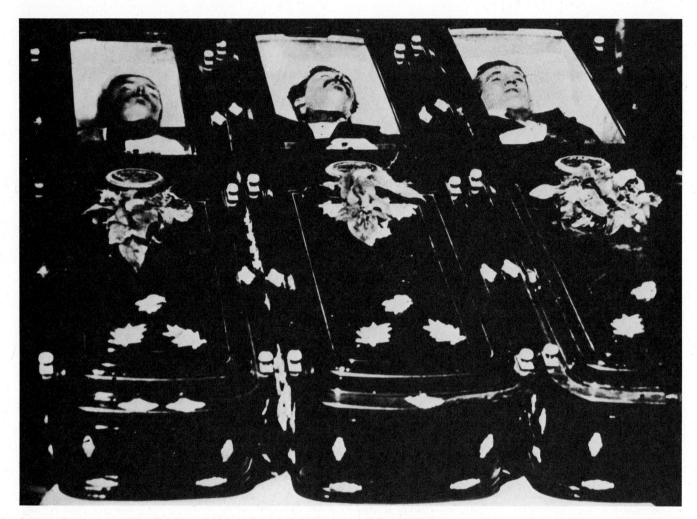

house; but even as his body sagged and slowly slid to the ground, he switched his pistol to his left hand. Lying there with his legs crossed, he rested the barrel across his arm and kept firing, though unsteadily.

By now Billy's brother was trying to save his own skin. Just after the first shots were fired, Ike had lunged at Wyatt Earp. Whether he hoped to wrest Wyatt's weapon or urge a truce is unclear. In any case, he grabbed Wyatt's arm and tried to get a grip around his shoulder. Seeing that Ike had no gun in his hand, Wyatt coolly pushed him away, saying, "Go to fighting or get away." Ike ran off toward Fly's front door. Doc Holliday sent a shotgun blast after him, but he made it inside untouched. Behan, who had been standing transfixed, abruptly leaped for cover too. He pulled Billy Claibourne around to the back door of Fly's and followed him in. Almost at once Ike came out the back

door and disappeared beyond the rear stalls of the O.K. Corral. He did not stop running until he reached a Mexican dance hall on Allen Street, where he took refuge.

Meanwhile, on the lot behind the corral, Frank McLaury's horse suddenly plunged into the street, exposing Tom McLaury. Doc Holliday aimed and fired at him. Doc's shotgun had failed him with Ike; not so now. The buckshot tore through Tom's vest and into his right side. He wobbled down Fremont Street to the corner of Third, where he collapsed, dying.

In a matter of seconds, Ike had fled and the three other cowboys had been wounded. But two of them did not count themselves out. The first of the foes to discover this was Virgil Earp. Virgil had taken no part in the shooting. When it began, he had shifted Doc Holliday's cane to his left hand and drawn a pistol to fire at Billy Clanton, but Morgan had gotten to Billy first. Now, standing in the lot, Virgil felt a bullet tear into his calf. He buckled to the ground—about 10 feet from where Billy lay firing across his arm.

Frank McLaury, despite his stomach wound, was not ready to quit either. As his horse came plunging from the lot, he tried to get his rifle from the scabbard on the frightened animal, but it shied and broke away. McLaury then drew his six-shooter—to find Doc Holliday eying him a few feet away. Doc had discarded Virgil Earp's cumbersome shotgun for his own pistol. As the two men fired simultaneously, a third shot came from the left—from Morgan Earp. McLaury crumpled, a bullet hole below his ear. But his own shot had pierced Doc Holliday's hip. Doc, it was said, would never make an easy target, for he was so wasted by tuberculosis and whiskey that if he turned sideways he could hardly be seen. Frank McLaury, in the final split second of his life, had disproved that.

It remained for Billy Clanton, who never wanted the shoot-out, to fire the cowboys' last shot. His target was Morgan Earp, and he managed to hit him in the shoulder. Morgan stumbled and fell. Billy tried to get to his feet. Morgan and Wyatt Earp fired together; hit below the ribs, Billy slumped down again.

Suddenly the shooting stopped; gun smoke drifted over a silent scene. Camillus Fly came out of his house and crossed the lot to where Billy Clanton lay dying, still trying to cock his six-shooter. "Give me some more cartridges," Billy pleaded. Fly pulled the pistol from his weakened grasp.

The gunfight was over. Of the eight participants, three men were dead, three were wounded and two—Ike Clanton and Wyatt Earp—were without a scratch. In less time than it took a minute hand to go round the clock, enmities had been resolved by a ritual obligatory for its proud performers. Yet, inevitably, a further reckoning was to come.

By late that afternoon, Tombstone was up in arms. At the nearby mines shrill whistles were sounded and the miners gathered weapons and marched into town to help keep order. Allies of the Earps watched their homes to protect them from friends of the Clantons and McLaurys who might ride into town to seek revenge. The bodies of the three dead men were delivered to Ritter and Ream, the undertakers. Two days after the

shoot-out the procession to the cemetery was led through the packed streets by members of the town's brass band. As the cortege passed one point, a friend of the victims held up an ominous sign bearing the words: Murdered in the Streets of Tombstone.

For weeks Tombstone debated questions of guilt or innocence. A coroner's jury rendered no clear verdict. After the inquest, Sheriff Behan jailed Wyatt and Doc Holliday on charges of murder. (Virgil and Morgan Earp, still recovering from their wounds, were not arrested, though Virgil was suspended as city marshal.) The case was heard before Magistrate Court Judge Wells Spicer—the same man who had detected a ray of hope in the presence of two Bibles in Tombstone. In the end, after 30 days of testimony, the judge decided that the defendants had been justified in their acts. They were, he ruled, "officers charged with the duty of arresting and disarming brave and determined men who were experts in the use of firearms, as quick as thought and as certain as death, and who had previously declared their intentions not to be arrested nor disarmed."

But Spicer did not wholly relieve the Earp faction of blame. He noted that Virgil Earp, as chief of police, had "committed an injudicious and censurable act" by calling on Wyatt and Doc to help him in arresting and disarming the Clantons and McLaurys. Still, Spicer went on, there were mitigating circumstances. His listing of them added up to a telling portrait of Tombstone: "When we consider the condition of affairs incidental to a frontier country, the lawlessness and disregard for human life; the existence of a law-defying element in our midst; the fear and feeling of insecurity that has existed; the supposed prevalence of bad, desperate and reckless men who have been a terror to the country, and kept away capital and enterprise, and considering the many threats that have been made against the Earps, I can attach no criminality to his unwise act."

The decision did not satisfy the victims' friends. Just two months after the shoot-out, Virgil Earp, now back on his feet, was blasted with buckshot as he crossed Fifth Street in the dark. The assailants got away without being seen. Virgil's left arm was shattered. He was taken to a room in the Cosmopolitan Hotel, where his wife, Allie, and some friends soon surrounded him. Virgil tried to console his wife. "Never mind," he told her, "I've got one arm left to hug you with."

Three months later, on a Saturday night in March 1882, Wyatt and Morgan Earp were at a billiard hall on Allen Street. As Morgan bent over a billiard table with a cue, two shots were fired through the glass of a back door. Morgan fell, his spine shattered by a bullet. He tried to be jocular about it, saying as he was carried to a couch, "This is the last game of pool I'll ever play." Within a half hour he was dead. Witnesses saw three men running from the scene—two of them were Pete Spence, the Clantons' friend, and Frank Stilwell, Sheriff Behan's deputy, whom Virgil Earp had arrested for holding up a stage the previous September; the third man was reported to be an Indian.

Three days later, Virgil and his wife boarded a westbound train to take Morgan's casket to California, where the Earps' parents had settled. Wyatt and Doc Holliday went along to guard Virgil as far as Tucson. As the train stopped in the Tucson station, Frank Stilwell was spotted in the shadows, armed with a pistol. Next morning a trainman found Stilwell dead, six bullets through his chest and both legs. He had been shot at close range; his clothes were covered with powder burns. By the time his body was discovered, Wyatt and Doc were on their way back to Tombstone.

That night Wyatt gathered a posse of friends to hunt down Pete Spence and the anonymous Indian who had killed his younger brother. As they rode into the Arizona back country, Sheriff Behan assembled his own posse to find and arrest Wyatt and Doc Holliday for the Stilwell murder. The next morning, March 22, Wyatt's men found and killed "the Indian"—actually a Mexican woodcutter—at Pete Spence's lumber camp in the Dragoons. Spence himself escaped Wyatt's wrath. With Behan's deputies roaming the hills in pursuit, Wyatt, Doc Holliday and a few of their companions took

flight. About a week later, weary and saddle-sore, they dismounted in Albuquerque, New Mexico—beyond the reach of the Arizona law.

For Tombstone, it was over at last: the feud, the gunfight, the aftermath. But the legend of those bloody days was just beginning. Accounts of the Earp war in Tombstone were published by newspapers across the West and picked up by the press back East. As much as any other shoot-out, the drama at the O.K. Corral secured the reputation of the Western gunfighters as figures of elemental force, rough-hewn knights whose daring—if not their virtue—was beyond question.

Many another frontier town that boomed later than Tombstone—or earlier—boasted of being the wickedest, most wide-open town in the West, largely basing its claims on the number of shoot-outs along its streets and in its saloons. The various attempts to enlarge the West's notoriety as a wild and violent land rose in part out of simple pride in living dangerously, in part out of self-serving appeals to potential patrons—cowboys, miners, buffalo hunters, soldiers. For them, a frontier community was a place to get gloriously drunk, to bed loose women and to win a bundle at the gaming table. To all this the prospect of gunplay added a heady spice.

Even cities that were more settled took pride in counting a few gunfighters among their inhabitants. "The gentleman who has killed his man is by no means a *rara avis* in Kansas City," observed a local newspaper with quiet pride in 1881. Such a person, the writer noted, might be seen serving at the bar of a Main Street saloon or standing behind the rosewood counter of a bank; he might be residing on "Quality Hill" or renting a room at 15 cents a night.

The gunfighter breed, whether operating in the name of the law or against it, sprang from every conceivable background. Jesse James and his equally lethal brother, Frank, were the sons of a Missouri preacher. The slums of New York City probably spawned Billy the Kid, a loner whose gunslinging exploits were heralded as heroic by some and as lunatic by others. Bill Tilghman, a deputy U.S. marshal whose guns helped bring peace to the Indian Territory, was a buffalo hunter before he began riding herd on outlaws. Mysterious Dave Mather, an itinerant gunfighter who served as marshal of several frontier towns—and spent as much time in their

jails—claimed to be a descendant of the famous Salem witch-hunter, Cotton Mather. John Ringo, a Texas desperado who, as part of Sheriff Behan's posse, helped drive Wyatt Earp out of Arizona, was rumored to be the black sheep of a genteel Southern family.

Yet different as all of these men were, the gun by which they lived and died gave them a shared identity. They were recognized—and recognized themselves—as a distinct fraternity in Western society; when any one of them made his appearance on a scene, his very presence could inspire awe and dread. And if a single gunfighter could stir fear, the arrival of several in the same town at the same time could set off tremors of terror throughout an entire region. Such was the case in Kansas in the spring of 1883, after a natty little gambler and saloonkeeper named Luke Short was driven out of Dodge City by business rivals. A few weeks later, while Short waited in Kansas City, a group of his gun-

fighter friends began drifting ominously toward Dodge.

A local newspaper, apprised of Short's threats of revenge, reported the impending influx with foreboding: "A brief history of these gentlemen who will meet here tomorrow will explain the gravity of the situation. At the head is Bat Masterson. He is credited with having killed one man for every year of his life. This may be exaggerated, but he is certainly entitled to a record of a dozen or more. He is a cool, brave man, pleasant in his manners, but terrible in a fight. Doc Holliday is another famous killer. Among the desperate men of the West, he is looked upon with the respect born of awe, for he has killed in single combat no less than eight desperadoes. He was the chief character in the Earp war at Tombstone, where the celebrated brothers, aided by Holliday, broke up the terrible rustlers.

"Wyatt Earp is equally famous in the cheerful business of depopulating the country. He has killed within

35

our personal knowledge six men, and he is popularly accredited with relegating to the dust no less than ten of his fellow men. Shotgun Collins was a Wells, Fargo & Co. messenger, and obtained his name from the peculiar weapon he used, a sawed-off shotgun. He has killed two men in Montana and two in Arizona, but beyond this his exploits are not known. Luke Short, for whom these men have rallied, is a noted man himself. He has killed several men and is utterly devoid of fear."

The gathering gunfighters had made no secret of their destination. Bat Masterson said he wanted to see old Dodge City friends. Earp and Holliday said the same. Shotgun Collins said he was just going to keep the others company. Luke Short let it be known that he would be returning to Dodge City on business. On the way there, the gunfighters' ranks were swelled by a half dozen less celebrated sympathizers, known to history only as Black Jack Bill, Cold Chuck Johnny, Dynamite Sam, Dark Alley Jim, Three-Fingered Dave and Six-Toed Pete. The panicked sheriff bombarded the state capitol with telegraphed pleas for help. The governor of Kansas, George Washington Glick, dispatched the state's adjutant general, Tom Moonlight, to try to prevent a war; a company of state militia stood ready to intervene. As the gunmen arrived in town wearing expressions that suggested deep thoughts on the frailty of human life, Short's business rivals suddenly turned conciliatory. They availed themselves of the good offices of Tom Moonlight and negotiated a settlement with Short. The gunfighters promptly melted away, their air of innocence still intact.

More remarkable than this peaceful outcome was Dodge City's readiness to believe everything it had heard about the gunfighters. In fact, their reputations were, in at least two cases, considerably inflated. Although Bat Masterson was supposed to have dispatched a dozen men as sheriff of Ford County, Kansas, there is no real evidence that he shot anyone. Wyatt Earp's record rested largely on the episode at the O.K. Corral.

Most gunfighters displayed not the slightest interest in setting the record straight, for notoriety gave them an edge in a duel with a nervous opponent. They often honed this edge by embellishing their past deeds. The most bald-faced liar among the Western gunmen probably was Wild Bill Hickok. As a U.S. Army scout, Hickok had seen action against the Indians and made some forays behind Confederate lines during the Civil War. Later he got into several shooting scrapes—though some said he tangled only with amateurs and drunks.

In 1867, Hickok was tracked down by an adventurous reporter named Henry M. Stanley—the same Stanley who later, in Africa, was to utter the famous words, "Dr. Livingstone, I presume." Apparently, on meeting Wild Bill, Stanley was uncharacteristically flustered: "I say, Bill, or Mr. Hickok, how many white men have you killed, to your certain knowledge?" Hickok blandly replied, "I would be willing to take my oath on the Bible tomorrow that I have killed over a hundred." The magnitude of the figure troubled Stanley not a whit. He repeated it without reservation in his newspaper article and indulged in a veritable wallow of hero worship. Wild Bill, he wrote, "is endowed with extraordinary power and agility. He seems naturally fitted to perform daring actions."

But not all gunfighters were given to overstatement. Some preferred to leave the scene of a fight with a minimum of fuss. Such was the case about one spectacular shoot-out that left six men dead at Newton, Kansas, in 1871. In Newton's brothel district, aptly named Hide Park, a group of cowboys had gathered outside a dance hall near the Atchison, Topeka and Santa Fe railroad tracks. Inside, an ex-railroad man named McCluskie, who had shot a cowboy in a quarrel some days before, was talking with employees of the road. Led by a Texan named Hugh Anderson, the cowboys moved into the hall, firing as they entered. McCluskie was shot in the neck, but as he fell, he kept firing his own revolver and wounded Anderson. At that moment, a gaunt youth—he looked to be no more than 18 —locked the dance-hall door and began blazing away at the cowboys, killing four of them. When the smoke cleared, McCluskie's avenger could not be found. No one knew anything about him, except that his name was Riley—and that he was dying of tuberculosis.

Even when they were not deliberately being men of mystery, the restless gunfighters of the West were hard to keep track of, and often were the subjects of phantom sightings and false reports. In March 1873 a Kansas City newspaper reported its confusion over the whereabouts of Wild Bill Hickok. Recent dispatches had variously reported that he had been killed in Galveston, Texas; that he was visiting relatives in Spring-field, Missouri; that he was "airing his long hair" back East in New York; that he had killed three Indians west of Omaha, Nebraska; and, again, that he had been shot to death but this time at Fort Dodge, Kansas. A few days later an indignant note from Hickok drew a promise from the press that "Wild Bill, or any other man killed by mistake in our columns, will be promptly resuscitated upon application by mail."

But Wild Bill was well aware that at another time, in another place, the report of his violent death might be true. Gunfighters, far more than ordinary men, passed their days in peril of dying with their boots on. The shoot-out, the ultimate test of their talent, was an event whose outcome might depend on a hairbreadth of difference between men's skills. And sheer luck could play almost as large a part as skill, considering the weapons with which shoot-outs were fought.

The single-action Colt revolvers (pages 42-44), the favorite handguns of the West, had to be cocked manually for each shot. Their ammunition—lead bullets propelled from black-powder cartridges—had some serious disadvantages. The black powder absorbed moisture, which sometimes caused misfiring. Each shot sent out a puff of dark gray smoke so thick that it impaired accurate aiming of the following shot. (Smokeless powder did not come into general use until about 1895.) When the smoke—and the legends—were cleared away, the fact was that experienced gunmen considered themselves proficient if, in an actual shoot-out, they could hit a man at a distance of 15 yards.

Aspirants to a gunfighter's career left as little as possible to chance and spent long hours refining their skills with weapons. In later life, Bat Masterson described the rigorous training that was necessary to enable a man to "throw lead" quick and straight, as though by instinct: "To accustom his hands to the pistols of those days, the man who coveted a reputation started in early and practiced with them just as a card sharp practices with his cards, as a shell game man drills his fingers to manipulate the elusive pea, or a juggler must practice to acquire proficiency. When he could draw, cock and fire all in one smooth lightning-quick movement, he could then detach his mind from that movement and concentrate on accuracy."

The gymnastics involved in that lightning-quick movement were enough to deter any but the most assiduous student. The gun had to be grasped by its handle with the wrist twisted downward, while the finger reached down at a 45° angle for the trigger and the thumb cocked the hammer. This art was so difficult as to cast a pall of improbability over the alleged achievements of men like Wild Bill Hickok; it was claimed that he once killed a gunman at his back by firing over his left shoulder and at the same moment, with his other gun, outshot a man in front of him.

Actually a gunfight was rarely decided by trick shooting. According to Wyatt Earp, it was an axiom among gunfighters that the man who won a shoot-out was the man who took his time. Shooting at someone who was returning the compliment, Wyatt said, meant "going into action with the greatest speed of which a man's muscles are capable, but mentally unflustered by an urge to hurry or the need for complicated nervous and muscular actions which trick shooting involves."

One gunfighting gambler, Turkey Creek Jack Johnson, was famous for taking his time. In 1876 in the heat of a saloon row in Deadwood, South Dakota, he invited two men to shoot it out with him in the road alongside the town cemetery. Each of his opponents strapped on two six-shooters. Johnson started toward them from one end of the cemetery fence. They started toward him from the other end, 50 yards away, and began firing. By the time they had gone 10 yards, each had emptied the chambers of one revolver and shifted to a second gun. Johnson, walking along with one Colt pistol drawn, still had not fired. At a distance of 30 yards, his first shot killed one of the men. Johnson stopped walking, waited until the second man came a few paces closer, allowed him two or three last shots — then fired once again. The dead man's finger was still on the trigger of his cocked six-shooter when someone rolled him over in the road.

Many shoot-outs occurred at closer quarters, with less chance for deliberation. At Dodge City's Long Branch Saloon one night in 1879, a gambler named Cock-Eyed Frank Loving got into a quarrel over a woman with a wagon driver named Levi Richardson. The two men chased each other around a gaming table, firing at such close range that their pistols almost touched. The wagon driver died of a chest wound. As was usual in such cases, Cock-Eyed Frank got off scot free with a verdict of self-defense after a quick coroner's inquest. The local newspaper offered this judicious comment on the affair: "Both, or either of these men, we believe, might have avoided this shooting if either had possessed a desire to do so. But both being willing to risk their lives, each with confidence in himself, they fought because they wanted to fight." Self-confidence was indeed an indispensable trait of the gunfighting breed, but such chaotic encounters, for all their ferocity, were somewhat at odds with the gunfighters' vision of their craft. When a Texas gunman, Clay Allison, defined himself with one simple statement — "I am a shootist" — the odd word carried all the professional status and pride of "artist" or "chemist."

From time to time, the most renowned gunfighters —all compulsive travelers — crossed paths as they moved through the lively towns of the frontier. Yet there were almost no instances of shooting exchanges between them. Outsiders might regard them as a predatory lot, but the gunfighters seemed to view themselves, collectively, as preyed upon by lesser men. When Jesse and Frank James, on the run from the law, slipped into Abilene, Kansas, in 1871, they soon came to an understanding with Marshal Wild Bill Hickok. They simply passed word to Wild Bill that they would make no "bad moves" while in town, but added that they had arranged for his funeral in the event that he attempted to capture them. Hickok did not come calling.

Yet gunfighters belonged to a species that courted its own destruction, readily—even eagerly—putting their lives on the line for any issue they deemed important. For all the romanticizing of their feats and the wishful upgrading of their motives, they did comport themselves with audacity, resourcefulness, and even a kind of grim humor that could scarcely be exaggerated by legend. A popular story of the 1880s offers a quintessential glimpse of these gunfighter traits. It told of a duel that was about to take place in a saloon. A space was cleared for the two antagonists. One of them was an unimposing little man, thin as a rail—but a professional gunfighter. The other was a big, bellicose fellow who tipped the beam at 200 pounds. "Now wait," the big man said, backing off. "He's shooting at a larger target. It ain't a fair fight." The little man quickly moved to solve the difficulty. Turning to the saloonkeeper, he said, "Chalk out a man of my size on the other fellow. Anything of mine that hits outside the line don't count."

Tools of the gunfighters' trade

"God did not make all men equal," Westerners were fond of saying, "Colonel Colt did." When it came to the use of shooting irons, however, some men were more equal than others—a fact gunfighters knew well. To improve the odds of landing on the right side of this equation, they exercised meticulous care in selecting their firearms from among the weapons available. As is evident here and on the following pages, they had a wide range of choices.

From service in the Civil War, thousands of frontiersmen inherited handguns like the three at right—revolvers whose rotating chambers held several rounds. They fired a kind of roll-your-own ammunition consisting of a ball, powder and a percussion cap. But the ammunition was all too fallible: unless carefully loaded, it might misfire or even set off chain-reaction detonations of the rounds in adjoining chambers.

The development of metallic cartridges soon solved these problems. The first metallic-cartridge revolver to be adopted as the standard sidearm of the postwar Army was the mordantly misnamed Colt's Peacemaker of 1873 (pages 42-43). Sold in enormous numbers on the open market and by mail, this single-action—i.e., manually cocked—pistol swiftly became the weapon most likely to be whipped from the holsters, waistbands or leather-lined coat pockets of Western gunfighters.

But the reliable Peacemaker, along with its imitators and successors, had a drawback. The relatively short barrel—eight inches or less—reduced the power and accuracy. While an expert might consistently hit a stationary man-sized target at 40 yards, effective revolver range in the chaos of combat was less than half that figure. Most gunfighters therefore enlarged their arsenals with a rifle or a shotgun.

Even with one of these bigger weapons for deadly firepower, and revolvers for close work, some gunfighters felt less than fully equipped, so they added a vest-pocket pistol to their array of iron. Although woefully inaccurate, a small, hidden firearm possessed a matchless potential for surprise, and more than once proved a trump in the hazardous games of men who lived by the gun.

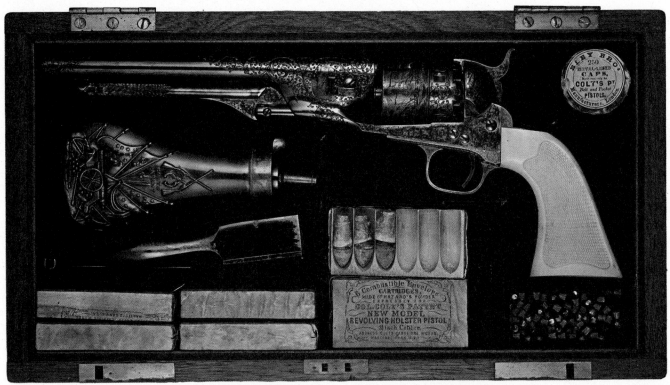

A deluxe kit for an 1860 Colt .44 includes an ornate powder flask, a bullet mold (the chisel-shaped object) and percussion caps (bottom right and in the container at top right). Also included were five boxes of prefabricated paper cartridges, one opened.

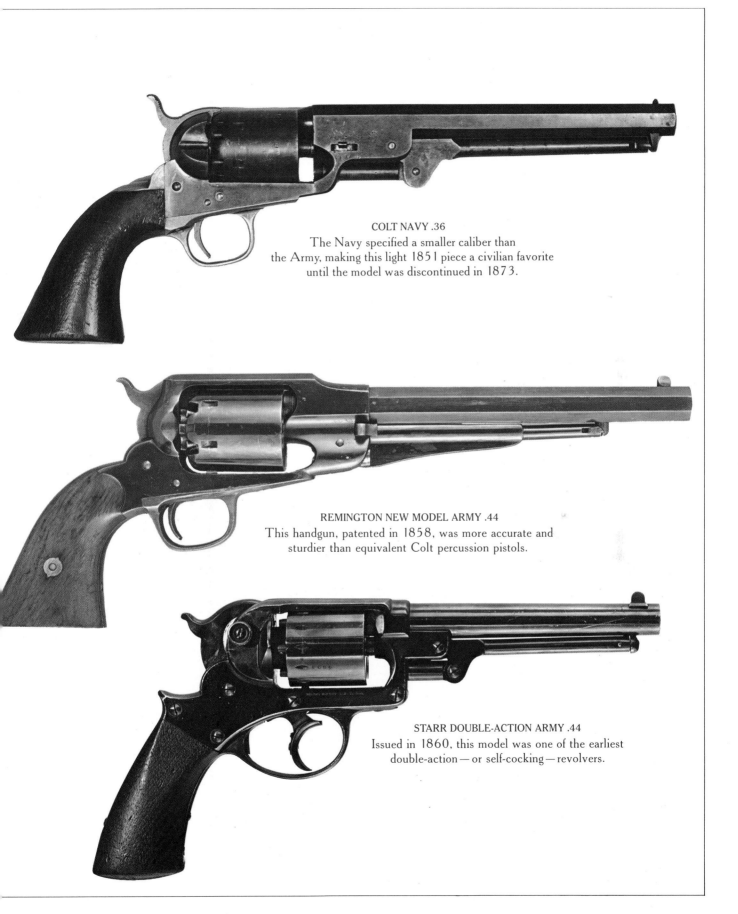

COLT NAVY .36
The Navy specified a smaller caliber than
the Army, making this light 1851 piece a civilian favorite
until the model was discontinued in 1873.

REMINGTON NEW MODEL ARMY .44
This handgun, patented in 1858, was more accurate and
sturdier than equivalent Colt percussion pistols.

STARR DOUBLE-ACTION ARMY .44
Issued in 1860, this model was one of the earliest
double-action — or self-cocking — revolvers.

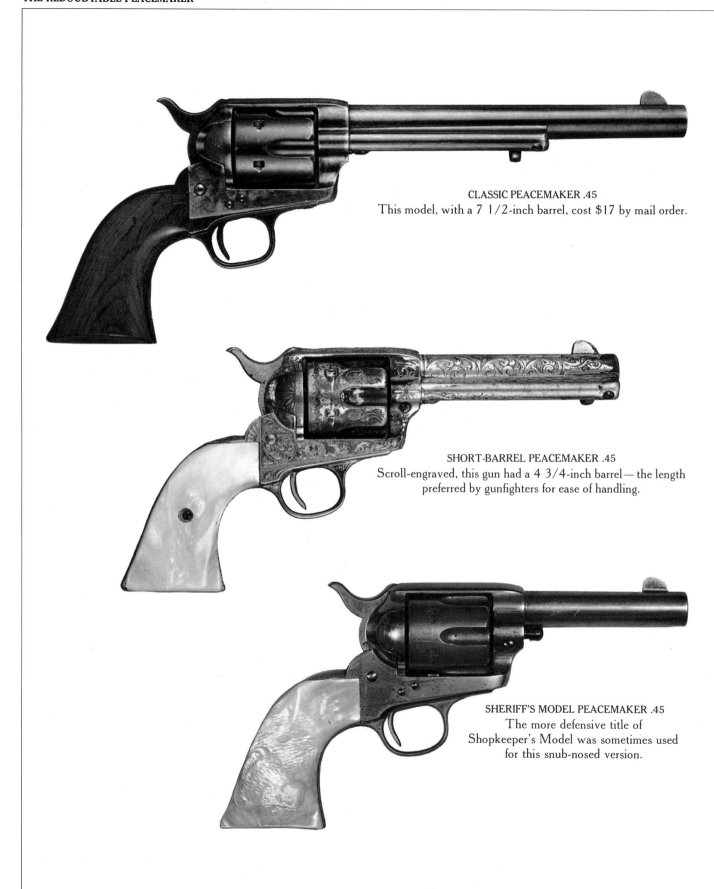

CLASSIC PEACEMAKER .45
This model, with a 7 1/2-inch barrel, cost $17 by mail order.

SHORT-BARREL PEACEMAKER .45
Scroll-engraved, this gun had a 4 3/4-inch barrel — the length
preferred by gunfighters for ease of handling.

SHERIFF'S MODEL PEACEMAKER .45
The more defensive title of
Shopkeeper's Model was sometimes used
for this snub-nosed version.

SMITH & WESSON SCHOFIELD .45
First produced in 1875, this single-action
revolver was Jesse James's choice.

An advertising display touts the Winchester Company's highly profitable line of cartridges for a variety of rifles, shotguns and pistols.

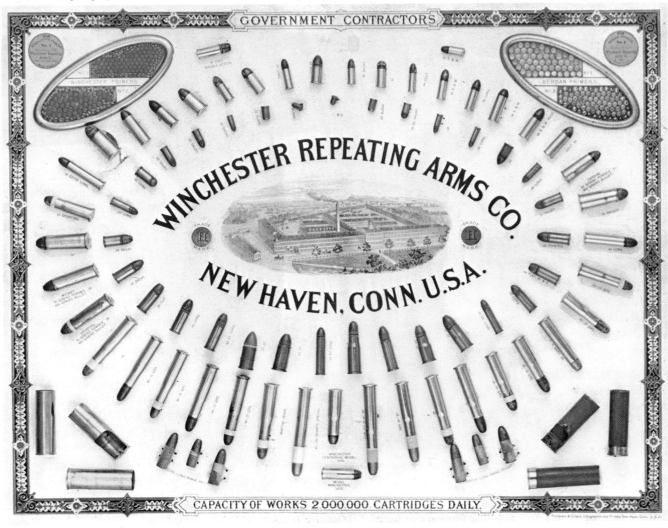

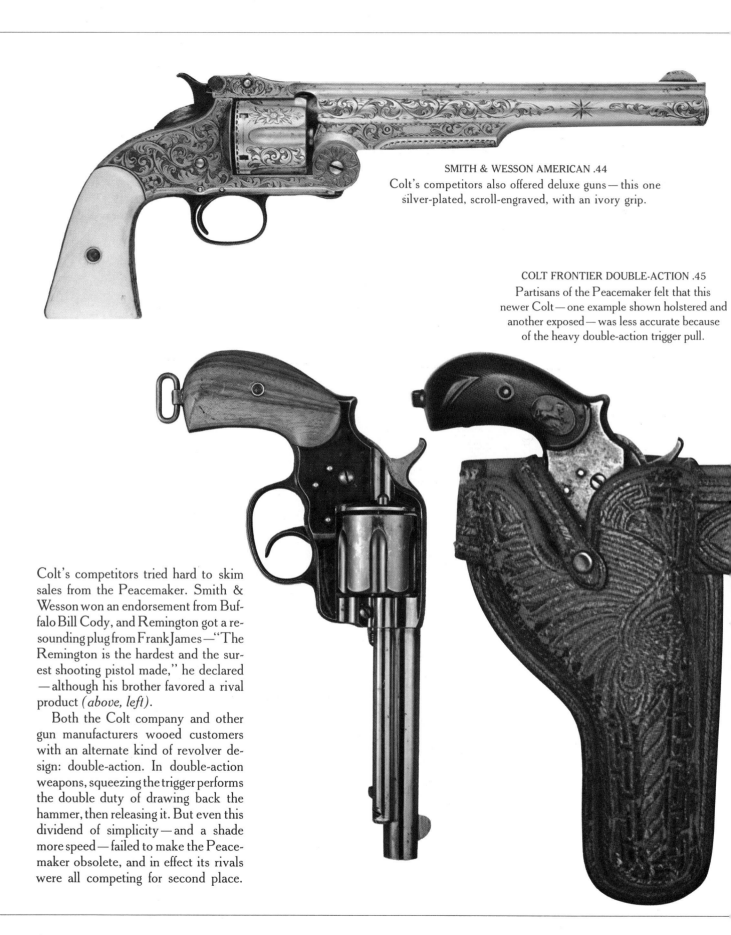

SMITH & WESSON AMERICAN .44
Colt's competitors also offered deluxe guns — this one silver-plated, scroll-engraved, with an ivory grip.

COLT FRONTIER DOUBLE-ACTION .45
Partisans of the Peacemaker felt that this newer Colt — one example shown holstered and another exposed — was less accurate because of the heavy double-action trigger pull.

Colt's competitors tried hard to skim sales from the Peacemaker. Smith & Wesson won an endorsement from Buffalo Bill Cody, and Remington got a resounding plug from Frank James—"The Remington is the hardest and the surest shooting pistol made," he declared — although his brother favored a rival product *(above, left)*.

Both the Colt company and other gun manufacturers wooed customers with an alternate kind of revolver design: double-action. In double-action weapons, squeezing the trigger performs the double duty of drawing back the hammer, then releasing it. But even this dividend of simplicity — and a shade more speed — failed to make the Peacemaker obsolete, and in effect its rivals were all competing for second place.

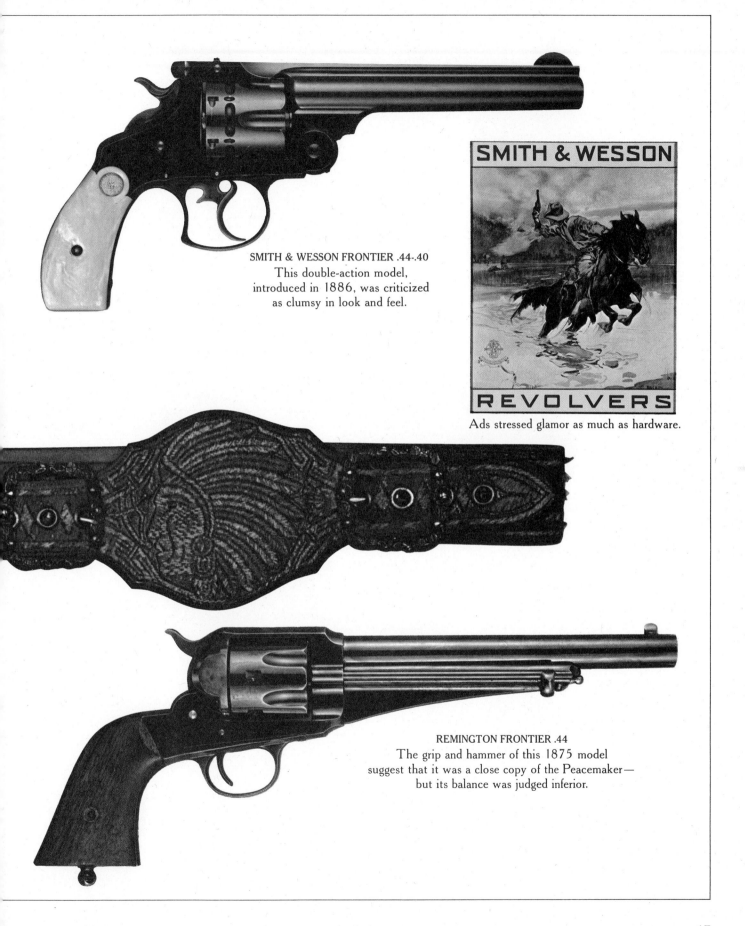

SMITH & WESSON FRONTIER .44-.40
This double-action model,
introduced in 1886, was criticized
as clumsy in look and feel.

SMITH & WESSON

REVOLVERS

Ads stressed glamor as much as hardware.

REMINGTON FRONTIER .44
The grip and hammer of this 1875 model
suggest that it was a close copy of the Peacemaker—
but its balance was judged inferior.

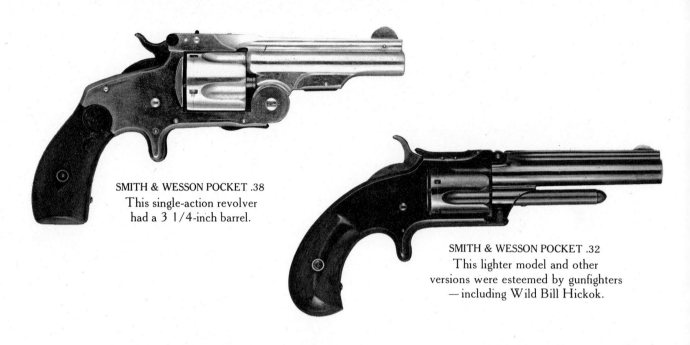

SMITH & WESSON POCKET .38
This single-action revolver
had a 3 1/4-inch barrel.

SMITH & WESSON POCKET .32
This lighter model and other
versions were esteemed by gunfighters
—including Wild Bill Hickok.

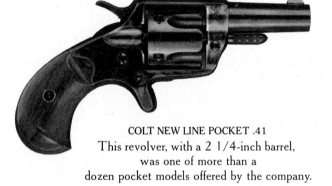

COLT NEW LINE POCKET .41
This revolver, with a 2 1/4-inch barrel,
was one of more than a
dozen pocket models offered by the company.

REMINGTON ELLIOT .22
The ring served as the trigger,
with a curved trigger stop behind
it, in this five-shot pistol.

REID'S "MY FRIEND" KNUCKLEDUSTER .32
Lacking a barrel, this model fired
direct from the revolver
chambers—and doubled as a bludgeon.

Easily stashed-away firearms—whether pocket revolvers or the one- or two-shot pistols known as deringers after the pioneering Philadelphia gunmaker Henry Deringer—often were hidden in bar girls' bodices and faro dealers' sleeves. Even the toughest gunfighters used them as back-up weapons. One Arizona lawman carried upward of half a dozen petite pistols on his person.

But the scaled-down size of these guns cost heavily in accuracy and range. Mark Twain, who packed a pocket-model Smith & Wesson .22 on his travels through the West, was guilty of only mild exaggeration when he wrote, "It was grand. It only had one fault —you could not hit anything with it."

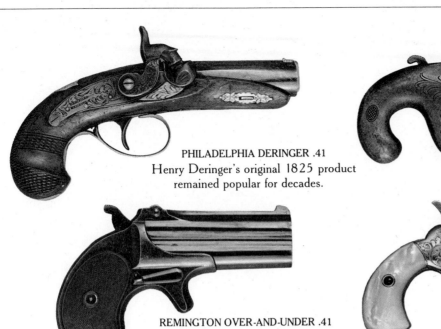

PHILADELPHIA DERINGER .41
Henry Deringer's original 1825 product
remained popular for decades.

COLT FIRST MODEL .41
This one-shot pistol was loaded by
pivoting the barrel downward.

REMINGTON OVER-AND-UNDER .41
More than 150,000 customers were
sold on this two-shot model.

COLT THIRD MODEL .41
Colt's best-selling deringer model
was loaded by turning the barrel sideways.

A pair of handy hiding places

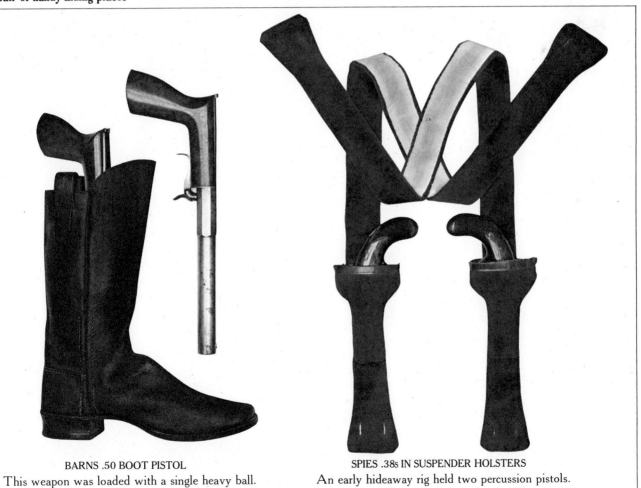

BARNS .50 BOOT PISTOL
This weapon was loaded with a single heavy ball.

SPIES .38s IN SUSPENDER HOLSTERS
An early hideaway rig held two percussion pistols.

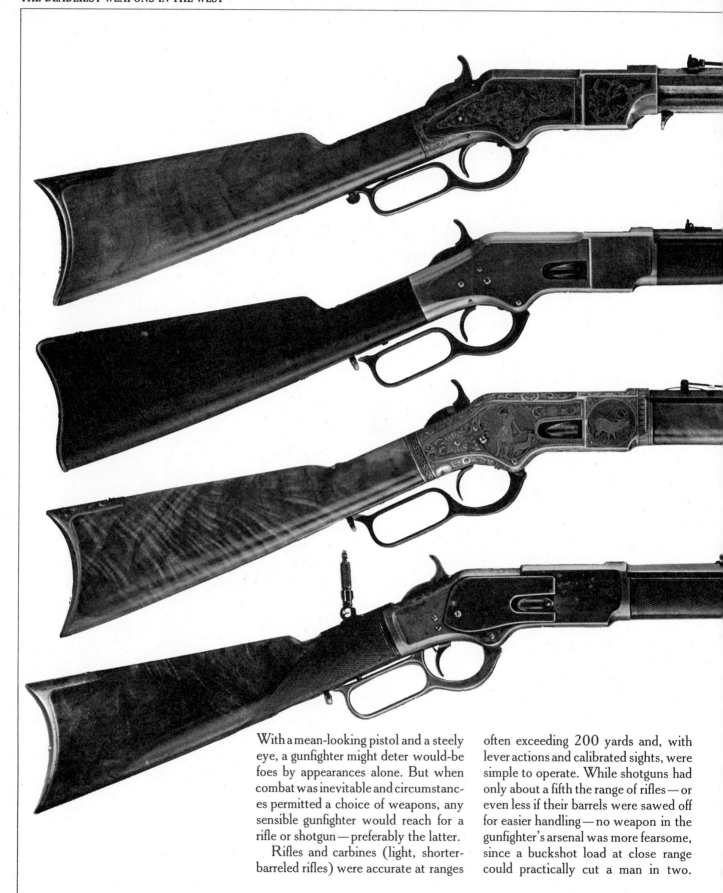

With a mean-looking pistol and a steely eye, a gunfighter might deter would-be foes by appearances alone. But when combat was inevitable and circumstances permitted a choice of weapons, any sensible gunfighter would reach for a rifle or shotgun—preferably the latter.

Rifles and carbines (light, shorter-barreled rifles) were accurate at ranges often exceeding 200 yards and, with lever actions and calibrated sights, were simple to operate. While shotguns had only about a fifth the range of rifles—or even less if their barrels were sawed off for easier handling—no weapon in the gunfighter's arsenal was more fearsome, since a buckshot load at close range could practically cut a man in two.

HENRY .44 RIFLE
Introduced in 1860, this model was the first
practical lever-action rifle.

WINCHESTER .44 CARBINE
With its 20-inch barrel, this 1866 carbine was four
inches shorter than the rifle model just below.

WINCHESTER .44 RIFLE
Fancily engraved to its owner's taste, this weapon's magazine
held 17 rounds, four more than the carbine.

WINCHESTER .44-.40 RIFLE
This example of the 1873 model, the best-selling rifle in the West,
boasted an extra rear sight for greater accuracy.

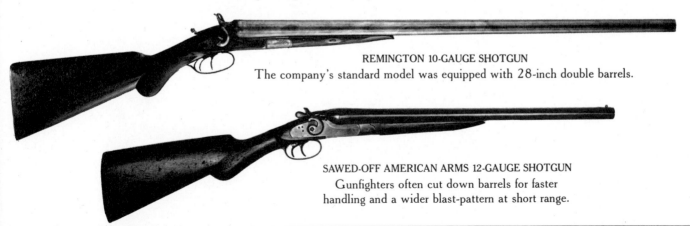

REMINGTON 10-GAUGE SHOTGUN
The company's standard model was equipped with 28-inch double barrels.

SAWED-OFF AMERICAN ARMS 12-GAUGE SHOTGUN
Gunfighters often cut down barrels for faster
handling and a wider blast-pattern at short range.

Among the several kinds of Western gunfighters, the most fearsome were the men who rode in outlaw gangs — swooping down on banks, trains and stages to seize booty that lay beyond the grasp of solitary gunmen. And no gang was bolder, more rapacious — or more renowned — than the one led by the James brothers, Jesse and Frank.

The James boys were well prepared for bandit careers. During the Civil War they had fought in Confederate guerrilla bands whose hit-and-run raids on Union troops terrorized the Kansas-Missouri border zone. With the coming of peace, the two young rebels organized fellow ex-guerrillas into a strike force, ranging in size from three to a dozen men at any one time, that made full use of the lessons learned in war. They planned assaults with commando precision, struck so swiftly they could paralyze an entire town, then vanished into the countryside with ghostly ease. The James gang flourished for 15 years, from 1866 to 1881, and executed 26 daring raids in and around Missouri for a total take of about half a million dollars.

Their success spawned scores of imitators — most of whom met a bloody end after a few precarious years. Still, the lure of quick money kept new gangs coming — and there were nonmaterial rewards as well. Gang leader Henry Starr, who operated in Indian Territory, evoked the appeal of bandit life this way: "Life in the open, the rides at night, the spice of danger, the mastery over men, the pride of being able to hold a mob at bay — it tingles in my veins. I love it. It is wild adventure."

By the 1870s, Jesse James *(far left)* was so proud of his gang — and so confident they could evade any pursuers — that he had a photographer brought to their cave hideout in Missouri to record this portrait.

53

The rampaging sons of the widow James

Shortly before 2 o'clock on a February afternoon in 1866, a dozen men rode into Liberty, Missouri, the seat of Clay County at the western edge of the state. It was St. Valentine's Day, but none of the horsemen looked like anybody's beau. All of them were muffled in long soldiers' overcoats, and some wore six-shooters strapped outside their coats. The first three riders dismounted in the deserted town square, taking up posts from which they could watch the surrounding streets. The others reined up in front of the Clay County Savings Association. Two of them dismounted and stepped into the small bank.

Inside, a clerk and a cashier were laboring over accounts at desks behind a wooden counter. The cashier, Greenup Bird, saw the two strangers stop to warm themselves at the stove. His son William, the clerk, went on writing. After a moment one of the men walked to the counter and slid a $10 bill across the polished wood. "I'd like a bill changed," he said. As William reached for the bill, the stranger drew a six-shooter and, almost as an afterthought, broadened his request. "I'd like all the money in the bank," he said.

No one had ever said that, or anything like it, to an American bank clerk before. Except for a raid on a small Vermont bank by a band of Confederate guerrillas during the Civil War, no one had ever robbed a bank during business hours. William Bird backed away in disbelief as the robbers hurdled the counter. One of them leveled a revolver at Greenup Bird. "Make a noise and we'll shoot you down," he warned. His part-ner struck William Bird with his gun and pushed him toward the bank's open vault. "Damn you, be quick," he said, shoving the clerk into the vault and following behind. There William gathered gold and silver coins from a shelf and stuffed them into a grain sack the robber had taken from under his coat.

The second robber, standing at Greenup Bird's desk, asked where the paper money was. "In the box," the cashier replied, pointing to a large tin container resting on a table. Six-shooter still in hand, the robber began to stack the contents—currency, bonds, bank notes and sheets of revenue stamps. When his partner emerged from the vault with a bulging sack, the legal tender was stuffed into it too; the total, it was later estimated, came to about $60,000. The cashier was then forced into the vault to join his son, and the door was slammed shut. "Stay in there," one robber called. "You know all Birds should be caged!" Clearly, the punster was familiar with the bank and its employees.

But the cage proved unconfining; the lock of the vault door had failed to catch. Father and son waited a moment, then pushed open the door and peered out. Through the bank's front window they saw several riders galloping past, whooping and shooting into the air. Opening the window to shout for help, the Birds witnessed a chilling sight. George Wymore, a 19-year-old student at Liberty's William Jewell College, had been walking down the street to his classes. As the mounted men swept toward him, he ran to take cover. One rider fired four times, and young Wymore fell to the frozen ground, killed instantly. The men who later examined his body found that any one of the bullets would have been fatal—an awesome display of accuracy.

A posse of enraged townsmen, armed with the few weapons they could muster on the spot, rode after the robbers. Scraps of bank paper were found at a country church in which the men had paused to divide their

A model of youthful decorum, Jesse James seems a lad his Baptist-minister father would have been proud of—and even as an outlaw he retained a streak of piety. This photograph and those on pages 57 and 70-71 are published here for the first time.

55

loot. From there the trail led to a Missouri River ferry crossing, but a blizzard forced the posse to turn back.

The search was later pressed westward into Kansas, but it never touched a run-down little farm at Kearney, Missouri, only a single railroad stop north of Liberty. The farm belonged to Mrs. Zerelda Samuel, formerly the widow James. Her two sons by her first husband had recently come home from their service as Confederate guerrillas. Jesse James was thought by his neighbors to be recovering from a war wound. His older brother Frank was reported to be spending his days with his nose in a book instead of attending to chores. That the James boys had become the leaders of an outlaw gang was not known to the public until almost four years later, after their sixth bank holdup.

They would remain at large for 15 years, amassing a record of depredations that included holdups of 12 banks, seven trains and five stages in 11 states and territories. During that time, other gangs would imitate them, but none lasted nearly as long, and none approached them in notoriety or hell-bent originality. Starting with the holdup in Liberty, the James boys and their ever-changing cast of gang members continually redefined what gunfighters might dare and get away with.

They were innovators, but in a sense they were merely applying to private ends the wartime lessons they had learned as guerrilla fighters in Missouri and neighboring states and territories. Missouri's Confederate troops had crumbled early, and Union forces ruled the state after 1862; but guerrilla bands harassed the occupiers and raided unguarded towns until the war's end. In one notably bloodthirsty action, in August 1863, four hundred fifty raiders under the command of William Clarke Quantrill descended at dawn on Lawrence, Kansas, a base for sporadic Union attacks on Missouri border communities. The guerrillas shot every man and boy in sight, then put the town to the torch. Among those taking part in the assault, which was unparalleled in its savagery, was Frank James.

Frank was 20 at the time, a hawk-nosed, blue-eyed, sandy-haired young man with a square jaw and distinctively wide ears. He was about five feet ten inches tall, slender in build, slow in movement, laconic in speech; and he already had the scholarly turn of mind that made him an avid reader of Shakespeare and Francis Bacon. In 1864 he temporarily left Quantrill's command and joined a guerrilla band led by Bloody Bill Anderson. That same year, Jesse, then only 17, signed on with Anderson. Jesse was the live-wire leader of the two brothers. Also blue-eyed, with an upturned nose and thin, mobile lips, he was said to have the face of a schoolgirl, and he often batted his eyes like one—the result of a childhood eye affliction. He was slightly shorter and sturdier than Frank, and he had the sudden energy of a coiled spring. Anderson said of him: "He is the keenest and cleanest fighter in the command."

The supreme moment of the James boys' wartime service came when Anderson's 225 guerrillas raided Centralia, Missouri, on September 27, 1864. After pillaging the town, they halted a train of the Wabash, St. Louis & Pacific Railroad, took $3,000 from the small packages stacked in the express car, then gunned down 25 Union soldiers who were aboard as passengers. Later that day the guerrillas rode against 200 Union troops that had set out after them, and in a single charge up a grassy ridge slaughtered the enemy force almost to the last man. Jesse James shot the commander of the Union troops, and Frank James would remember the charge as one of the great events of his life. "The only battles in the world's history to surpass Centralia," he said years later, "are Thermopylae and the Alamo."

At the war's end, the Missouri guerrillas were denied amnesty; unlike regular Confederate soldiers, they went home as outlaws. Three and a half months after Lee's surrender at Appomattox, Frank James gave himself up at a federal army depot and was soon paroled. Jesse also tried to surrender but was shot in the chest by federal soldiers as he rode toward Lexington, Missouri, carrying a white flag to signal his intentions. Badly wounded, he escaped into a stand of woods. A farmer brought him into Lexington, where the federal commander in local charge paid a wagon driver to cart him home to die in peace. Back in Kearney, however, Jesse gradually healed. Within a few months he was attending Sunday services with his mother (even as a child he had a religious bent, once rising in church to ask the congregation to pray for his brother's soul). On weekdays Jesse passed the time with other guerrilla veterans, nursing grievances against the former enemy, telling tales of wartime daring—and planning a career of crime.

The three topics seemed to be related. The sense of grievance was deep-seated, for Union rule had been

Still neophytes at banditry, Frank and Jesse James flaunt their long-barreled revolvers. Frank *(left)*, the older by three years, was quiet and bookish, while Jesse, as a friend put it, was "reckless and devil-may-care."

In a ferocious assault on the pro-Union town of Lawrence, Kansas, in 1863, William Clarke Quantrill's Confederate guerrillas—Frank James among them—slaughtered 150 civilian men and boys, set homes ablaze, then got drunk amid the ruins. The terrorists were denied amnesty at war's end.

harsh in western Missouri. To rid the region of guerrillas, the Union commander had issued his notorious Order No. 11 *(page 60),* giving Confederate sympathizers in four border counties 15 days to quit the region. In their absence, their houses were razed, their crops burned and their possessions destroyed.

Yet the guerrillas had survived these drastic measures. Operating hundreds of miles from the nearest Confederate lines, outnumbered and ruthlessly hunted by Union troops, they had staged one successful raid after another. Recalling those exploits, the James boys and their friends realized that the same tactics could be put to the uses of an outlaw gang in peacetime.

Quantrill and Anderson had been masters of guerrilla warfare. Recruiting country boys already familiar with horses and guns, they had drilled their irregulars relentlessly in riding and marksmanship — until all of them could shoot as straight as the murderer of George Wymore at Liberty. Quantrill and Anderson had maintained elaborate intelligence networks to spot the enemy's concentrations and movements; the bank robbers at Liberty even knew the identities of the men who worked there. And the basic method of executing a guerrilla raid proved ideally suited to bandits on horseback: hit the target by surprise, with lightning swiftness, then scatter into the surrounding countryside and hole up in refuges that had been scouted in advance. After the James boys embarked on their career in crime, they never forsook their guerrilla habit of searching for hidden valleys where hunted men could pasture horses, and they kept an eye out for caves in which bands of men could, if necessary, live concealed for weeks.

Perhaps the most important requisite for guerrilla warfare was to win the support of people in the countryside — and the James brothers were to enjoy such support in abundance. Not only were they farm boys themselves, but they seemed to the Southern farmers to stand for the lost Confederate cause, gallant and defiant. The postwar years found these farmers desperately in need of loans to restore their ravaged lands; they came to hate the town bankers for tight money policies and high interest rates. When the James boys rode out against the banks, the best wishes of many Missourians went with them.

At the start it was not all easy going. After the St. Valentine's Day triumph at Liberty, the gang discov-

Order No. 11 and its legacy of hatred

Just four days after Lawrence, Kansas, was ravaged by Quantrill's Confederate guerrillas *(page 56),* the district Union commander, Brigadier General Thomas Ewing, retaliated by a drastic measure designed to cut off the raiders' grass-roots support in the bordering Missouri counties. Ewing's Order No. 11, issued on August 25, 1863, was an eviction notice of stunning scope. It gave civilians in three counties and part of a fourth just 15 days to leave their homes and quit Ewing's command, unless they could prove their loyalty to the Union cause —and few of them could.

Scarcely able to grasp what was happening to them, Missourians piled possessions into wagons and set off into the unknown. Chaos was compounded by nightmare when pro-Union guerrillas swept in from Kansas and, joined by some of General Ewing's troops, embarked on an orgy of looting, burning and murder. One Union officer, the painter George Caleb Bingham, was so sickened by the carnage that he told Ewing he would use his brush to make him infamous; five years later he produced the poignant scene below. (Frank James, who was a hidden witness to the sufferings of his fellow Missourians, saw Bingham's painting in later life and commented, "That is a picture that talks.")

Ewing's decree virtually wiped out an entire region: the population in Cass County dropped from 10,000 to 600, and Bates County was left all but empty. Yet his strategy of vengeance failed. The Confederate guerrillas subsisted easily on stray cattle and chickens; they retired from Missouri a few months later, but only because of the onset of cold weather. The following year the irregulars returned to operate with undiminished ferocity, enjoying more sympathy from outraged Missourians all across the state than ever before. And at the end of the Civil War, the natural heirs to this sympathy were the ex-guerrillas in the James gang, in whom many aggrieved citizens of the countryside were disposed to see a last unquenchable flame of the Confederate cause.

Smoke drifts over a scene of murder and pillage as General Thomas Ewing, mounted at left center, observes the execution of his Order No. 11.

ered that Missouri banks could be almost as stingy with robbers as with farmers. In October 1866 in the town of Lexington, four members of the gang, two with revolvers drawn, sauntered into the banking house of Alexander Mitchell & Company. They took some $2,000 from the cash drawer, then demanded the key to the vault. The cashier protested. There was less money in the vault than they thought, he assured them, and in any case he did not have the key. The outlaws checked his pockets, found no key, decided that shooting the cashier would not unlock the vault, and rode off with their disappointing haul.

The gang met resistance of a deadlier sort in Richmond, Missouri, the following May. By now word of their tactics had spread, and so when they galloped into the town square, yelling wildly and firing pistols in the air, a teller inside the Hughes & Wasson Bank hastily locked the bank door. While six of the gang held the town under siege, six others dismounted and splintered the lock with a bullet. Inside the bank, they quickly filled a sack with $4,000 in gold. But the getaway proved a problem. First, the Mayor of Richmond ran toward the bank with revolver in hand; the horsemen outside shot him down. Then the invaders rode toward the town jail, where a few former guerrillas were being held for continuing to advocate a Confederate secession. They came under fire from the jailer and his son. Hiding behind a large elm tree in the courthouse yard next to the jail, the jailer's son got off a few shots, until several horsemen sped past and caught him in their crossfire. Seeing him fall, the jailer made a desperate run toward him. Riddled with bullets, he died sprawled across his son's body. By then townspeople had begun shooting at the gang from nearby windows. With a final fusillade, the robbers drove them back from their windows and rode off—$4,000 richer.

All business in Richmond was suspended for three days as the dead were buried and heavily armed posses set out in pursuit of the outlaws. The hunt continued on and off for months, with night raids and gunfights as the hunters tracked down one or another suspect. The James boys themselves got away, but at least three of their comrades were caught and lynched.

The lynchings infuriated James sympathizers everywhere. When Bud Pence, a young suspect in the bank robbery, was arrested in his home in Kentucky at the re-

quest of Richmond officials, the *Louisville Courier* urged the Governor to refuse extradition. "If the Governor of Missouri cannot protect our citizens," the newspaper thundered, "then it is high time for the Governor of this State to refuse to surrender them." And by the time a Missouri sheriff arrived to take charge of the prisoner, Bud Pence had mysteriously escaped.

Perhaps because of this show of Kentucky tolerance, the James boys decided to visit the state. Early in 1868 they appeared at their uncle George Hite's farm, 11 miles from Russellville, seat of Logan County. George Shepherd, a friend from guerrilla days, lived nearby. When Shepherd showed Jesse and Frank around Russellville, the main point of interest turned out to be the bank. The three men decided to rob it and Shepherd rode off to Missouri to "get up a crowd."

The three recruits he brought back included another former companion-at-arms, a fleshy six-footer named Cole Younger. Now 24, Cole had taken part with Frank James in the Lawrence massacre; he was also said to have tested an Enfield rifle one day by firing it into the backs of several Yankee prisoners tied together and stacked against a tree—simply to see how many bodies one bullet would penetrate. He was on his mother's farm near Lee's Summit, hard at work, when George Shepherd came calling. Lee's Summit offered little excitement for a young war hero; Cole changed his overalls for a proper suit and headed for Kentucky.

Jesse and Frank James were delighted to see him, and picked him to lead the way into the Russellville bank. On March 20, 1868, wearing his city clothes, he presented the bank's aged president, Nimrod Long, with a $50 bill to change. As the banker examined the bill—a counterfeit—Cole drew a gun and held the muzzle to his head. "Surrender!" he snapped.

Long broke for the back door. Another member of the gang creased his scalp with a shot, then beat the old man to the floor with the barrel of his gun. "I cooked his hash," he said as he joined his companions in the vault. He was wrong. Long got to his feet, made it out the back door and ran to the front of the bank. The gang lookouts posted there fired at him, but he kept going down the street, shouting for help. A few armed citizens came on the run and firing, but the James gang easily shot their way out of town. As they galloped off, George Shepherd coolly took time to call to a bystander: "You needn't be particular about seeing my face so well you'd remember it again."

It was a warning he would have cause to regret. Russellville's first quick response was to form a large posse, with horses borrowed from buggies, wagons and hitching posts. The posse's search proved fruitless, but Russellville's bankers were a stubborn lot. Taking a novel tack, they hired a Louisville detective, D. G. Bligh, to investigate the crime — the first time the James gang had faced this experience. Bligh's sleuthing resulted in a raid by the law on the home of George Shepherd. Not one to give up easily, Shepherd was taken only after a gunfight and went off to jail for three years. But Frank and Jesse went home free to their mother in Clay County.

Widowed some years before the Civil War, and since remarried to a doctor from Kentucky, Zerelda Samuel was by all accounts an impressive woman. A reporter who interviewed her in later years described her as "graceful in carriage and gesture, calm and quiet in demeanor, with a ripple of fire now and then breaking through the placid surface." She was also pious and, soon after the Russellville robbery, she had the pleasure of seeing Jesse baptized in the Kearney Baptist Church. In preparation for this ritual, her son had prayed long and hard for the forgiveness of his sins. If any in the congregation questioned his resolve, they did not have to wait long to have their doubts confirmed. Within a year he had strayed from the path of righteousness, tempted by the prospect of a fine haul from the Daviess County Savings Bank at Gallatin, Missouri.

This robbery, in December 1869, was engineered by the two James boys alone, without benefit of a gang. While Frank held the horses outside, Jesse walked in and asked the cashier to change a $100 bill. The technique had worked in the past, but this time things went awry. As the cashier was changing the bill, Jesse's customary cool mien changed to black anger; he noticed that the man resembled the Yankee officer whose troops had killed Bloody Bill Anderson in the war. This unlucky coincidence cost the cashier his life. Jesse furiously wrenched the bill from the man's hand, shot him, scooped up $700 from the open safe and the cash drawer, and rushed into the street. Frank was exchanging shots with a dozen Gallatin citizens who had sped to the scene. As Jesse came out, Frank took off; but Jesse's mare, panicked by the gunfire, bolted just as he was springing into the saddle. His heel held fast in the stirrup, and he was dragged along the street about 30 feet, head downward, before he could get free. As the mare ran off, Frank wheeled his horse and galloped back into the face of the townspeople's fire, and Jesse leaped up behind him. It was the closest call yet for the brothers. A mile out of town they relieved a farmer of his horse and headed home in more comfortable fashion.

Jesse's wayward mare was soon identified, and the James boys — up to now only suspected — were openly branded as outlaws. A week after the Gallatin affair, they received their first mention by name in the Missouri press. Noting their careers as guerrillas, the *Kansas City Times* described them as "desperate men, having had much experience in horse and revolver work." Yet, though rewards totaling $3,000 were offered for their capture, Frank and Jesse were still at large six months later. Jesse even sent a letter to the *Times* denying that he had held up the Gallatin bank. Ever since the war, he wrote, "I have lived as a peaceable citizen, and obeyed the laws of the United States to the best of my knowledge."

With this dignified declaration of innocence, the James family launched what was, in effect, a public-relations campaign to keep popular opinion on their side. Each of the gang's subsequent exploits was followed by formal disclaimers, written by Jesse and sometimes personally delivered by his mother to the offices of Missouri newspapers. The editor of the *Kansas City Times,* a staunch Confederate sympathizer, obliged with editorials depicting Jesse and Frank as ex-heroes hounded by the authorities because of their wartime guerrilla activities.

Jesse and Frank also set out to enhance their public image by feats of showmanship worthy of their great contemporary, P. T. Barnum. Early in June 1871 the James gang robbed a bank at Corydon, Iowa, while most of the townspeople were outside a nearby Methodist church, listening to some political oratory. Having enriched themselves to the tune of $6,000, Jesse, Frank, Cole Younger and the rest of the gang then masked their faces with kerchiefs and rode over to the church. Jesse broke into the oration to inform the crowd: "We've just been down to the bank and taken every dollar in the till." As Corydon's citizens stood thun-

Like the James boys, the Youngers — Cole *(left)* and Jim — learned outlaw strategy as wartime Confederate guerrillas. Later, along with two other brothers, they proved to be the James gang's most reliable recruits.

derstruck, Jesse and his companions politely lifted their hats, gave out a few wild whoops and galloped off.

Jesse and Frank and 18-year-old Bob Younger — who had come to join his brother Cole — played to an even larger crowd at the Kansas City fairgrounds the following year. On the fair's biggest day the trio seized a cashbox from the ticket seller near the gate, then spurred their horses right through the throngs, shooting into the air as they went. When the pandemonium died down, it was reported that the robbers had made off with the day's receipts of $10,000, and that they had either shot or trampled a 10-year-old girl.

Even so, for the editor of the *Kansas City Times,* this escapade provided the occasion for an orgy of adulation. A front-page story proclaimed the holdup "a deed so high-handed, so diabolically daring and so utterly in contempt of fear that we are bound to admire it and revere its perpetrators." In a subsequent issue an editorial on "The Chivalry of Crime" hailed the gang as Missouri's version of the Knights of the Round Table.

Later the *Times* carried the usual letter from Jesse, with its bland denial that he or Frank had been anywhere near the fairgrounds at the time of the crime.

The James boys' wooing of the press and public had its desired effect: a growing army of detectives ran up against a stone wall of silence. By now the bankers of several states had called in the Pinkerton National Detective Agency *(page 73)* to aid in the hunt, but the men sent from Pinkerton headquarters in Chicago were poorly received in rural Missouri. As far as the farmers were concerned, the Pinkertons had been used by the Union armies to spy on Confederates and by the big corporations to spy on workers; now they were being used by the banks to spy on the James brothers. It was not a reputation likely to quell country people's ingrained suspicions of city slickers.

To make matters worse for the Pinkertons, they had no idea of what the James boys or the other members of the gang looked like. They had no photographs of Jesse or Frank, and the descriptions of the gang by their victims or by witnesses of their holdups were sketchy, inaccurate or conflicting. The hunters would not have recognized their quarry even if they had met face to face. Indeed, many a Clay County cracker-barrel session was enlivened by stories of how Jesse or Frank had stopped a detective along some road to strike up a casual conversation, then had offered a snippet of false information to lead the pursuer astray.

When Allan Pinkerton's operatives came up empty-handed in their initial efforts to nab the James gang, the head of the celebrated agency took it as a personal affront, and he soon set up a branch office in Kansas City to supervise the manhunt. In the summer of 1873, however, the James boys branched out too. Drawing on their guerrilla experience in halting and looting the train at Centralia in 1864, they decided to expand their operations from banks to railroads. On a curving stretch of the Rock Island line's tracks near Council Bluffs, Iowa, Jesse, Frank and five members of the gang pulled a rail out of line. Just as a train approached, the engineer, John Rafferty, spotted the sabotage and tried to stop, but the engine toppled off the tracks and was wrecked. The coaches piled into each other, injuring a dozen passengers, and Rafferty himself was crushed to death. The outlaws ransacked the coaches and the express car without finding what they were after; the big

Curiosity seekers of 1890 inspect a sandstone cave that was a boyhood haunt of the Younger brothers and a favored hideout during their outlaw days. Even as fugitives, the Youngers boldly ventured into the nearby Missouri resort town of Monegaw Springs to savor the spa's high life.

Secure in a forest fastness, the James gang plots a new robbery in this illustration from *Outlaws of the Border,* one of many 19th Century books that catered to the public's appetite for accounts of Western banditry.

shipment of gold they were looking for came through 12 hours later, on another train. For once, the gang had failed in advance intelligence work.

Allan Pinkerton found no satisfaction in the inadvertent foiling of the James boys. He was infuriated; the Iowa hijacking struck him as a direct and intolerable challenge. The James boys were well aware of the fact. Six months later, when the gang held up a train at Gads Hill, Missouri, one robber brought faint smiles to the frozen faces of the passengers by asking the conductor, "Where is Mr. Pinkerton?" And this time, the outlaws displayed considerably more expertise than they had on the first train job.

Gads Hill consisted of a few rude dwellings, a depot and a sawmill huddled beside the tracks of the Iron Mountain Railroad. Late in the afternoon of January 31, 1874, five men came riding in; their faces were masked by shoulder-length sheets of thin white cloth, secured by scarves wrapped round their necks and tied, turban-like, over their heads. They seized the station

agent, then pulled a switch that would send the soon-due southbound express onto the sawmill siding. To prevent the train from crashing into the end of the siding, one of the gang slowed its approach by waving a red flag, while the others hid nearby.

The engineer braked the locomotive just as it lurched onto the siding. The conductor jumped off to see what the trouble was and was promptly surrounded by outlaws with drawn revolvers. Sizing up the situation through the windows of the train, a railroad agent and the porter locked themselves in with the first-class passengers in the sleeping car. Fearful lest the robbers shoot down the door, the passengers insisted that it be opened. It was, and the first robber to enter went directly to the railroad agent, warning him to "dish out or be shot." The agent got the message and quickly produced his key to the baggage-car safe. Turning next to the passengers, the robber proved more forbearing—and unusually garrulous. He announced that he would examine each man's hands before taking his money, and that

66

His flanks protected by two confederates, a member of the James gang shoots down a fleeing clerk during a bank holdup. Another employee lies dead on the floor, while a third seeks escape through a back door.

only "plug hat gentlemen" would be robbed. "Hard-handed men have to work for their money," he explained, "the soft-handed ones are capitalists, professors and others that get money easy."

The train was on the siding for 40 minutes before the robbers were ready to leave. As they prepared to mount up, one of them had a final word with the conductor. "Give this to the newspaper," he said, and handed the conductor a note. It was, in effect, a news release written by Jesse in advance, deliberately misleading as to the robbers' physical appearance and with the amount of the haul understandably left blank, but otherwise surprisingly accurate:

THE MOST DARING ROBBERY ON RECORD

The southbound train on the Iron Mountain railroad was boarded here this evening by five heavily armed men and robbed of_____dollars. The robbers arrived at the station a few minutes before the arrival of the train and arrested the station agent and put him under guard, then threw the train on the switch. The robbers were all large men, none of them under six feet tall. They were all masked and started in a southerly direction after they had robbed the express. They were all mounted on fine, blooded horses. There is a hell of an excitement in this part of the country.

The sheer effrontery of this communiqué left the Pinkerton men with no doubts as to the culprits' identities. Five weeks after the holdup, a 26-year-old Pinkerton agent named John W. Whicher stopped at the town of Liberty, on his way to the Samuel farm at Kearney. He called on a local banker and a former sheriff to ask directions, explaining that he was going to seek work from Mrs. Samuel as a farm hand, then surprise her boys when they showed up. The two men tried to dissuade him. "The old woman will kill you if the boys don't," one warned. But Whicher caught a train to Kearney and was seen there that evening setting off on the four-mile walk to the farm. His body was found the

In a scene from *Life and Times of Jesse and Frank James,* their men round up valuables from train passengers. The book's author said it had been dictated by Jesse's wife and mother, a claim both denied.

following day, shot through the head and the heart.

Within a week, a shoot-out near Monegaw Springs, Missouri, claimed two more Pinkerton men. Three of them had paused at a house near the Springs, hoping to pick up a lead on the Youngers. Their queries were overheard by two men visiting there—none other than John and Jim Younger, who had joined their brothers Cole and Bob at the outlaw trade. When the three strangers rode off, the Youngers went after them and ordered them to halt. John Younger, 28, was carrying a double-barreled shotgun; Jim, 26, held a revolver. One of the detectives put spurs to his horse and fled down the road to safety; the other two stopped and dropped their revolvers to the ground.

"What are you doing in this part of the country?" one of the Youngers asked. "Just rambling around," replied detective Louis Lull of Chicago. "You've been at the Springs, asking for us," the outlaw snapped. "We've been at the Springs, but we weren't asking for you 'cause we don't know you," the detective protested.

Lull's partner, Edwin Daniel, broke in to insist that he was no detective. (He was, in fact, a former sheriff's deputy from Osceola, Missouri, hired by the Pinkertons for his knowledge of the countryside.) "Then what in hell are you riding around here with all them pistols for?" Jim Younger asked.

Suddenly, Lull reached behind his back, drew a spare pistol and shot John Younger through the neck. John's shotgun roared almost simultaneously; Lull dropped from his saddle into the bushes at the roadside, fatally hit. A moment later John Younger toppled from his horse and lay, unmoving, in the road. Daniel spurred his horse; Jim Younger raced after him and killed him with a single bullet. He then galloped back to the house where he and his brother had been staying, asked his hosts to bury John's body, and vanished.

The murder of three Pinkerton men within a single week created a political crisis for Missouri officialdom. Republicans who ruled neighboring Kansas howled about the "disgrace of Missouri." In reply, Missouri's

Democratic press could only rake up resounding but well-worn political clichés. "Robbers in Democratic Missouri are outlaws," complained the *Kansas City Times,* "while robbers in Radical Kansas are elected to the highest offices in the State."

But something more than rhetoric was clearly needed. The Missouri legislature appropriated $10,000 for a force of armed secret agents, directly responsible to Governor Silas Woodson and dedicated solely to the pursuit of the James gang in Missouri. This decision for law and order was by no means clear-cut; more than a third of the legislators refused to vote on the appropriation. Another appropriation, for pensioning the widows and orphans of anyone "who shall hereafter be killed in attempting to arrest the Younger and James brothers," was not even put to a vote; and a bill to mobilize the state militia against the gang failed to pass.

Still, Governor Woodson now had his secret agents. What he did not know was that the quarry had left the state. In April 1874, Cole Younger and his surviving brothers went to Dallas, Texas. The Youngers were not unknown there. On a visit eight years earlier, Cole had caused a scandal by his dalliance with 18-year-old Myra Belle Shirley, daughter of a prominent horse breeder who had been expelled form Missouri during the Civil War as a Confederate supporter. Myra Belle had borne Cole a daughter. By the time he reappeared in Dallas, she had been twice married—first to a Texas horse thief, then, after he was killed, to a dashing Cherokee desperado named Sam Starr—and now she was riding her way to notoriety as Belle Starr, the Bandit Queen of the Indian Territory *(page 162).*

Despite Cole's earlier peccadilloes, the Youngers acquired a gloss of respectability during their two-year stay in Dallas. On several occasions, needing money, they returned to Missouri to take part in the James gang's raids on banks and trains. But the Dallas County district attorney, in an affidavit for the Pinkertons, attested to the propriety of the Youngers' way of life in Texas. "Cole, Bob, and Jim Younger sang in the choir

69

Standing amid their recruits, Jesse *(right)* and Frank James take a breather between holdups on an Iowa farm owned by ex-Missourians.

70

of the Baptist Church," he avowed. "The boys were often called on by the sheriff to assist in the arrest of desperate characters and they always responded."

After the Pinkerton slayings in 1874, Jesse and Frank James also disappeared from Missouri, returning only long enough to attend their own weddings. In April, Jesse married a childhood sweetheart, his cousin Zee Mimms, culminating a nine-year engagement that at times had seemed almost to have escaped his attention. Jesse and his bride went off to Texas for their honeymoon. Meanwhile, Frank was courting Annie Ralston, the daughter of a Missouri farmer. In June, Annie took a train to Kansas City—to visit relatives, she said—and soon a letter arrived at the Ralston home. It was the tersest of wedding announcements: "Dear Mother, I am married and going West."

Though Frank James liked to quote Francis Bacon's celebrated observation that a man with a wife and children has given hostages to fortune, domesticity made little difference in the lives or reputations of the James brothers. In the two years following their marriages, they were credited with holding up stages in Texas and Missouri, trains in Kansas and Missouri, and banks in Mississippi and West Virginia. That they personally presided at all these affairs was not proved, but their names—as well as those of the Younger brothers—inevitably came up when any other known member of their gang was identified or suspected. By now, the gang had become a large, loose fraternity of former guerrillas who converged from Missouri, Kansas, Kentucky, Arkansas and Texas whenever the James boys sent word that they were ready to make a "raise." Undoubtedly these gunmen were not averse to doing an occasional job on their own, but the public was interested in them only as bit players in the riveting saga of the James and Younger boys.

Just when it seemed that the gang could do no more to increase their fame, or their legions of admirers, the Pinkertons did it for them. The agency finally planted a "farm hand"—a Pinkerton agent named Jack Ladd—on a property owned by one Daniel Askew across the road from the Samuel place at Kearney. From his employer's porch Ladd could see Mrs. Samuel's front yard. In January 1875 he spotted the James boys there; and on January 26th a special night train brought in a force of detectives. Surrounding the Samuel house, they

tossed a round metal object into it. The nature of the object was never positively determined. James partisans insisted it was a grenade; the Pinkertons said it was merely a flare, intended to illuminate the interior of the house. What is certain is that a member of the family shoveled the object into the fireplace and that it exploded with a blinding flash. Mrs. Samuel's right forearm was all but torn off, later requiring amputation; her son by her marriage to the doctor, nine-year-old Archie, was killed by a fragment of the metal casing.

Zerelda Samuel fought back with her own special weapon—skillful propaganda. She let it be known far and wide that Jesse and Frank had not even been at home when the Pinkertons attacked. An outraged public saw the James boys in a new light—as martyrs. Not helpless martyrs, however: a few months after the raid, farmer Askew was shot to death on his doorstep.

If the James boys could do no wrong, the Pinkertons could do no right. Increasingly hated, they dropped all pretense of stealth. After the gang held up the Missouri Pacific Railroad at Rocky Cut, Missouri, in July 1876, the detectives carried out raids in several parts of the state, surrounding possible houses of refuge, routing out the inmates, and in one case causing the death of a woman when a Pinkerton gun went off accidentally. Missourians viewed such desperation tactics with mounting ire and sometimes with contempt. Such was the case when 12 Pinkertons descended on the farm of Annie Ralston's father, hoping to nab Annie's husband, Frank James. They burst into the house at daybreak and conducted a search. It was not only a futile search but, as everyone except the Pinkertons knew, a pointless one. Ralston would hardly have harbored Frank James; he was not even on speaking terms with the man who had stolen his daughter.

Still, the Pinkertons' increasing harassment of friends, neighbors and relatives of the James boys—as well as of the Younger brothers—helped bring the gang to a fateful turning point: they decided to expand their operations farther afield. In August 1876, Jesse, Frank and the three Youngers—Cole, Jim and Bob—boarded a train for Minnesota, some 370 miles from Clay County, and farther north in Yankee country than the travelers had ever before ventured. Accompanying them were three outlaws: Clell Miller and Charlie Pitts —both veterans of Quantrill's guerrilla force—and a na-

ALLAN PINKERTON, PRINCIPAL.
GEO. H. BANGS, Gen'l Sup't.
Robert A. Pinkerton, Sup't., 66 EXCHANGE PLACE NEW YORK.
Benj. Franklin, Sup't., 45 SOUTH THIRD STREET. PHILADELPHIA
F. Warner, Sup't., 191 & 193 FIFTH AVENUE. CHICAGO.
W. A. Pinkerton, " " "
Clarence A. Seward, Attorney and Counsel for the Agency, 29 NASSAU St. NEW YORK.

PINKERTON'S NATIONAL
We never sleep.
DETECTIVE AGENCY.

Allan Pinkerton in 1867

When the desperate bankers of the border states hired Allan Pinkerton to pit his army of sleuths against the James gang in 1871, they figured their troubles with holdups were over. In the detective business, Pinkerton had no peer. He once wrote to an aide, "I do not know the meaning of the word 'fail.' Nothing in hell or heaven can influence me when I know that I am right."

Pinkerton had honed his skills for this epic manhunt in a variety of secretive pursuits. In his native Scotland he had been a revolutionary agitator for workingmen's reforms, escaping arrest only by emigrating in 1843. Settling in Illinois, he turned ardent abolitionist and smuggled many a runaway slave to safety in Canada. His relish for undercover work next prompted him to join the Chicago police force as its first detective; after cracking a counterfeit ring and scoring other successes, he formed his own detective force in 1850.

The agency quickly won fame for daring new methods, including a form of psychological warfare against its quarry. In one case, the murder of a bank teller in 1856, Pinkerton assigned a detective who startlingly resembled the dead man to shadow a suspect named Drysdale. Hounded day and night by this specter, Drysdale broke down, confessed and committed suicide. Such tactics caused criminals everywhere to fear Pinkerton. They dubbed him "The Eye," a name suggested by the agency's symbol (above) — and that later gave rise to the term "private eye."

Another innovation — supplying the Illinois Central Railroad with a guard force — led to a dream assignment for the agency chief. Pinkerton's contacts with the railroad included an ambitious executive and a backwoods lawyer, later better known, respectively, as General George McClellan and President Abraham Lincoln. Through their offices, a Major E. J. Allen — one of Pinkerton's many aliases — was appointed in 1861 to set up a secret service for the Union Army. He deployed his spies skillfully and, when they sniffed out a plot to assassinate Lincoln on a train from Baltimore to Washington, Pinkerton personally thwarted the attempt by putting the President on an earlier train.

In the wake of these activities, the Pinkerton agency came to be widely regarded as a minion of Northern big business and an unofficial branch of the federal government. The Pinkerton men were especially loathed by poor and unreconstructed Confederates of the border states, who balked the hunt of the James gang at every turn — and, for once, Allan Pinkerton learned the meaning of failure.

Despite the agency's inability to break up the James gang, its list of successes lengthened steadily, even after the founder's death in 1884. His sons William and Robert, whom he had trained to continue the detective dynasty, enjoyed a particularly satisfying triumph in 1896, when Pinkerton men bested the infamous Wild Bunch in a shoot-out; later, the leaders of the gang, Butch Cassidy and the Sundance Kid, would have to flee to South America. And the organization William and Robert left to their own sons in time was to serve as a model for a new federal agency — the F.B.I.

tive Minnesotan, Bill Chadwell. Indeed, the idea for the trip had come from Chadwell, who had described his home state's banks with contagious enthusiasm.

In Minnesota the gang made a grand tour, mostly by rail, visiting at least 10 cities. They posed as a party of land speculators and cattle traders, a cover that enabled them to size up banks and explore routes of escape. But they were in no particular hurry; in St. Paul, Jesse took the boys to a brothel run by Mollie Ellsworth, who remembered him from earlier days in a St. Louis establishment, and the outlaws also visited a gambling house. They dropped $200 at the tables, but the loss was evidently no problem. Shopping around at several livery stables, they produced enough money to buy the best horses, saddles, bridles and bits they could find. Then the gang left the city in pairs, making a long, lazy horseback trip southward along the Minnesota River to the town of Mankato, a thriving county seat.

Jesse and three of the other outlaws rode into Mankato together. One of them visited the First National Bank and reported favorably on its prospects as a target. The bank was spared, however, by an unexpected turn of events. As Jesse rode down the main street, a laborer who had once lived in Missouri hailed him. "Hallo, Jesse, what are you doing up here?" he called. Jesse paused, and smiled. "Hell, man, I don't know you," he said, and—signaling his cohorts to follow him —rode on, leaving Mankato behind. Instead, the robbers made their way toward the town of Northfield —and the biggest shoot-out of their lives.

Cole Younger and Bill Chadwell went ahead to survey the situation. Asking around as to whether the town had any gun shops, they were told there were none. They then visited the town's two hardware stores and examined their meager stocks of weapons, took a quick look at the First National Bank, and departed. At a rendezvous that night at an inn outside of Northfield, the gang agreed that the time and place were right.

On the morning of September 7, 1876, the men set out for Northfield, trotting at a leisurely clip, clad in the linen dusters that cattlemen customarily wore. Jesse on a striking white-legged sorrel, and Bob Younger and Charlie Pitts on handsome bays, were the first to reach town. They dismounted in Mill Square, at the foot of a small iron bridge that spanned the Cannon River, and looked around. Dominating the far end of the square

was a two-story stone building called the Scriver Block. One of the stores it housed, facing the square, was the big general merchandise firm of Lee & Hitchcock, its sign proclaiming "Good Goods Cheap!" Another Scriver Block tenant was the First National Bank; but only its small back door led to the square—the front entrance was around the corner on Division Street. The three outlaws walked around to the front of the bank and surveyed the places across the street from which trouble might come: Wheeler & Blackman's drugstore, a small hotel called the Dampier House and a row of commercial buildings.

Satisfied that Younger and Chadwell had not overlooked any potential hazards the day before, Jesse, Bob and Charlie repaired to J. G. Jeft's restaurant across the bridge. They ordered ham and eggs—four eggs per man —and lingered over the meal. Shortly after two in the afternoon they rode back across the bridge.

This time the three outlaws dismounted on Division Street, hitching their horses directly in front of the bank. For a few minutes they stood at the door; then, suddenly, three more horsemen came clattering over the bridge, through Mill Square and onto Division Street, shooting and whooping as they rounded the corner. From the opposite end of Division Street came two more horsemen, charging. As terrified bystanders scattered, Jesse, Bob and Charlie rushed into the bank, shouting "Throw up your hands!" The cashier, Joseph Heywood, and the clerks, A. E. Bunker and Frank Wilcox, turned to see the three climbing the counter with revolvers in hand. Heywood ran for the vault; Charlie reached it first. Heywood tried to slam the vault door shut on Pitts, but at that instant Jesse got there and spotted the safe inside.

"Open it," he demanded.

"It has a time lock. It can't be opened," the cashier protested.

"That's a damned lie," Jesse shouted, and with his revolver he struck Heywood to the floor.

Bob Younger, meanwhile, had ordered the two clerks to get down on their knees, demanding the whereabouts of the cash drawer. Bunker pointed to it. Then, while Younger examined the rolls of coins and loose bills in the till, Bunker made a dash for the bank's back door. Whirling from the vault, Charlie Pitts took a shot at him, missed, rushed to the door and fired again, winging

In 1870, six years before the James gang's bungled bank holdup, Northfield, Minnesota, wears the air of a tranquil mill town. Citizens on routine errands cross the bridge that would be used by the invading bandits, while others chat near the bank, housed in the building with arched windows.

Beset on all sides by unexpectedly combative townsmen, members of the James gang gallop about Northfield in confusion. Two bandits lie dead, and a third—his horse shot—takes cover beneath a staircase.

A souvenir card of the battle of Northfield memorializes a trio of townsmen (top) killed in the fray; the three Younger brothers, all taken alive; and three less lucky cohorts, who were photographed in death.

Bunker as he raced down a stairway to the back alley.

At the front of the bank, on Division Street, the five mounted lookouts found themselves under unexpected fire. Their blazing six-shooters had failed to cow Northfield's citizens; despite the shortage of weapons, the townsfolk were putting up a stiff fight with a few rifles and shotguns hastily commandeered from the two hardware stores. One man, Elias Stacy, raced to Division Street and fired at Clell Miller. In the excitement Stacy had loaded his shotgun with light bird shot, but the blast knocked Miller from his horse. His face badly bleeding, the outlaw mounted again and charged.

It looked like certain death for Stacy, but young Henry Wheeler intervened. A medical student on vacation from the University of Michigan, Henry had been in his father's drugstore across from the bank when the shooting started. Remembering an old army carbine that was in the baggage room of the Dampier House next door, he ran into the hotel, found the gun and carried it into an upstairs front room. From there he saw Clell Miller riding hard at Stacy. Henry fired, and the

outlaw again fell from his horse. Cole Younger galloped up, dismounted and spoke to him. Miller tried to raise himself on his arms, then rolled over, dead. Younger seized his cartridge belt and pistols and sped off.

In the midst of the shooting a Swedish immigrant, newly arrived in Northfield, blundered up Division Street toward the bank. One of the horsemen shouted at him to get out of the way; uncomprehending, the Swede plodded on and was shot through the head. Suddenly a single shot shattered the silence inside the bank. On the way out, Jesse had passed the cashier lying dazed on the floor. He abruptly turned back, put his revolver to the man's temple and blew his brains out.

As the robbers rushed out and mounted up, it was plain that the usual quick getaway was out of the question. Northfield's citizens were seeing to that. Elias Stacy had run up an outside stairway at the corner of the Scriver Block, ducked inside and, from a window on Division Street, was still blasting bird shot at the invaders. From the stairway itself, hardware merchant A. E. Manning leveled a Remington repeating rifle at

Bill Chadwell as he rode down the street. Manning took aim—"as cool as though he was picking off a squirrel," one witness later said—and toppled Chadwell from his saddle with a bullet through the heart. Another shot from Manning's rifle hit Cole Younger in the shoulder at the same time young Henry Wheeler, firing from the hotel window, blew the hat off Cole's head.

By now the gunfire on Division Street had become general. Frank James was hit in the leg and Jim Younger in the face; blood gushed from his mouth. Still, the gang went on riding up and down the street, shooting into doors and windows. Bob Younger leaped from his horse, took cover behind it and aimed at merchant Manning on the Scriver Block stairway. Manning drew a bead on the head of the handsome bay and shot it down. Younger dodged behind a stack of boxes, but he was still in the view of Henry Wheeler in his perch upstairs at the Dampier House. Henry fired his carbine and hit Younger in the right thigh.

Suddenly an outlaw shouted, "We are beat, let's go!" Bob Younger limped out into the street, calling "Hold on, don't leave me! I'm shot!" Cole Younger wheeled back just as another Northfield man discharged a load of buckshot that shattered Bob's right elbow. Lifting Bob onto his own horse, Cole raced after his friends as they clattered across the Cannon River bridge.

In about 20 minutes, the people of Northfield had virtually destroyed the gang that had held the nation spellbound for a decade. Six of the eight robbers had escaped alive—but a further reckoning impended. After the shoot-out, telegrams alerted the entire state and hundreds of Minnesotans set out to finish the job Northfield had started. The outlaws were soon spotted riding through the nearby village of Dundas. Bob Younger had his shattered elbow in a sling. Jim Younger was bandaged about the mouth with strips torn from his linen duster. Frank James had tied a cloth around his leg.

With posses combing the woods, guards posted at bridges and mounted men patrolling the roads, the gang made only halting progress. Four days after the raid, when a posse flushed them from a wooded ravine, they had covered only 15 miles. Still, they held off their pursuers. After a few more days and several inconclusive skirmishes, they were reported in the Blue Earth Woods, heading for Mankato. At that point the gang split up. Jesse—who had come through the Northfield

episode unhurt—took off with Frank late at night on a single horse, breaking through a line of armed pickets. One of the pickets fired a shot that passed through Frank's knee and lodged in Jesse's thigh. They rode on, stole two horses from a farmer and headed toward the Dakota Territory. Once, when they stopped for a meal at an isolated farmhouse, they were so stiff-legged that they were able to remount only by climbing a fence and sliding sideways onto their horses.

A few days after the James boys left, the Youngers and Charlie Pitts were trapped in a thicket of willows and plum trees near Madelia, about 25 miles west of Mankato. They fought on until only Bob Younger was left standing. Finally he cried out, "The boys are all shot to pieces. For God's sake, don't kill me!" Charlie Pitts was dead; all three Youngers were wounded. The brothers were taken into custody, sure that they would be lynched. They seemed almost grateful when a Minnesota judge sentenced them to life imprisonment.

Jesse and Frank James made it to the Dakota Territory; their trail vanished near Sioux Falls. There the fiasco of Northfield had an appropriate sequel. The James boys stole two horses from a farmer's yard. One of the horses was blind in one eye, the other blind in both eyes. Nevertheless the brothers escaped on them.

After that wry finish to their Minnesota venture, Jesse and Frank adopted an underground way of life. They tried to revive their gang with new recruits and did manage to rob three trains in later years, but their great days were over. Their chief feat was simply to remain at large year after year, still possessing a certain flamboyance, a certain style.

A few months after the Northfield raid, Jesse turned up in his home state. At Fulton he visited Dr. Martin Yates to be treated for the gunshot wound in his thigh. The doctor and the outlaw dined that evening at Fulton's Whaley Hotel—sharing a large table with several Pinkerton men on the hunt for Jesse James. For Jesse, it was a characteristic bit of bravado, the kind that always delighted him. Later, in Louisville, Kentucky, he ran into D. G. Bligh—the first detective ever hired to hunt the James gang. Jesse chatted with the unsuspecting Bligh and subsequently sent him a postcard, informing him that he had met up with Jesse James at last.

For years, detectives and secret state agents searched for the James brothers in Kentucky, Texas and their na-

80

While his brother stands ready to help, turncoat Bob Ford murders Jesse James as the unarmed outlaw tidies a picture in his home. This re-creation of the scene erred in one respect: the killer fired while seated.

JESSE JAMES AS AN ANGEL.

tive Missouri. The sheriff of Clay County spent more nights than he cared to count shivering behind bushes near the Samuel farm. But Jesse and Frank generally avoided their former haunts. When they did visit Missouri, they usually stayed in Kansas City. "The best hiding place in the world for a man with money is some big city," Frank James told a newspaper interviewer long afterward. "Most people look alike there."

For everyday living the brothers chose Nashville, Tennessee. Jesse and his wife rented a house on Boscobel Street, in East Nashville, where he was known as J. D. Howard and thought to be a wheat speculator. As B.J. Woodson, Frank lived with his wife on a small farm nearby. Mr. Howard and Mr. Woodson were sometimes away from home for weeks at a time, but their absences never aroused suspicion among their neighbors, for both seemed respectable family men. Soon after settling in Nashville, Jesse and Zee had their first child, a son they named Jesse Edwards; Annie bore Frank a son, Robert, in 1878. A year later Zee gave birth to a daughter, named Mary.

In October 1879, Jesse returned to Missouri to attempt a comeback. At a farm east of Clay County, he expounded on the art of robbing trains to a hastily recruited gang and handed out shotguns and masks. On the night of October 8 the outlaws held up the Chicago & Alton Railroad at Glendale, Missouri, making off with $6,000. Jesse then returned to Tennessee —but a dirt-poor farmer who had joined in the raid was identified and arrested. He soon confessed to his part in the robbery and named Jesse James as his leader.

The confession signaled the beginning of the end for the James boys. When they could no longer inspire fear or loyalty in their own confederates, the result was inevitable. In 1881 they made a last, desperate effort to revive their reputation in Missouri. That July they held up a Chicago, Rock Island and Pacific train near Winston, killing the conductor and a passenger. Two months later they halted and held up a Chicago &

Alton train at Blue Cut, Missouri, beating the railroad agent senseless after he opened the safe for them. Before he left the train, Jesse—still showing the old flair—pressed two silver dollars into the engineer's hand and said, "Here is two dollars for you to drink the health of Jesse James tomorrow morning."

Several members of the gang were tracked down and talked freely. From them, the authorities began to get a picture of rivalries and disarray in the new James ranks. Missouri's Governor Thomas Crittenden set out to exploit the opportunity. He persuaded the railroads to put up a $5,000 reward for any member of the gang—with an additional $5,000 each for Jesse and Frank. The offer soon had its effect on two brothers who had become recent recruits of the gang.

Early in 1882 one of them, Bob Ford, told Governor Crittenden that he was an acquaintance of Jesse James and wanted to assist in his capture. He had met Jesse through a mutual friend, Dick Liddil, another gang member who was quietly negotiating his own surrender terms and was soon to give himself up. Bob Ford, a wiry 21-year-old, met with the sheriff of Clay County and together they formed a plan. Ford was to stay in Jesse's confidence for the time being. That might not be easy; when the news got out that Dick Liddil had surrendered, Jesse was certain to become suspicious of Liddil's friend Bob Ford. But before that happened—if the plan worked as it was supposed to—Ford would tip off the sheriff on the time and place of the gang's next job.

In November of 1881, Jesse, still under the pseudonym of Howard, had moved his wife and children to St. Joseph, Missouri, where they settled into a small hilltop house with a commanding view of the street approaches. Jesse was restive; perhaps he sensed that the law was closing in on him. When, in late March of 1882, two friendly faces appeared—Bob Ford and his brother Charlie—he welcomed them warmly and put them up at his home. Charlie was in on Bob's plan, and eager to help. But he was to be only an onlooker on April 3, when the incredible finally happened. ◉

Though right-handed himself, Bob Ford strikes a left-handed pose with a revolver in imitation of Jesse James, whom he had recently slain. Ten years afterward Ford was shot to death by a James partisan.

This bank and another across Coffeyville's main street were the Daltons' twin targets.

Bloody fiasco at Coffeyville

Even after justice of one sort or another caught up with the James gang, the celebrity they had achieved inspired a slew of imitators. Among them were the Dalton brothers—Bob, Emmett and Gratton. Cousins of the Youngers, the Daltons grew up outside the sleepy burg of Coffeyville, Kansas, where their famous kinsmen and the James boys were the local heroes.

Forming a gang of their own in 1890, the Daltons pulled off a number of unspectacular train robberies, then hatched a scheme that seemed certain to win them headlines: they would be the first gang to rob two banks simultaneously—and in their own hometown. When the brothers and two henchmen rode into Coffeyville on October 5, 1892, their plan went awry immediately. The street where the two banks stood was under repair, and they had to hitch their horses half a block away. They donned stage mustaches and goatees as disguises, but townspeople recognized them nevertheless. Hardware dealers began handing out firearms to merchants and passersby.

At the First National Bank, two of the Daltons extracted $20,000 from employees. But across the street at Condon & Co., the three other robbers were balked by a wily teller who persuaded them that the vault had a time lock and could not be opened. As the two contingents ran for their horses, they were met by withering gunfire. Though the gang managed to kill four townsmen, two of the Daltons and both henchmen were cut down, and a third Dalton brother was badly wounded. They had earned their headlines at last —a cascade of them *(left)*, recording a debacle no gang would ever surpass.

84

Shattered windows and pocked walls attest to the fire power directed at the bandits even before they emerged from Condon & Co.

The gang's corpses lie piled in the street, a morbid spectacle for passersby. Sole survivor Emmett Dalton served 15 years in prison.

Cole Younger, paroled after serving 25 years in a Minnesota prison for the botched Northfield robbery, enjoyed a lucrative second career as a lecturer on penitent themes like the one advertised in this handbill.

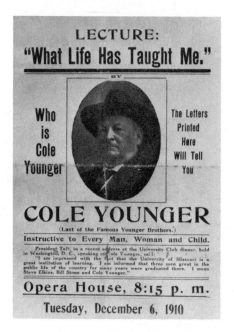

LECTURE:
"What Life Has Taught Me."
BY
Who is Cole Younger

The Letters Printed Here Will Tell You

COLE YOUNGER
(Last of the Famous Younger Brothers.)
Instructive to Every Man, Woman and Child.

Opera House, 8:15 p. m.
Tuesday, December 6, 1910

With a surprising gift for simple graphic narrative, Bob Ford later described the event in a report to Governor Crittenden. No one has ever bettered his account:

"On the morning of April 3, Jess and I went downtown, as usual, before breakfast, for the papers. We got to the house about eight o'clock and sat down in the front room. Jess was sitting with his back to me, reading the St. Louis *Republican.* I picked up the *Times,* and the first thing I saw in big headlines was the story about Dick Liddil's surrender. Just then Mrs. James came in and said breakfast was ready. Beside me was a chair with a shawl on it, and as quick as a flash I lifted it and shoved the paper under. Jess couldn't have seen me, but he got up, walked over to the chair, picked up the shawl and threw it on the bed, and taking the paper, went out to the kitchen. I felt that the jig was up, but I followed and sat down at the table opposite Jess.

"Mrs. James poured out the coffee and then sat down at one end of the table. Jesse spread the paper on the table in front of him and began to look over the headlines. All at once Jess said: 'Hello, here. The surrender of Dick Liddil.' And he looked across at me with a glare in his eyes.

"'Young man, I thought you told me you didn't know that Dick Liddil had surrendered,' he said.

"I told him I didn't know it.

"'Well,' he said, 'it's very strange. He surrendered three weeks ago and you was right there in the neighborhood. It looks fishy.'

"He continued to glare at me, and I got up and went into the front room. In a minute I heard Jess push his chair back and walk to the door. He came in smiling, and said pleasantly: 'Well, Bob, it's all right, anyway.'

"Instantly his real purpose flashed upon my mind. I knew I had not fooled him. He was too sharp for that. He knew at that moment as well as I did that I was there to betray him. But he was not going to kill me in the presence of his wife and children. He walked over to the bed, and deliberately unbuckled his belt, with four revolvers in it, and threw it on the bed. It was the first time in my life I had seen him without that belt on, and I knew that he threw it off to further quiet any suspicions I might have.

"He seemed to want to busy himself with something to make an impression on my mind that he had forgotten the incident at the breakfast table, and said: 'That picture is awful dusty.' There wasn't a speck of dust that I could see on the picture, but he stood a chair beneath it and then got upon it and began to dust the picture on the wall.

"As he stood there, unarmed, with his back to me, it came to me suddenly, 'Now or never is your chance. If you don't get him now he'll get you tonight.' Without further thought or a moment's delay I pulled my revolver and leveled it as I sat. He heard the hammer click as I cocked it with my thumb and started to turn as I pulled the trigger. The ball struck him just behind the ear and he fell like a log, dead."

Bob Ford was quickly tried before a jury of St. Joseph citizens. He pleaded guilty and was sentenced to death. Two hours after the sentencing, a telegraphed pardon arrived from Governor Crittenden. A few months later Frank James, certain that he too would be assassinated, sent a letter to the Governor offering to surrender in exchange for a pardon. The Governor pointed out that he could not pardon Frank for crimes of which he had not been convicted but gave his assurance of a fair trial and settled down to wait.

On October 5, 1882, Crittenden summoned reporters and aides to his office for an important announcement. When all were assembled, Frank James calmly walked into the room. "Governor," he said, "I am Frank James. I surrender my arms to you. I have removed the loads from them. They have not been out of my possession since 1864. I now give them to you personally. I deliver myself to you and the law."

Frank was taken by train to a jail at Independence. Cheering crowds thronged the stations along the route.

An equally canny merchandiser of his past, Frank James—here a spry 70—plays host at his birthplace. Tourists plunked down money not only to see the outlaw shrine but to buy pebbles from Jesse's grave.

A St. Louis newspaper wondered whether Frank had surrendered to Missouri or the state had surrendered to him. He was arrested for the murder of a passenger during the train robbery at Winston, and was tried in a packed opera house at Gallatin—scene of the gang's bank holdup 14 years earlier. The state that had failed to capture Frank failed to convict him. For the last time, the people of Missouri sheltered the man they remembered as a hero in the war for the Confederacy.

Even before testimony was taken, Prosecutor William Wallace saw how his case would go. Looking at the jury panel, he said: "The verdict of the jury that is being selected is already written." The trial contained an element of farce. When Confederate General Joseph O. Shelby, summoned as a character witness, was asked to identify Frank, he called loudly, "Where is my old friend and comrade in arms? Ah, there I see him! Allow me, I wish to shake hands with my fellow soldier who fought by my side for Southern rights!" After so

stirring a declaration, mere facts seemed trivial—in rural Missouri, at least—and facts were all the prosecutor had to offer. Frank James was acquitted.

He was 40 at the time and lived for 32 more years, long enough to see many other outlaws try to emulate the exploits of the James gang. The West was still alive with badmen, eager to prove themselves more daring than the first and most notorious outlaws. But Frank James had nothing more to prove. The only shots he ever fired again came from the gun he used as a starter at race tracks and county fairs—one of a variety of jobs he took to earn his livelihood.

In time he emerged as a minor political philosopher, berating the bankers and corporations he had once so effectively robbed. "If there is ever another war in this country," he said in 1897, "it will be between capital and labor. I mean between greed and manhood. And I'm as ready to march now in defense of American manhood as I was when a boy in defense of the South."

87

By the 1890s, plays about the James gang were being churned out by the dozen, most of them as cavalier with the truth as the one

advertised by this poster, in which Jesse (*left*) holds lawmen at bay with the aid of a black accomplice and a gun-toting blonde.

Butch Cassidy's Wild Bunch: last of the old-time gangs

In 1866, the same year Jesse James led his gang's first raid against a Missouri bank, a child who was to be the last of the Western gang leaders was born in Beaver, Utah. His name was Robert LeRoy Parker, later changed to Butch Cassidy in token of admiration for a friend, Mike Cassidy, who had taught him the fine arts of rustling and horse theft. Like the James boys, he came from a family with a devout religious tradition, but grew up observing few strictures of his faith.

As a youth, Butch joined a gang whose members included Bill McCarty, rumored to have been a James gang veteran. After participating in train and bank holdups, the neophyte drifted off on his own. In 1893 he was arrested for stealing a horse and spent a year and a half in the Rawlins, Wyoming, penitentiary—without chastening effect. Released at the age of 30, Cassidy promptly formed his own gang. After Cassidy's men had robbed a bank, lifted a mining camp payroll and pulled off a series of rustling successes, local newspapers honored their prowess by calling them the Wild Bunch.

In one sense, the label was misleading, for Cassidy himself made it a lifelong point to avoid needless violence. When pursued by posses, he shot at the horses, never at the riders. He said, apparently truthfully, "I have never killed a man." He ran his gang dem-ocratically, asking members' advice on projects. Even the wanted posters described him as "cheery and affable."

But in the flair they displayed in action, the Wild Bunch lived up to their name—particularly after they turned their attention to trains. At 2:30 a.m. on June 2, 1899, near Wilcox, Wyoming, they used a warning lantern to halt the Union Pacific's Overland Limited. The gang detached the express car and set a stick of dynamite underneath—enough to open it like an egg crate but not enough to maim the stubborn guard inside. More dynamite blew the safe apart, sending currency wafting through the night air. The outlaws scooped up $30,000 and rode off.

Cassidy (*seated at right*) and cohorts assemble in Fort Worth in 1901 to have a portrait made "as a good joke." Adding insult to injury, they sent a copy to a bank they had recently robbed in Winnemucca, Nevada, along with a note of thanks.

Photographed during a brief stay at Wyoming State penitentiary, Cassidy looks like a tough customer. Actually, he abjured the homicidal use of weapons — as befitted the grandson of a Mormon bishop.

The safe that Cassidy's men plundered in their first train robbery stands amid the splintered wreckage of the express car, demolished by charges of dynamite after it was carefully separated from passenger cars.

469 R

FORM 55-3-'01-10M-AE.

P. N. D. A.　　No.

NAME......George Parker.　No. 469 R
ALIAS......"Butch" Cassidy; George Cassidy; Ingerfield.
NATIVITY...United States.　**COLOR**......White
OCCUPATION...........:......Cowboy; rustler
CRIMINAL OCCUPATION.........Bank robber, highwayman, cattle and horse thief
AGE....37 yrs (1902).　**HEIGHT**....5 ft. 9 in
WEIGHT....165 lbs...　**BUILD**...... Medium
COMPLEXION......... .... Light
COLOR OF HAIR..........................Flaxen
EYES..........Blue.　**NOSE**.....................
STYLE OF BEARD.....Mustache; sandy, if any
REMARKS:—Two cut scars back of head, small scar under left eye, small brown mole calf of leg. "Butch" Cassidy is known as a criminal principally in Wyoming, Utah, Idaho, Colorado and Nevada and has served time in Wyoming State penitentiary at Laramie for grand larceny, but was pardoned January 19th, 1896. Wanted for robbery First National Bank, Winnemucca, Nevada, September 19th, 1900 See Information No. 421.

470 R

FORM 55-3-'01-10M-AE.

P. N. D. A.　　No.

NAME......Harry Longbaugh.　No. 470 R
ALIAS......"Kid" Longbaugh; Harry Alonzo; Frank Jones; Frank Boyd; the "Sundance Kid"
NATIVITY...Swedish-American.　**COLOR**..White
OCCUPATION............. ....Cowboy; rustler
CRIMINAL OCCUPATION .... Highwayman, bank burglar, cattle and horse thief
AGE....35 years.　**HEIGHT**.......5 ft. 10 in
WEIGHT....165 to 175 lbs.　**BUILD**....Good
EYES....Blue or gray.　**NOSE**.....Rather long
COMPLEXION................ .... Medium
STYLE OF BEARD......Mustache, (if any), natural color brown, reddish tinge
FEATURES.............................Grecian type
COLOR OF HAIR......Natural color brown, may be dyed; combs it pompadour
IS BOW-LEGGED; FEET FAR APART.
REMARKS:—Harry Longbaugh served 18 months in jail at Sundance, Cook Co., Wyoming, when a boy, for horse stealing. In December, 1892, Harry Longbaugh, Bill Madden and Henry Bass "held up" a Great Northern train at Malta, Montana. Bass and Madden were tried for this crime, convicted and sentenced to 10 and 14 years respectively; Longbaugh escaped and since has been a fugitive. June 28, 1897, under the name of Frank Jones, Longbaugh participated with Harvey Logan, alias Curry, Tom Day and Walter Putney, in the Belle Fourche, South Dakota, bank robbery. All were arrested, but Longbaugh and Harvey Logan escaped from jail at Deadwood, October 31, the same year. Wanted for robbery First National Bank, Winnemucca, Nevada, September 19th, 1900. See Information No. 421.

Mug shots and lengthy descriptions of Cassidy *(left)* and the Sundance Kid were distributed by Pinkerton's National Detective Agency.

The Wild Bunch followed up its first thunderous train job with three more. Although Pinkerton men were on the gang's trail, the Union Pacific considered a business-like approach to the problem — offering to buy out Cassidy with a pardon and a position as an express guard "at a good salary."

After the deal fell through and Cassidy robbed another train, the railroad organized its own gang of gunfighters, outfitted them with high-powered rifles, and sent them out in a high-speed train to bring in the Wild Bunch. Cassidy, realizing that such determined pursuers would eventually catch up with him, decided to transfer his operations to South America. He journeyed to New York sometime in late 1901, accompanied by a trusted confederate, Harry "Sundance Kid" Longbaugh of Sundance, Wyoming, and by Longbaugh's lady love, Etta Place. After taking in the city sights, they sailed to Buenos Aires and new opportunities.

During the next decade, Cassidy, the Sundance Kid and Etta robbed banks and trains all across South America. Pinkerton men continued to keep track of them; one dossier entry noted: "As soon as Cassidy entered an Indian village he would be playing with the children. When hard pressed by local authorities, he would always find a hideout among the native population."

The ultimate fate of the trio remains a mystery. Stories circulated that they were killed in a battle with troops in Bolivia or Uruguay, but more reliable reports indicated that they returned to the U.S. and lived to a ripe old age. Whatever the outcome, Longbaugh had foreseen the future accurately when he said, during the glory days of the Wild Bunch: "I'll never be taken alive."

A grim squad of Union Pacific riflemen rides the rails in a specially assigned train, under orders to hunt down the Wild Bunch and bring an end to their depredations.

Before sailing for South America with Cassidy, the Sundance Kid *(right)* and his sharpshooting mistress, Etta Place, stop by a New York studio for a stylish portrait.

Gang member Ben Kilpatrick found time to romance Laura Bullion, a "soiled dove."

Rifle and six-shooter in readiness, Deputy U.S. Marshal Joe Cheeseman sets out on a manhunt in the Indian Territory.

3 | The man with the badge

The guardians of Western law and order held a variety of titles: town marshal, county sheriff, state or territorial ranger, federal marshal. But whatever their status, their colleague, Sheriff Bat Masterson, saw them as "just plain ordinary men who could shoot straight and had the most utter courage and perfect nerve—and, for the most part, a keen sense of right and wrong."

Perhaps out of courtesy, Masterson left a number of things unsaid. The peace officers' keen sense of right and wrong did not keep some of them from the pursuit of second careers as practicing outlaws. His description of them as "ordinary men" was probably closer to the mark, for they spent most of their time at such prosaic tasks as paper work and tax-collecting.

Yet on numerous occasions they did indeed display valor and skill with a gun, and collectively they left a deep and decisive imprint on frontier justice.

A star-and-crescent badge signals the authority of the reigning lawman of El Reno, Oklahoma Territory, believed to be John Marshall.

Joe Mason, deputy marshal of Dodge City, began as an Army scout.

Deputy U.S. Marshal T. Thompson roamed Oklahoma Territory.

T. J. Carr served six years as a sheriff in the Wyoming Territory.

In Dodge City, L. C. Hartman was a low-ranking deputy policeman.

98

Deputy Sheriff C. H. Farnsworth *(left)* and Ranger W. K. Foster patrol a pass in Arizona's mountainous wilds.

99

Frontline forces of law and order

Not all citizens of the frontier complained when law and order proved a little late arriving in their midst. Some, in fact, welcomed the delay. In 1878 an editor in the half-civilized territory of New Mexico looked eastward toward the still less civilized plains of Texas and wrote with frank envy about the kind of law enforcement that Texans practiced. "There are no county officials in Potter County in the Panhandle of Texas," he observed. "Better yet, there are no state officers to interfere with the unalloyed liberty which the inhabitants of that county enjoy. When any horse thieves or bad characters make their appearance they are strung up to the cottonwoods."

Such improvised frontier justice gave way to constituted authority only bit by bit, and sometimes with marked informality. When the early settlers of Cheyenne, Wyoming, were troubled by brigands and bandits, they formed a vigilante force headed by Nathaniel Kimball Boswell, who had come all the way·from New Hampshire to open a drugstore in the territory. With the full blessing of right-thinking elements in the community, Old Boz, as they fondly called him, took it upon himself to arrest rustlers and keep a curb on a population made up for the most part, according to one newspaper, of "gamblers, thieves, highwaymen, ruthless cutthroats and women of the underworld." Boswell's initiative so charmed the governor of the Wyoming Territory, John Campbell, that he decided to appoint him county sheriff. Campbell was undeterred by Wyoming's lack of official forms for such purposes. He simply took a sheet of paper and in his own hand wrote: "Know Ye: That reposing special trust and confidence in the

patriotism, integrity and ability of N. K. Boswell, I, John A. Campbell, in pursuance of and by virtue of authority vested in me, do appoint him Sheriff of the county of Albany." At the time—May 1869—Wyoming had four counties in all, each extending the full length of the territory, north to Montana and south to Colorado and Utah. Thus, by a few strokes of a pen, Nat Boswell became the chief law enforcer of a bailiwick that covered 16,800 square miles.

An equally casual air often attended official arrangements within the frontier towns themselves. When a settlement grew big enough to acquire a town charter, choosing peace officers for the newly incorporated community generally was the first order of business. In at least one case the action was decidedly premature. After Ellsworth, Kansas, got its charter in 1871, the Mayor and council promptly appointed a marshal to enforce the laws. In their haste, the city fathers neglected to adopt laws for the marshal to enforce. A week later they sheepishly reconvened to remedy the oversight.

Even with laws on the books and a duly authorized officer patrolling the streets, keeping order in frontier towns remained at best a shaky proposition. It often depended on the courage and gunslinging skill of a peace officer rather than on any widespread respect for authority. The lawman lived in a world imbued with the frontier psychology of self-reliance—and a world in which firearms were available to everyone. In such a powder-keg situation, the law was best enforced when the man with the badge was skilled with the gun. When he disarmed a group of overexuberant cowboys or separated a pair of quarreling gamblers or held off a howling lynch mob at the door of a jail, the citizenry knew that his six-shooter stood for peace—or else.

In a society where saloonkeepers and owners of gambling halls counted as reputable citizens—and sometimes served as mayors or town councilmen—it was not

Assorted badges worn by frontier peace officers range from the dazzlingly ornate to the starkly simple—with the plainest belonging to the highest rank, U.S. marshals.

George Ruffner, sheriff of Yavapai County, Arizona, in the 1890s, takes his ease in an office complete with a newfangled typewriter. Many sheriffs concentrated on paper work and left rougher tasks to deputies.

surprising that gunslingers and gamblers could become peace officers. Sometimes, indeed, they continued their parallel careers. Wild Bill Hickok *(page 123)* spent a good part of his term as marshal of Abilene, Kansas, at the poker table. Anyone who sought him on official business had to come to his headquarters at The Alamo, with its huge bar, its array of gaming devices, its orchestra and the oil paintings of nudes on its walls. Like most gunfighters turned lawmen, Hickok saw no reason to abandon his private pursuits while keeping the peace. He held office at the pleasure of the Mayor and city council, and knew he was likely to lose his post when the next mayor named his own man.

Compared with some other town marshals, Wild Bill was a paragon of propriety. Citizens of Laramie,

Wyoming, felt impelled to hang their head lawman when it was discovered that in his simultaneous capacity as saloonkeeper he was drugging and robbing his patrons. A number of county sheriffs—who were a cut above town marshals in the peace-keeping hierarchy —met similar ends as a result of their extracurricular activities. Irate vigilantes disposed of the sheriff of Ada County, Idaho, by rope when he was found to be moonlighting as a horse thief.

Such men were exceptions, but the dilemma posed for peaceable citizens of the frontier was widespread. Often the choice they faced when selecting a guardian of law and order lay between an upright but ineffectual fellow townsman and a newcomer of dubious past but iron nerve. Wild Bill Hickok's own bailiwick of Abilene provided a case in point. In 1870, when it ranked as one of the first of the rowdy Kansas cattle towns, the provisional town government named a reluctant grocer as marshal and also proceeded to erect a jail. It was still under construction when a bunch of hell-bent cowboys arrived in town after their long, tedious cattle drive from the plains of Texas. They sized up the new lawman, correctly decided that he was a weak reed, and expressed their sentiments by tearing down his partially built headquarters. Eventually, however, the townsmen managed to complete a jail, and a skylarking chuck-wagon cook was housed in it. The reluctant grocer appeared to have scored his first triumph. But then the prisoner's allies, converging on the scene, shot the lock off the jail door and set their friend free.

Stung by such humiliating displays of official ineptitude, frontier communities that yearned for a firm hand in law enforcement occasionally went to extremes to obtain it. In exchange for a measure of stability, they were sometimes ready to accept even a known badman as marshal, presumably on the theory that such a man was best equipped to deal with his own kind. Few citizens worried about how he had erred in the past, or how he might err in the future. So long as he kept local troublemakers in check, respectable folk could only approve — and fervently hope that his conversion to law and order was a lasting one.

Dime novels to the contrary, the frontier peace officer was seldom the solitary figure he was painted to be, stalking malefactors against superior odds. The Old West had an impressive number and diversity of lawmen, and a basic framework of jurisdictions. Occasional overlaps, as well as rival ambitions and personal feuds, often caused conflicts between men in different jurisdictions — the clash between the Earps of Tombstone and Sheriff Behan of surrounding Cochise County was a notable example — but just as often there was cooperation. And within each jurisdiction the head lawman was as a rule able to call upon various sources of help, both trained and amateur, when things threatened to get seriously out of hand.

At the town level, the marshal — in effect, the chief of police — usually had at his disposal a small force made up of an assistant marshal and a few policemen; in addition, he could call upon ordinary citizens in an emergency to serve as temporary policemen. On the county level, law enforcement rested in the hands of a sheriff, an undersheriff and a group of deputy sheriffs, aided now and then by posses of impromptu deputies.

There was also a third level of lawmen, in the form of a corps of federal officials operating on a state- or district- or territory-wide basis. These United States marshals and their deputies were technically charged with enforcing only federal laws and pursuing such criminals as mail robbers and Army deserters, but the deputies often held additional commissions as town or county lawmen and lent a hand — and a gun — in support of their local counterparts.

In the wildest reaches of the Southwest, where county government was rudimentary or nonexistent, a special breed of lawmen flourished: the rangers or mounted police. Cattle thieves and other miscreants who operated along the Mexican border in Texas, New Mexico and Arizona had particular reason to fear these pursuers, who were direct agents of the state or territorial government. Usually they were recruited from the ranks of the toughest candidates available — men who could not only shoot straight and fast, but also ride hard and long, since they had to patrol great distances on horseback. Rangers in the three states were organized in quasi-military fashion, but they exercised their own judgment as to methods of law enforcement. Once, when Captain Burt Mossman was asked just how he and his rangers meant to go about ridding Arizona of rustlers, he put it this way:

"If they come along easy, everything will be all right. If they don't, well, I just guess we can make pretty short work of them. I know most of them, and the life those fellows are leading in the mesquite shrub to keep out of reach of the law is a dog's life. They ought to thank me for giving them a chance to come in and take their medicine. Some of them will object, of course. They'll probably try a little gunplay as a bluff, but I shoot fairly well myself, and the boys who back me up are handy enough with their guns. Any rustler who wants to yank on the rope and kick up trouble will find he's up against it."

Collectively, the town, county, territorial or state, and federal lawmen made up a sizable hierarchy, with the U.S. marshal at the top of the pecking order. In large part he owed his preeminence to the fact that he alone had the honor of being directly appointed by the

The first lawmen of Guthrie, in Oklahoma territory, line up with other citizens under a sign misspelled by the craftsmen next door. The town zoomed from zero residents to 10,000 during the land rush of 1889.

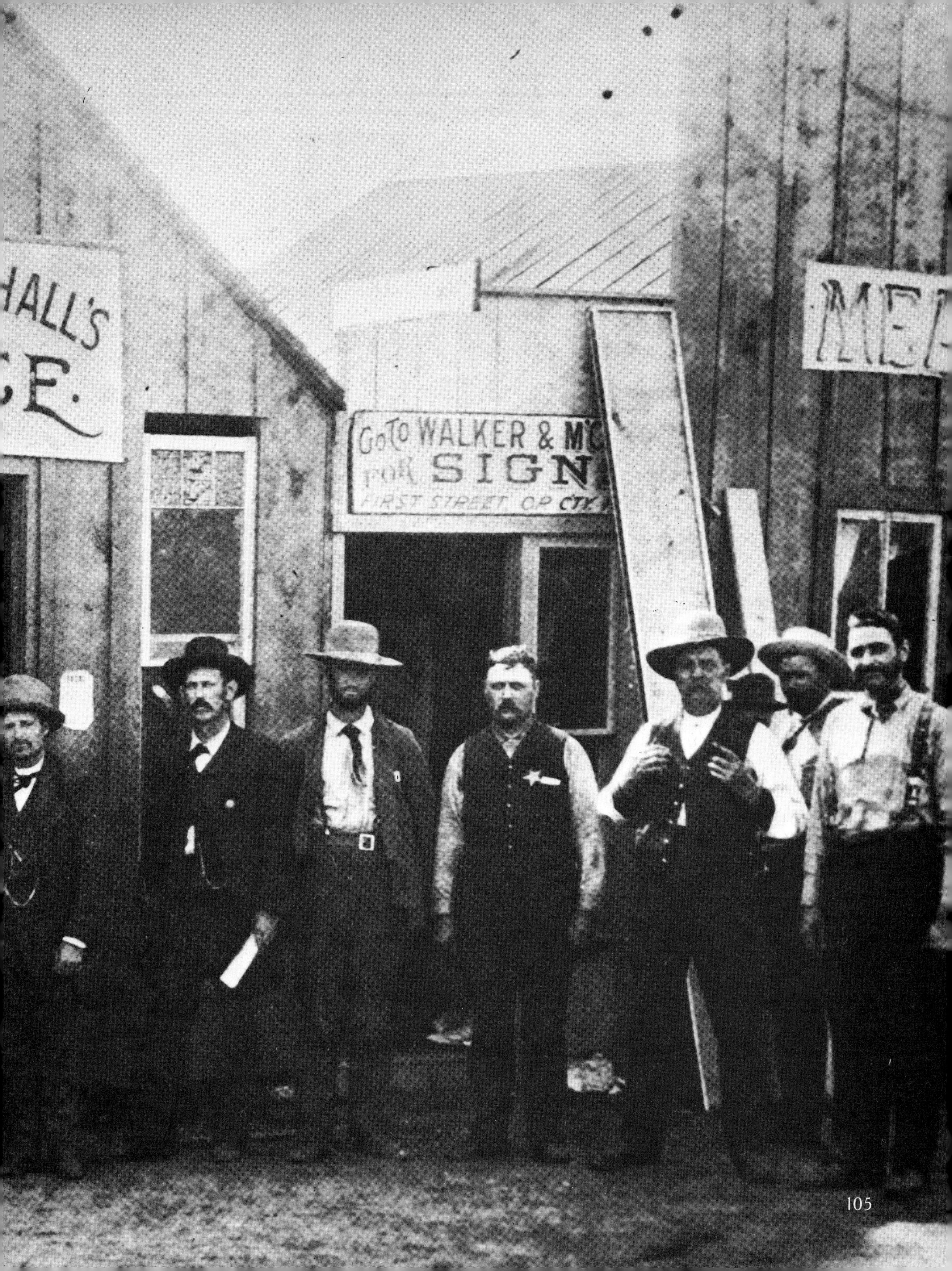
HALL'S
CE.
GO TO WALKER & M'C
FOR SIGN
FIRST STREET, OP CTY.
ME

President of the United States, with the advice and consent of the Senate. Since party patronage dictated his selection, his talents at gunfighting were of considerably less import than his talents at politicking. He in turn had the power to dispense patronage by selecting his own deputies. As a result, the post of U.S. marshal was so profitable that when it fell vacant it tended to attract a flood of aspirants. In 1882, three weeks after a vacancy occurred in New Mexico, an Albuquerque newspaper reported: "The President is still holding off the appointment of a U.S. marshal. It is understood there are fifty-one applications, with sixty-four bushels of petitions and seventy-three barrels of recommendations on hand."

The men who won in such scrambles for office were sometimes conspicuously lacking in integrity or experience in law enforcement. Among the U.S. marshals who held sway in the state of Colorado were a wholesale liquor dealer, a real estate agent, a bank appraiser and a manufacturer of soft drinks. During its earlier days, as a territory, Colorado had fared even worse in the selection of a chief peace officer. Its first U.S. marshal, appointed in 1861, was arrested for embezzling federal funds. The second, an ex-judge of the Denver municipal court, was better behaved. But the third resigned his office facing charges of larceny and of passing counterfeit money. The fourth was convicted of fattening his purse by making fraudulent claims against the federal government, and served two years in Leavenworth penitentiary.

Skulduggery in high places either amused or enraged the average citizen of the West, but naturally his chief concern with law enforcement, or the lack of it, lay closer to home. When he had complaints to register, he might send a letter to some august official with an office hundreds of miles away, remote and unreachable, but the official he saw face to face was one of two men with whom, like as not, he had more than a nodding acquaintance: the town marshal or the county sheriff. Between them, these two men served as the real mainstays of frontier law.

Of the two, the sheriff had the edge in power as well as prestige. He was the county's chief peace officer and sometimes its chief executive. Many sheriffs took pride in personally tracking down and apprehending the lawless; but many others, like most U.S. marshals, pre-

ferred to leave this job to gunfighting deputies and devote most of their time to politics and money-making. In almost every county, the sheriff won his post by a hotly contested election, and he needed a politician's craft and flimflam. There were exceptions, of course; when Bat Masterson ran for sheriff of Ford County, Kansas, he told the voters, "I have no pledges to make, as pledges are usually considered mere clap-trap." But, once a sheriff attained office, he could scarcely avoid finding it profitable, for much of his time was spent collecting county taxes, and often he received a percentage of the take. Combined, in some states, with a certain amount of judicious graft from road-building and other county contracts he dispensed, that sort of income could make a man wealthy: Sheriff John Behan, the Earps' enemy in Tombstone, was reputed to have raked in $40,000 a year during his term.

Such bonanzas aside, a host of practical everyday duties went with the sheriff's job. All sheriffs were expected to maintain the county jail, serve court orders and sell the property of tax delinquents. In addition, some sheriffs had to take on a variety of odd jobs created by problems peculiar to their areas. In Wyoming they inspected the owners' brands on all horses that were to be driven out of the state, to guard against their theft. Utah's sheriffs maintained not only the county jails but also the county dog pounds. In Colorado, sheriffs had to help fight forest fires, in Texas they helped to eradicate prairie dogs and in New Mexico they went out in search of straying livestock.

At the third level of law enforcement—the town—these extra assignments multiplied; indeed, town marshals often had more duties than they could keep track of. Lethal showdowns and shoot-outs made some of these lawmen famous far beyond their localities, but work of a less heroic nature took up most of their time. In many places, a town marshal carried out the functions of a health inspector, a fire inspector and a sanitation commissioner. Sometimes he collected town taxes, as well as the license fees that were required of saloons, places of prostitution and owners of pet dogs; the experience thus gained occasionally enabled him to earn a few dollars on the side as a bill collector for some private entrepreneur. Other typical demands on the town marshal's time included serving subpoenas, presiding over the local jail, keeping official records of arrests and of the property taken from prisoners in his custody, giving evidence at trials and maintaining order in his town's police court.

Some of the most celebrated gunfighters of the West carried out these mundane tasks and more. In Abilene, Wild Bill Hickok kept the streets clear of litter as well as unruly cowboys; to supplement his $150-a-month salary, he also got 50 cents for every unlicensed dog he shot within the city limits. In Tombstone, Virgil Earp had to hunt down an "accordion fiend" who kept the townspeople awake at night.

Even when a marshal exercised his most vaunted power and made an arrest, it usually turned out to be a pretty prosaic affair. In one typical month at Tombstone, for example, Virgil Earp and his deputies made 48 arrests. Of the total, 18 stemmed from drunk-and-disorderly charges, and 14 were for disturbing the peace. Only eight involved violence or the threat of violence: four for assault, three for carrying concealed weapons and one for resisting an officer. The remainder dealt with a miscellany of such misdeeds as petty theft and reckless buggy driving.

But that record is deceptive. It does not accurately reflect the tinderbox instability of a frontier town, or the sudden deadly flare-ups that brought lawmen running, their guns at the ready. Many such episodes occurred in the towns of Texas or Kansas or Montana when cowboys arrived from the range dusty, tired and lonesome. Within a few hours—cleaned up and liquored up, with full pockets and weeks of boredom to work off—they would be out on the streets, ready for fun and looking for trouble. Their day might end in tragedy—in a gunfight with a crooked gambler or a fatal quarrel over the shopworn favors of a prostitute. Even comparatively harmless horseplay could turn dangerous, especially when cowboys "hurrahed" a town by riding through at a full gallop, yelling and yipping and shooting into the air. A typical incident of this sort took place in Dodge City, Kansas, on a steamy July night in 1878.

A man named Charles Bassett was town marshal at the time; Wyatt Earp was assistant marshal; Bat Masterson's younger brother Jim was a policeman on the city force, and Bat himself was sheriff of the surrounding county. At about 3 a.m., two cowboys drifted out of the Lady Gay saloon, by now presumably ready to return to their camp just outside of town. What happened next was reported by the *Dodge City Times.* The cowboys "buckled on their revolvers, which they were not allowed to wear around town, and mounted their horses. All at once one of them conceived the idea that to finish the night's revelry and give the natives due warning of his departure, he must do some shooting, and forthwith he commenced to bang away, one of the bullets whizzing into a dance hall nearby, causing no little commotion among the participants in the 'dreamy waltz' and quadrille."

The famous vaudevillian Eddie Foy was performing at Dodge City that week and happened to be in the Lady Gay on the night of the hurrah. When some bullets strayed into the saloon, Foy recalled, "everybody dropped to the floor at once, according to custom. Bat Masterson was just in the act of dealing in a game of Spanish monte with Doc Holliday, and I was impressed by the instantaneous manner in which they flattened out like pancakes on the floor."

Outside, on the dark street, the affair suddenly changed from a prank of two cowboys who were letting off steam to a dead-serious duel between a pair of armed, mounted men and a pair of lawmen on foot. Hearing the shooting, Jim Masterson and Wyatt Earp had raced to the scene and they now began to exchange volleys with the galloping riders. In no time at all a fifth man injected himself into the fray. According to the *Times,* "some rooster who did not understand the situation perched himself in the window of the dance hall and indulged in a promiscuous shoot all by himself." After a few chaotic moments, the lawmen drove the cowboys off. As they clattered over a bridge leading out of town, either Masterson or Earp—no one ever learned which —winged one of the riders and brought him down.

Except for the wounded cowboy, a young Texan named George Hoy, nobody had even been hit. The Lady Gay had a few new bullet holes to join those that already pocked its walls and ceiling. Eddie Foy also sustained damage to some clothes that were hanging in his dressing room. "I had just bought a new eleven-dollar suit," he wrote. "When I went back to get it after the bombardment, I found that it had been penetrated by three bullets, and one of them had started a ring of fire smoldering around the hole." Dodge City's residents agreed that the wounded cowboy had received his just

Guthrie residents betray mixed feelings as U.S. Marshal
W. C. Jones (center), charged with enforcing the Oklahoma territory's dry laws, holds a jug of booze he seized
from a local toper and smashed. At his right, a town wag
tries to nip at a bottle despite a friend's restraining hand.

ie Ok. May 28.

deserts, though somewhat to their surprise they found themselves genuinely sorry when George Hoy died a few weeks later. "George was nothing but a poor cowboy," wrote the *Ford County Globe,* "but his brother cowboys permitted him to want for nothing during his illness, and buried him in grand style when dead, which was very creditable to them."

If the people of Dodge felt any remorse, it was fleeting. Ornery cowboys were the bane of all cattle towns, and local lawmen were to be applauded for keeping them from shooting up the place. Four years after George Hoy's premature death, Dodge acquired a tough new town marshal, a Kansas gunfighter named Jack Bridges. The members of the city council were so pleased with his handling of the cowboy problem that within a year they raised his salary from $100 to $150 a month; a joking newspaper editor implied that they also added a fringe benefit by which Bridges and his assistant marshal were now "entitled to kill a cowboy or two each season."

The appointment of Bridges set off a sharp little flurry of civic controversy between Dodge City and the neighboring town of Caldwell over the relative merits of their lawmen. Such arguments were not uncommon in an era of bursting local pride. A Caldwell newspaper fired the opening shot when Bridges was named to the job: "Jack," it said, "belongs to the killer class, and it is only a question of time when he will lay down with his boots on." The Dodge folks seethed. "Caldwell, through her newspapers, is jealous of Dodge City," retorted the *Dodge City Times;* then the paper moved in for the counterattack: "Caldwell is incapable of self-government. Three city marshals have been cowardly slain in that city." The *Times* heaped fresh coals on the fire when it published a letter from a reader declaring that the editor of the Caldwell paper possessed "the venom of the reptile, the sliminess of the toad and the odoriferous qualities of the skunk."

Even an impartial observer would have conceded that Caldwell's experience with lawmen had been at best ill-starred. The *Dodge City Times* had not exaggerated in pointing out that three of Caldwell's town marshals had been "cowardly slain"—though in fact only one of them had died while in office. George Flatt had been a drunken braggart, but a superb gunfighter nevertheless—one of the few men who really could shoot to kill with both hands. Before winning his appointment as the marshal of Caldwell he had made his reputation while serving on a posse, when he shot down two badmen almost simultaneously though under fire himself. Soon after leaving office, while strolling down Caldwell's Main Street at one o'clock in the morning, Flatt was ambushed by a gang of assailants and cut down in a hail of bullets and buckshot.

The mayor of Caldwell, a saloonkeeper named Michael Meagher, and six other men were arrested on suspicion of the crime, but in the absence of any evidence they were eventually released. Later, Mike Meagher served briefly as town marshal—and, in his turn, was shot down in a gunfight with five cowboys on a spree. The third ill-fated marshal, a young fellow named George Brown, died in the line of duty. Hearing that an armed man had entered the Red Light Dance Hall, he and a constable hurried to the scene to take his guns away. But inside the hall, they found themselves opposed by four men. The inexperienced marshal took them all on. A single bullet brought him down before he could even get his bearings on a target; the constable fled to safety.

In July 1882, two weeks after George Brown's death, a man named Henry Brown—so far as is known, no relative of the slain marshal—rode into Caldwell. A short, hard, blue-eyed man, he had come alone up the Chisholm Trail from the south, packing two ivory-handled six-shooters and a well-worn Winchester rifle. Soon after his arrival in town, he dropped into the Mayor's office to ask for a lawman's job. "All right," the Mayor was reported to have said. "It's your funeral." Henry Brown became assistant marshal of Caldwell. He was to prove a classic example of the gunfighter turned lawman—but with an ending that rocked decent citizens everywhere.

In announcing his appointment, the *Caldwell Post* could divulge little about Brown except that "it is said that he is one of the quickest men on the trigger in the Southwest." In fact, though the good people of Caldwell did not know it, their mayor had unwittingly hired one of the Southwest's most unregenerate hardcases. In Texas and New Mexico, Henry Brown was famous as a desperado. He was with Billy the Kid and some other friends during New Mexico's notorious Lincoln County War of 1878 when they murdered the county

sheriff and cold-bloodedly slaughtered two deputies who were being held as prisoners. Brown had also stolen horses in the Pecos valley and run them into the Texas Panhandle. He had squandered his loot in one saloon and gambling hall after another. Then, about 1880, his life took a sudden turn when he served a short hitch as a deputy sheriff in Oldham County, Texas. Thus, when Brown hit the Chisholm Trail for a look at the cattle towns of Kansas, he was a seasoned gunfighter with

Date	Name of Prisoner	Offence
Oct 16 brought from Old Record	Jose Juan Confined Sept 20	Petty Larceny
Oct 6 brought from old record	Jeaus Molino Confined Sept 23	Murder
Oct 6	Theodore Brown Confined Oct 16 1877	Murder
Oct 18	Jesus Cruz Confined Oct 17 1877	Petit Larceny
Oct 22	Otto Von Reichenbach Confined Oct 22	Drunk & disorderly
Nov 11	Francisco Valenzuela Confined Nov 11	Disturbing the peace
Nov 14	Juan Figaroa	Drunk & disorderly (awaiting exam)
Nov 20	Juan Jose Preciado (Papago) Confined Nov 20	Petit Larceny

...tted By		Penalty	
...n J.P.	To be confined in County Jail One Month from Sept 20th	Discharged Oct 19 Term Expired	
...as J.P.	Held to Appear before the Grand Jury and Indicted	Sent to Penitentiary Prison Nov 11th 1877	
...nbush	Re-examined by J. Burgass J.P. and committed on the charge of Manslaughter Oct 19th		
...en J.P.	To be Confined in County Jail twenty days from Oct 18th 77	Discharged Nov 6 Term Expired	
...table	Taken before Myres J.P. by Constable Dutton Oct 23rd and not returned		
...es J.P.	Fined $10 in default of which to be confined 10 days in County Jail	Paid fine & discharged November 12th 77	
...table	No charge preferred	Discharged November 18th	
...s J.P.	To be confined in County Jail for One Month, commencing November 21st 1877	Discharged Dec 20 Term Expired	

a growing taste for the lawman's side of the business.

In Caldwell, Henry Brown proved to be a superb peace officer and won the abiding affection of the citizens. Within six months the Mayor and city council moved him up from assistant marshal to acting marshal to marshal. In the latter capacity he killed two men—an Indian named Spotted Horse who was foolish enough to resist arrest, and a gambler, Newt Boyce, who was idiotic enough to try a shoot-out with Brown. But it was the mere fact of Brown's presence in Caldwell that counted most. With his own hand-picked deputy, a huge Texan named Ben Wheeler, he dominated the once-wild streets of the town. The incongruous pair —the sawed-off marshal and his towering right-hand man—rarely had to use their guns.

Caldwell rejoiced in its head lawman—an exemplar of virtue who did not drink, did not gamble, and did not even smoke or chew tobacco. At one point, to replace his worn rifle, the townspeople presented him with a shining new, elegantly engraved, gold-mounted Winchester bearing the inscription: "For valuable services rendered the citizens of Caldwell." In March 1884, he further gladdened their hearts by marrying a Caldwell girl, Maude Levagood. Apparently she pronounced it "Lee-va-good," for in announcing the marriage, the *Caldwell Journal* noted the event with an atrocious pun ("he did not Lev a good girl at all, but took her unto himself for better or for worse"), before adding that the newspaper staff collectively "throws its old shoe after the young folks and wishes them a long and prosperous life." The newlyweds took an important step when Henry bought a house—an act that was rare indeed among Western gunfighters.

Then, in late April, Henry decided to turn outlaw again—why, no one will ever know. Perhaps he needed money; perhaps married life was constraining; perhaps Caldwell had become too tame for him. In any case, at the end of April, Brown and his deputy, Ben Wheeler, rode out of town. Somewhere on the open range they picked up two Texas cowboy friends, Bill Smith and John Wesley. Together the four men headed west.

Their destination, Medicine Lodge, was a settlement about 55 miles from Caldwell. It was a tiny place with few of the attractions of the rowdy cattle towns along the railroads—but it had a small bank with no one of the likes of Henry Brown to protect it. Medicine Lodge had undergone some bad days, according to an account by a local newspaper editor, when "a few swaggering ruffians took virtual possession of the town, howled about the streets and fired their revolvers until their wild and woolly spirits were satisfied and then left unharmed and went unpunished." After that demonstration of unopposed tyranny, the editor added, the place became known as a town whose "white-livered inhabitants" ducked into their houses when despera-

111

Crude as it was, this wooden jail in Larned, Kansas, could claim superiority over some frontier lockups. One sheriff confined his prisoners by simply throwing a cowhide over them and pegging it to the ground.

does showed up. It must have seemed the ideal spot for a quick, quiet, easy bank holdup.

It turned out to be nothing of the kind. Though one newspaper described Brown's raid on the bank as an attempt at robbery that "for cold-bloodedness and boldness of design, was never exceeded by the most famous exploits of the James gang," actually it was a botched job. Neither Brown nor any of his confederates had ever robbed a bank. While Bill Smith acted as lookout, the other three entered the bank shortly after opening time. Within minutes they killed the cashier and mortally wounded the president. But the dying cashier locked the bank vault, and soon the empty-handed bandits were hightailing it out of town with a posse at their heels. Brown and his men knew little about the surrounding countryside. In a few hours they were trapped in a blind box canyon. They fought off their pursuers for a while, then gave up the futile battle. The aftermath was quick and brutal. At 9 o'clock that night a

mob broke into the Medicine Lodge jail, overpowered the sheriff and his posse and swarmed over the prisoners. The four men made a break for freedom; Brown ran only a few yards before falling dead, riddled with buckshot and bullets. Wheeler, Smith and Wesley were hanged later that night from an elm tree east of town. Then the "white-livered inhabitants" of Medicine Lodge went home. Soon afterward they read this judgment of their behavior in the local newspaper: "Mob law is to be deplored under almost any circumstance, but in this case the general sentiment of the community will uphold the summary execution of justice by the taking of these murderers' lives."

Caldwell, of course, was shattered. "When the news came," the *Journal* reported, "it fell like a thunderbolt at midday. People doubted, wondered, and when the stern facts were at last beyond question, accepted them reluctantly." After a detailed account of the affair, the *Journal* editor addressed himself to the difficult task of

Built in 1874 at a cost of $11,000, the Helena, Montana, jail was the envy of turnkeys everywhere. Behind its imposing facade were six cells, an exercise hall, and a kitchen and sleeping quarters for the guards.

composing an obituary for Caldwell's late lamented marshal. He conceded that Henry Brown had one fault as a peace officer—but only one: "He was too ready to use his revolver or Winchester." On the other hand, the editor went on, "He had gained the entire confidence of the people," and Brown and Ben Wheeler "had made two as good officers as the city has ever had. They had been given credit for honor and bravery." The obituary also quoted from a letter Henry Brown had written to Maude Brown a few hours before his death:

Darling Wife:—I am in jail here. I want you to come and see me as soon as you can. I will send you all of my things, and you can sell them, but keep the Winchester. This is hard for me to write this letter but, it was all for you, my sweet wife, and for the love I have for you. Do not go back on me; if you do it will kill me. If a mob does not kill us we will come out all *right after awhile. Maude, I did not shoot anyone, and did not want the others to kill anyone; but they did, and that is all there is about it. Now, good-bye, my darling wife.*
                                                      H. N. Brown

The people of Caldwell had hired Henry Brown in all innocence, ignorant of his past and his proclivities. The same could not always be said of other Western communities. Some towns not only accepted but frankly admired marshals who openly acknowledged their seamy records. Austin, Texas, was one such place. The citizens of the state capital never stopped boasting of their chief law enforcer in the early 1880s, Ben Thompson, one of the most ruthless gunmen in Western history —and proud of the fact.

Bat Masterson, a connoisseur in these matters, considered Thompson the best gunfighter of them all. "Others missed at times," Bat wrote, "but Ben Thompson was as delicate and certain in action as a Swiss

113

Flanked by grim-faced townsmen, light-mustached Marshal
Henry Brown of Caldwell, Kansas, and his deputy, Ben
Wheeler (right), share shackles with two cowboy cronies
after bungling a bank holdup in 1884. A mob later shot
Brown as he tried to flee, then lynched his accomplices.

watch." Jovial, well-mannered, easily spotted by his silk stovepipe hat, dapper suits and carefully waxed mustache, Thompson had cut a wide and lethal swath across the West, spending winters gambling in Texas, summers gambling in Kansas. At a point in his career when he had already killed at least five men and had once been indicted for murder (and exonerated), he settled permanently in Austin, quickly acquiring the lucrative concession to operate the faro tables upstairs at the Iron Front Saloon. In December of 1880 he turned lawman, winning election as marshal of Austin in a field of five candidates.

Thompson gave the town a brand of law enforcement that delighted it. From the moment he took office the crime rate dropped, and so did the number of arrests; his appearance on the streets was enough to keep things peaceful. Citizens forgave him his peccadilloes —when things got *too* quiet he liked to get drunk and shoot out the street lamps—and they happily reelected him to a second term in 1881. Only when he gunned down an old enemy in a shoot-out in San Antonio did they feel that he had finally gone a little too far, and reluctantly accepted his resignation. But Thompson continued to ride high in Texas. Though he was no longer Austin's head lawman, his very presence could still inspire both awe and fear, and he could clear a room simply by stepping into it.

He did just that at a banquet of the Texas Live Stock Association held at Simon's Cafe in Austin in 1884. A friend of his, a lawyer named L. E. Edwards, had been turned away because he had received no formal invitation to the affair. Inside the cafe, 20 cattlemen of the association were laughing and whooping as a Texas Ranger, sitting precariously on the back of a chair, delivered a comic speech. One leather-lunged guest, a cattle baron named Shanghai Pierce, having bellowed in vain for someone to pass him a platter of turkey, had just climbed up onto the banquet table and was stumbling over the dishes and tureens toward the desired sustenance at the far end. Suddenly Ben Thompson burst into the room, drew his six-shooter and shouted, "Show me the rascal that don't like L. E. Edwards!" The cattlemen stampeded for the exits. Shanghai Pierce dived through the nearest window, taking out the sash as he went. Within seconds, only the Texas Ranger was left to face Thompson, and his tac-

Bad day at Blackwell, Oklahoma

For all their fame as resolute bands bent on tracking down violators of the law, Western posses occasionally covered themselves with more embarrassment than glory. One such episode—reconstructed the next day by an enterprising local photographer *(below and right)*—took place on December 4, 1896, at Bert Benjamin's ranch near Blackwell, Oklahoma Territory.

Before dawn that day a posse slipped into position around a shack in which two men suspected of planning a robbery of the town's bank were holed up.

When they emerged at sunrise, Deputy Sheriff Alfred Lund bellowed: "Throw up your hands!" Instead, the suspects reached for their guns. As the first shots rang out, three members of the posse —half the total force—took to their heels. Lund stood his ground, wounding one gunman, killing another—and inadvertently riddling one of Bert Benjamin's livestock.

The wounded man proved to be a hardcase named Ben Cravens, but the dead man seemed an even bigger prize. Since he was missing three fingers, the lawmen confidently identified him as the vicious outlaw Dynamite Dick Clifton, who was said to have lost the same number of appendages during a gunfight. It turned out that the dead man "had been invested in a notoriety of which his corpse was unworthy," as a newspaper commented later. He was, in fact, only a petty thief named Buck McGregg. Despite this disappointment, the press managed to find a happy note; it reported that Blackwell's encounter with crime had caused "a marked advance in the local real estate market."

In a rare photographic reconstruction of a manhunt, members of a posse surrounded a shack *(right)* from which they flushed two gunmen.

The outlaws' mounts were saddled and loaded with weapons, but were out of their reach.

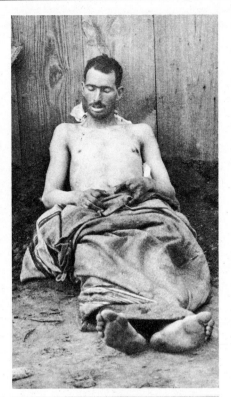

Bemused citizens view the cow killed by Deputy Sheriff Lund *(white shirt, rear row)*.

Shown propped against a wall in Blackwell, dead bandit Buck McGregg *(top)* was at first identified as another outlaw, train and bank robber Dynamite Dick Clifton, who had a $3,500 reward on his head. The posse's real catch turned out to be Ben Cravens *(above)*, a rustler and killer who was wounded during the shoot-out. Cravens returned to crime after a jail break.

tical position (he was still squatting on the chair back) was plainly bleak. But Ben mercifully departed, satisfied that he had made his point.

One of the few gunfighters who might have matched that feat was Bat Masterson. Like Ben Thompson, Bat had a wide and well-earned reputation — one so overwhelming that lesser men usually gave way without forcing him to draw his guns. Like Thompson, too, Bat was something of a prankster, who loved to be in trouble or on the edge of it. But there the resemblance ended. Except for his disreputable younger brother Billy, Ben Thompson never teamed up with anyone. Nor did he seem to mind his lone-wolf way of life; the year and a half he spent as a lawman was no more than a pleasant interlude in a lifetime dedicated to gambling and gunfighting. Bat Masterson belonged to a lawman clan, a trio of brothers who were as loyal to one another as the three musketeers and who, together, committed themselves wholeheartedly to taming one of the wildest of all cattle towns, Dodge City.

There were five Masterson brothers in all, sons of a Kansas homesteader who settled on a prairie farm near Wichita in 1871. The youngest of the boys, George and Tom, would never have any particular claim to fame. But Ed, the eldest brother, eventually became the marshal of Dodge City; Bartholomew, the second-born, called "Bat" for short, served as the sheriff of Ford County, which had Dodge City as its county seat; and Jim, the third brother, followed Ed as Dodge's marshal. Of the three, Bat always figured as the leader, the maker of big plans.

In 1872, when he was 19, Bat talked Ed and Jim into leaving the boring life of the farm for a fling at buffalo hunting in the wilds of southwestern Kansas. Ed and Jim returned to the farm for a while, but except for a few brief visits Bat never did go back. He followed the great buffalo herds from Kansas down through the Indian Territory and into the Texas Panhandle, meeting adventures enough to satisfy the most foolhardy of farm boys. At a Panhandle town called Adobe Walls (if it could be called a town: it consisted of two stores, a blacksmith's shop and a saloon), he had his first taste of Indian-fighting. Actually it was considerably more than a taste. For five days, in a company of 35 hunters, Bat helped to hold off a determined attack by 500

Marshal Ben Thompson of Austin, Texas, admitted to 32 killings as a private citizen. Though he always "killed openly and manly," according to Bat Masterson, he met his own end in an ambush by hired assassins.

Kiowa, Comanche, Cheyenne and Southern Apache warriors who were spreading havoc in the region. Later, he rode as a scout for Colonel Nelson Miles during a full-scale Army campaign in the Texas Panhandle against the same tribes. In 1876, in Sweetwater, Texas, he had his first real gunfight.

The details of that fight were never fully unraveled. What seems certain is that Bat took a Sweetwater girl named Molly Brennan from under the nose of her former lover, a U.S. Army sergeant named Melvin King, and when King found them together one night in a saloon, he opened fire on Bat. As the story goes, Molly threw herself in front of Bat to protect him; King's bullet passed through her body, killing her instantly, and lodged in Bat's pelvis. But as he fell, with the sergeant cocking his pistol for another shot, Bat fired back. King died at an Army camp the following day. As for Bat, he suffered a slight permanent limp from his wound, and took to carrying a cane—at first out of necessity, later for adornment alone.

Tested and proven as a buffalo hunter, scout and gunfighter, Bat Masterson arrived in Dodge City in the spring of 1877 to settle down—in his own way. He was 23, strikingly handsome with his mop of black hair, slate-blue eyes and compact body, and something of a dandy in the frontier fashion. When he first came to town, he sported a Southwestern sombrero with a rattlesnake-skin band, a scarlet silk neckerchief and Mexican sash, gleaming silver-plated six-shooters in silver-studded holsters and a pair of gold-mounted spurs; an observer on Front Street suggested that all this finery might give Bat an edge in a gunfight by blinding his opponent. But Bat had come to Dodge bent on business, not gunfighting.

His brothers Ed and Jim, who had preceded him to Dodge, were already well ensconced. Jim was the co-owner of a combination saloon-dance hall that had been well reviewed by the *Dodge City Times* ("The graining of the bar is finely executed. Charley Lawson's orchestra are mounted on a platform tastefully ornamented with bunting"). Ed, the steadygoing elder brother, had just been appointed assistant marshal of Dodge.

Almost at once after Bat's arrival in town he ran afoul of the law. In a burst of good cheer, probably stimulated by bad whiskey, he got himself arrested. The trouble started when Marshal Larry Deger, a whale of a man at about 300 pounds, began to march a diminutive deadbeat named Bobby Gill off to jail for disturbing the peace. According to the *Times,* "Bobby walked very leisurely"—so much so that Larry felt it necessary to assist him along with a few kicks in the rear. This act was soon interrupted by Bat Masterson, who grabbed the marshal around the neck, giving the prisoner a chance to escape. Deger then grappled with Bat, at the same time calling upon bystanders to take Bat's gun. With the help of half a dozen men Bat was disarmed; then Deger pistol-whipped him about the head until the blood flowed, and dragged him to jail. "Every inch of the way was closely contested," said the *Times* in its account of the affair, "but the city dungeon was reached at last, and in he went. If he had got hold of his gun before going in, there would have been a general killing."

That afternoon Ed Masterson performed his first official act as assistant marshal: he arrested Bobby Gill without any special difficulty, and tossed him into the clink to join Bat. Next day Bat and Bobby stood up together in police court. Bobby Gill got off with a five-dollar fine—and later received a free railroad ticket out of town, provided by the marshal. Bat, who had made the mistake of resisting arrest, and was the brother of a substantial citizen, was ordered to pay $25 plus costs. He left the courtroom with an understandable and abiding dislike for Larry Deger.

In this dislike he was joined by an unexpected ally—Dodge City Mayor James "Dog" Kelley (the nickname was not a personal slur; it arose from the fact that Kelley proudly kept a pack of greyhounds that once belonged to no less a hero than George Armstrong Custer). Kelley's quarrel with Deger was purely a business matter. Like many a cattle-town mayor, he was a saloonkeeper; he owned a modest but promising establishment on Front Street. Like many a marshal, Deger had business ambitions; during his term of office he bought into a rival Front Street saloon. In the summer of 1877, at the peak of the cowboy influx into Dodge—the most profitable time of year for saloons—the marshal attempted to use the powers of his office in a highhanded coup against the Mayor.

At 2 o'clock one morning Deger waddled into Kelley's saloon and arrested the Mayor's bartender on a minor, trumped-up charge. Dog Kelley soon came run-

Top lawmen in Dodge City from 1877 to 1881, the Masterson brothers—Jim, Ed and Bat *(from left to right)*—met varying fates. Ed was murdered—and his brothers fell from favor for their excessive gunplay.

ning to the jail and ordered his bartender released; when the marshal refused, the Mayor announced that he was suspended from office. Deger simply ignored him. Now Mayor Kelley ordered Assistant Marshal Ed Masterson and Policeman Joe Mason to arrest their boss. The marshal promptly drew his gun and warned the officers not to come near him, but after some palaver Ed talked Deger into letting himself be locked up for the moment. Ten minutes later, released without bail, Marshal Deger lodged a complaint against Kelley for interfering with a lawman in the discharge of his duty—and now the Mayor found himself arrested. Not until late afternoon did other officials manage to restore the status quo. The city council reinstated Deger as marshal; the police court dismissed the charge against the Mayor.

Clearly, Dog Kelley did not have enough backing in the city council to fire the marshal. But a group of ambitious young newcomers to Dodge, sympathetic to the Mayor, were at that moment planning a political takeover that would give Kelley and his supporters undisputed control of the city after the next election. The newcomers hung out at the office of the young county

attorney, Mike Sutton, who had come to Kansas fresh from a Missouri law school with only a single shirt to his name. Sutton's office was furnished with chairs so fragile that they had to be held together with baling wire, and visitors prudently preferred to stand. Nevertheless, the atmosphere proved congenial. The budding politicos welcomed such recruits as Mayor Kelley, Lloyd Shinn, the 22-year-old editor of the influential *Dodge City Times,* and Bat Masterson, who had just been appointed undersheriff of Ford County. Opposition forces began to call the members of these assemblies "the Gang," and they promptly adopted the name for themselves.

In the fall of 1877, Larry Deger, the Gang's prime target, announced that he would run for county sheriff that year. Immediately, the Gang put Bat Masterson forward for the office. The *Times* gave him a wholehearted endorsement: " 'Bat' is well known as a young man of nerve and coolness in cases of danger. He is qualified to fill the office and if elected will never shrink from danger." Soon afterward Bat won the endorsement of a "People's Mass Convention," which held its

A county check repays Bat Masterson for $35 in expenses—a drop in the bucket for the free-spending sheriff. He once irked Kansans by charging $4,000 for five months' care and feeding of seven prisoners.

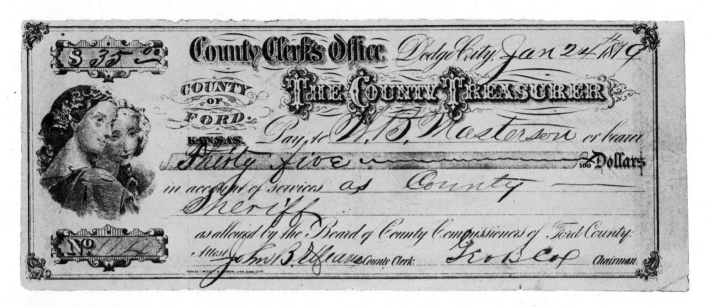

session at the Lady Gay saloon. In the election he beat Deger by three votes. The city council knew and respected a political landslide when they saw one. At Mayor Kelley's request, the council members finally fired Larry Deger as marshal of Dodge. In his place, after consulting the new movers and shakers of the town, they appointed Ed Masterson.

Less than six months earlier Ed and Bat Masterson had been inexperienced deputy lawmen. Now, by luck and skillful politicking, they were powerfully ensconced respectively as marshal of Dodge City and sheriff of Ford County. Ed was 25 years old, a year older than Bat. Though both had a lot to learn, only Ed really had the time to do so; a cattle town in winter was a quiet place, and Ed's services would not be much needed until the cowboys roared into town the following summer. But Bat's county-wide duties required that he be a quick learner—and he was. He started by changing his personal style to something more respectable. The sombrero and sash were abandoned; as he made his rounds of the county in a buggy and team, he wore a tailor-made black suit and a smart bowler hat with a high curled brim. Eddie Foy, who met him during this period, described him as "a trim, good-looking young man with a pleasant face and carefully barbered mustache, well-tailored clothes, hat with a rakish tilt, and two big silver-mounted, ivory-handled pistols in a heavy belt."

Only two weeks after assuming office, Bat got the chance to launch his term in a blaze of glory. At Kins-

ley, about 35 miles from Dodge City in neighboring Edwards County, six bandits tried to rob a train, were foiled and fled into the countryside. The sheriff of Edwards County and a detachment of troops from Fort Dodge set off in separate pursuits. Bat ignored both operations. Anticipating the bandits' movements, he led a posse through a driving blizzard to Crooked Creek, 55 miles from Dodge, and hid his men in an abandoned drovers' camp. When two of the outlaws approached seeking shelter from the storm, Bat sent one man out as a decoy to lead them into the camp. Before they could brush the snow from their coats the sheriff sprang forward, his two six-shooters cocked, and ordered them to throw up their hands. One did; the other reached for his revolver. The hammer click of another gun behind him changed his mind, and he surrendered too.

After turning over his prisoners to Edwards County officials, Bat took up the pursuit of the other four bandits, leading his posse 80 miles south to the neck of the Indian Territory. This hunt failed, but a month later two of the fugitives turned up in Dodge, hoping to learn the whereabouts of the sheriff's posse. One was soon spotted at a dance hall. Before dawn, Bat summoned his brother Ed and another lawman and took the outlaws without a gunfight.

The fifth bandit eluded capture for half a year more, and the sixth man was never caught. But Bat's triumph was splendid enough. Three of the prisoners were convicted after a short trial when the fourth, a border ruf-

Wild Bill Hickok: the saga of a dubious Galahad

When the glorifiers of the West began casting about for a single figure who could symbolize the lawman as hero, the most conspicuous—and eager—volunteer for that honor was James Butler Hickok. He had all the right attributes: courage, good looks, a sharpshooter's eye and a peerless appreciation of his own ferocity.

Born in 1837 in Illinois, Hickok emigrated to Monticello, Kansas, as a young man. There the ready belligerence that earned him the nickname Wild Bill also won him a brief job as a constable. Later, after serving as a Union scout in the Civil War, Hickok became a professional gambler and, in his best-known confrontation, outshot a fellow cardsharp in the public square of Springfield, Missouri. Eastern journalists began to seek him out after this classic duel, and Hickok obliged them with some out-and-out whoppers: he claimed that, among other feats, he had once picked off 50 Confederates with 50 bullets and a wonder-working rifle.

Still, some of Hickok's deeds were real and heroic. As an Army scout in 1868, he rescued 34 men from an Indian siege in Colorado by galloping through the attackers to summon help. He subsequently kept the peace in Hays City and Abilene, Kansas, killing four men in the line of duty. He cut an awesome figure in these towns; one visiting cowboy remembered him standing "with his back to the wall, looking at everything and everybody from under his eyebrows—just like a mad old bull."

But Wild Bill's glory was short-lived. In 1871 in Abilene, he loosed

Wild Bill sports a mass of long hair as a contemptuous challenge to scalp-seeking Indians.

a fusillade at a group of quarrelsome drunks, killing one troublemaker—and one policeman. The city council fired him, and his career slid downhill to a squalid chaos of booze, gambling and arrests for vagrancy. By 1876, plagued by eye trouble and the threatened loss of his marksman's gifts, he had wandered to Deadwood in Dakota Territory. One afternoon a saddle tramp named Jack McCall, convinced that Hickok had killed his brother in Kansas, sneaked up behind him at a poker table and shot him in the head. The very cowardice of the act testified to Wild Bill's potent reputation. Before he was hanged, McCall reportedly said he had not dared to meet Hickok face to face because "I didn't want to commit suicide."

fian named Dave Rudabaugh, tes-tified against them. Turning state's evidence was rare in those times and among such men. The *Kinsley Graphic* reported, almost wonder-ingly: "Rudabaugh testified that he was promised entire immunity from punishment if he would 'squeal,' therefore he squole. Some one has said there is a kind of honor among thieves. Rudabaugh don't think so."

For Bat Masterson, it was clear sailing from then on. The dapper young lawman became a familiar sight as he whipped his team and buggy around his bailiwick, an enor-mous area stretching 100 miles from east to west and 75 miles from north to south. Horse thieves and other outlaws wisely began to give this new hard-working sheriff a wide berth, and the plains of Ford Coun-ty were at relative peace. But in Dodge City, as the spring of 1878 drew on, Ed Masterson's work load as the city marshal grew heavier. Sa-loon rows among incoming cow-boys, con men and restless soldiers visiting from Fort Dodge kept him busy on both sides of the Santa Fe tracks; midnight robberies on the streets of Dodge increased in num-ber. Ed had courage enough and he enjoyed the respect of the citizenry, but Bat warned him that his easy-going manner and inborn gentle-ness would never inspire fear among the rapidly swelling number of hard-cases in town.

The differences between Bat and Ed Masterson were of life-or-death importance to a frontier peace of-ficer. Bat had the instincts and the reputation of a gunfighter; Ed did not. Bat rarely had to fire his re-volvers in a fight, for the simple rea-

THE PISTOL.

Murder of Edward J. Mas-terson City Marshal.

THE ASSAILANTS SHOT—ONE OF THEM DEAD.

DOLGE CITY IN MOURNING.

On Tuesday evening, about 10 o'clock, Edward J. Masterson, Marshal of Dodge City, was murdered by Jack Wagner and Alf Walker, two cattle drivers from near Hays City. The two cow boys were under the influence of bad whisky and were carrying revolvers. Early in the evening Marshal Masterson disarmed Wagner; later Marshal Masterson and Deputy Marshal Nat Harwood tried the second time to disarm Wagner. While in the act Master-son was shot in the abdomen. Walker in the meantime snapped a pistol in the face of Officer Haywood. Masterson fired four shots, one of them striking Wagner in the bowels from the left side. Walker was struck three times, one shot in the lungs and his right arm horribly shattered with the other shots.

The shooting occurred on the south side of the Railroad track. Marshal Master-son coolly walked over to the business side of the street, a distance of about 200 yards, and upon reaching the sidewalk he fell exhausted. He was taken to his room where he died about 40 minutes af-terwards.

Wagner and Walker were removed to Mr. Lane's room, where the former died at about 7 o'clock Wednesday evening. Walker is lying dangerously wounded, with no hopes of his recovery.

Some of the flying shots grazed the faces of one of our citizens and a cattle man. The shots were fired almost simultaneous-ly, and the wonder is expressed that more death and destruction did not ensue, as a large crowd surrounded the scene of the shooting.

The officers were brave and cool though both were at a disadvantage, as neither desired to kill the whisky crazed assail-ants.

The death of Marshal Masterson caused great feeling in Dodge City. The business houses were draped in mourning, and bus-iness on Wednesday generally suspended.

Elsewhere we give the expression of sympathy and ceremonies following this terrible tragedy.

son that most of his adversaries didn't dare shoot it out with him. In the absence of such encounters, he maintained his reputation and his ex-pertise by constant practice. As his public—and his potential opponents —looked on, Bat would spend hour after hour shooting at empty cans and "sweetening" his guns. "We used to file the notch of the ham-mer," he later recalled, "till the trig-ger would pull sweet, which is another way of saying that the blamed gun would pretty near go off if you looked at it."

Ed Masterson never nursed his six-shooters and never felt the need to. His method was to talk—or try to talk—his adversaries into submis-sion, and he wanted to go about cleaning up Dodge in his own way. Toward the end of March 1878, the *Times* carried this brief report: "City Marshal Masterson contem-plates organizing a tramp brigade for the purpose of clearing the streets and alleys of the filth and rubbish that has been accumulating for a year or so. There are about thirty tramps now sojourning among us, all of whom have no visible means of support and are liable to arrest un-der the vagrant act."

Ed's tramp brigade never got into action. One night only a week or so after he proposed it, the marshal tried to disarm two drunken cow-boys outside a saloon—with his own gun, as always, in its holster. Both men raised their revolvers, and Ed pinned one of them to a wall. At that point Bat Masterson came run-ning across the Santa Fe tracks, tak-ing a quick shot at the second cowboy as he did so. Not knowing it was Bat who was shooting, Ed let go of his man to draw his gun at last — and the freed cowboy got out his own six-shooter and fired. In seconds, the Mastersons shot both men, one fatally, but Ed stumbled off with a mortal wound. According to the *Ford County Globe* account, "His clothes were on fire from the discharge of the pistol, which had been placed against the right side of his abdomen and 'turned loose.'" A man standing nearby completed the story. "I saw him coming and in the darkness of the evening he seemed to be carrying a lighted cigar in his hand. I remarked to a friend that the cigar burned in a remarkably lively manner, but as the man drew near we saw that the fire was not at the end of a cigar but in the wadding of his coat. He fell dead at our feet."

Ed Masterson may not have been the gunfighter his brother was, but Dodge City perhaps loved him all the more for that. The next day, every business in town closed down and most doors were draped with black crepe. The young marshal's body lay in the parlor of the Dodge City Fire Company, to which he had belonged; the firemen claimed the honor of conducting his funeral. A choir stood at the coffin to sing a somber dirge: "Lay him low, lay him low, In the clover or the snow; What cares he, he cannot know." That afternoon almost every buggy and wagon in town joined the cortege bearing Ed Masterson to the military cemetery at Fort Dodge. The city council preceded the hearse, Bat Masterson rode alone behind it, and behind Bat came the 60 uniformed volunteers of the fire company.

The Mastersons were not yet finished in Dodge City. Later that spring the third brother, 23-year-old Jim, joined the city marshal's force as a policeman. In the fall of the following year, Jim moved up to become marshal of Dodge. On the day he took office, Bat Masterson was defeated for re-election as sheriff.

Bat's gunfighting hand had lost none of its skill; his opponent, a dull-witted saloonkeeper named George Hinkel, won the election on an economy platform. An opposition newspaper gloated, "The 'Gang' is no more in existence. It has lost its grip forever." Less than two years later, in 1881, that statement finally came true: Dog Kelley lost the mayoralty and Jim Masterson went out of office with him.

By then Bat had traveled far from Dodge. He came back now and then, especially when his brother needed him. Once, when Jim got into a shooting scrape with a saloonkeeper named Peacock and a bartender named Updegraff, Bat came all the way from New Mexico to lend a hand. A few minutes after he got off the train, he saw Peacock and Updegraff across the street. "I have come over a thousand miles to settle this," Bat called. "I know you are heeled; now fight!" The shooting lasted three or four minutes, with Bat sheltered behind an embankment. One bullet came so close that it threw some of the embankment dirt into his mouth. Another bullet passed through the Long Branch saloon, and another passed through Updegraff's lung. Both the saloon and the bartender were later repaired; Bat paid a $10 fine and left on the train the same night he arrived.

He continued his travels, flitting about the boomtowns of the West. In Colorado, he turned up as a gambler in Leadville, as town marshal in Trinidad. In another Colorado town called Creede, he combined both roles. As the manager of a gambling house, he patrolled his own premises in a lavender corduroy suit. As Creede's marshal, he kept such order in the streets that a Denver newspaper reported: "All the toughs and thugs fear him as they do no other dozen men in camp. Let an incipient riot start and all that is necessary to quell it is the whisper, 'There comes Masterson.'"

It could not last forever. As the years took their toll, Bat's reflexes slowed, his eye dimmed — and he knew that he could not live on his reputation alone. So he turned from the lawman's life, the gunfighter's life. One year, in Denver, he managed a saloon that featured a variety theater, and he married one of the actresses. He turned to promoting prize fights, lost his bank roll on bad bets and began drinking heavily. Denver was glad to see him go. He wound up in New York City — of all places — earning his living as a sports writer.

Bat Masterson was now a national celebrity, but he had unbuckled his gun belt for good. In 1905, when President Theodore Roosevelt offered to appoint him the U.S. marshal for the Oklahoma Territory, Bat turned him down in a letter that combined sadness with common sense. "I am not the man for the job," he wrote the President. "Oklahoma is still woolly, and if I were marshal some youngster would try to put me out because of my reputation. I would be a bait for grown-up kids who had fed on dime novels. I would have to kill or be killed. No sense to that. I have taken my guns off, and I don't ever want to put them on again."

Oases of pleasure and dens of iniquity

A tenderfoot once observed that Wyatt Earp's most vivid recollections of his days as a frontier lawman involved people who were entering, occupying or leaving saloons. Earp replied tartly, "We had no Y.M.C.A.'s."

There were good reasons why the watchful eye of the law was needed in the saloons of the West. Beyond their primary function as purveyors of drink, many of them provided facilities for gambling and for consorting with fast women — activities that frequently sparked gunplay. But the saloon was also a social club, an art gallery of sorts and a haven of relaxation and repartee. One standard joke stemmed from the ritual that called for customers to pour their own drinks from a bottle into a shot glass. If the customer spilled a single drop, the bartender was likely to inquire, "Do you want a towel?" implying that the drinker had wasted enough whiskey to take a bath in it.

Some saloons dispensed rotgut but others, notably in rich mining towns, were stocked with the finest liquors and wines, and could supply almost any mixed drink known to man. At the better establishments Buffalo Bill Cody had no trouble getting his favorite, a Stone Fence: a shot of rye and a twist of lemon in a glass of cider.

Bartenders often were hired not just for their mixing skills but for their ability to handle rowdies. Yet beneath a stern exterior many a barkeep concealed a sentimental heart. "Don't forget to write to mother," read a sign in a Montana saloon. "She is thinking of you. We furnish paper and envelopes free, and have the best whiskey in town."

Patrons, fiddlers and a lone female gather in 1888 at the Elephant Saloon in Beer City, near the Oklahoma territory. Seated at far right is Marshal Lew Bush, later killed by a madam named Pussycat Nell.

126

At the Cosmopolitan Saloon in the affluent mining town of Telluride, Colorado, the marshal leans benignly against the gleaming mahogany bar as

midafternoon gambling goes on apace across the room. Other diversions are suggested by the nude on the far wall—a portrait of a local Jezebel.

Determined to keep peace on his modest premises, a bartender in Albany County, Wyoming, has his pistol stashed in a glass within handy reach as a visiting gambler stacks chips and awaits his next prospect.

FARO CUE BOX

Sliding counters *(top and bottom)* kept track of the cards pulled from the deck.

CARD PRESS

Made of uncoated paper, cards were tightly stored in such boxes to prevent curling.

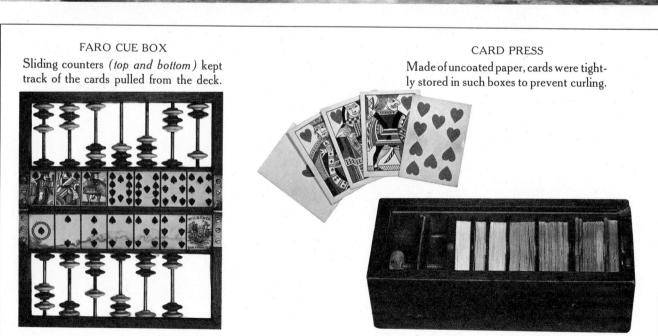

Oblivious to kibitzers, poker players prepare to ante up at a New Mexico hangout. Though poker pots often exceeded $1,000, such games as faro *(opposite, below)* and keno *(below)* also had devotees.

KENO GOOSE
This urn, or "goose," released numbered pellets one at a time in a game like bingo.

CARD CUTTER
A device to trim off the worn, fuzzy edges of cards helped to extend their lifetime.

To the accompaniment of a banjo, cowboys while away the hours at poker and pool in a Montana Territory saloon. Frontiersmen were no

slouches with a cue; one denizen of Western dives, Jacob "The Wizard" Schaefer, won a series of national billiards crowns beginning in 1879.

Dodge City's Long Branch saloon, a favorite haunt of Bat Masterson and Wyatt Earp, kept customers happy with a host of inspirational art works — including this aptly titled painting, *The Cowboy's Dream.*

A whiskey advertisement *(left)* that graced a wall of a Tombstone barroom depicts a high-stakes faro game. Playing against the faro bank was known as "bucking the tiger" — the motto printed at the upper left.

The brewery ads hanging in countless saloons functioned somewhat like bar snacks: just as salty pickles made men drink more, visions of noble womanhood turned them tearful — and also made them drink more.

Judge, attorney and aides convene at Tombstone's new courthouse in the mid-1880s.

The ultimate responsibility for maintaining order in the Old West belonged to men armed not with guns but gavels —the judges. At first, the brand of justice they dispensed was as makeshift as the towns that sprang up along the frontier's far edges. Many early judges were tradesmen on the side and had little or no lawbook learning. Lacking courthouses, they were often obliged to hold trials in stores or saloons; and even when they had a courtroom, formality was often absent. At the police court in Dodge City, a judge opened one session with the declaration: "Trot out the wicked and unfortunate, and let the cotillion commence."

But continuing violence forced communities to elect qualified judges and build facilities like the one shown here —places where justice could reign with the dignity and authority it deserved.

Judgment days for a rambunctious land

Charles Jackson, a politician in Shelby County, Texas, had no intention of starting a ruckus that warm fall day in 1840. When he raised his rifle, took careful aim, and shot a man named Joseph Goodbread through the heart, he only wanted to do right by a friend whom Goodbread had cheated in a business deal. But Jackson's notion of right touched off a war that raged for four long years and spread through five counties. And as it raged it exposed a weakness in frontier life that few people were willing to admit: the system of justice on which Americans elsewhere depended had taken only a tenuous hold in the West.

Jackson's act triggered a monumental feud between his own allies and Goodbread's friends. The two factions, augmented by outlaws and opportunists of every sort, and operating as vigilante teams under the high-flown titles of the Moderators and the Regulators, embarked on a protracted orgy of shooting and looting, lynching and burning that left at least 50 men dead and ravaged the countryside.

Clearly, the crimes that were committed called for justice to be meted out, and from time to time one judge or another appeared on the scene to try to temper gun law with lawbook law. The difficulty of this task was discovered at considerable personal cost by the judicial troubleshooter who was sent to conduct the mur-

der trial of Charles Jackson himself.

The first sight that greeted District Court Judge John Hansford upon arrival in the town of Pulaski was the presence in the streets of some 150 armed men, ominously lurking about. He was followed into the courthouse by 20 of them, along with the sheriff and the defendant —also armed. Not yet completely cowed, Hansford fined the sheriff for letting his charge come into court with his weapons. The defendant was outraged; it so happened that the sheriff was the friend for whom he had committed murder. He removed his pistols, threw them on the judge's bench, took off his coat, and demanded that the trial commence.

Hansford managed to get through a turbulent day, even choosing a panel of jurors, but overnight he had unnerving second thoughts about the matter. Next morning he was gone, leaving the sheriff this plaintive note: "Being unwilling to risk my person in the courthouse any longer where I see myself surrounded by bravos and hired assassins, and no longer left free to preside as an impartial judge at this special term of court called for the trial of Charles W. Jackson, I order you to adjourn the court tomorrow at eight o'clock by proclamation without delay."

In the absence of the judge, Jackson was given a mock trial by his cronies; he pleaded self-defense, and was acquitted. Judge Hansford was not so fortunate. A few days later, some miles outside of Pulaski, he was found shot to death by a party or parties unknown.

Hansford's fate was exceptionally harsh, probably because he had the bad luck to be dealing with Texans at a time and place of unusual turmoil; Texas itself was then still an independent republic and, though its leaders had adopted the U.S. system of justice as a model,

Minutes before his execution for a double murder in 1898, ranch hand Billy Calder grimaces as the hangman in Lewistown, Montana, inspects the noose. Hangings were often heralded by invitations (*above*) to the press and other interested parties.

Sheriff's Office,
Missoula County.
Missoula, Mont., Nov. 22, 1892.
Mr. *B.F. O'Neil*

Your presence is requested at the execution of
JOHN BURNS,
FOR THE MURDER OF MAURICE HIGGINS.
To take place in the yard of the Missoula County Jail on
Friday, December 16, 1892.
WM. H. HOUSTON, Sheriff.

With a white-haired elder presiding *(left)*, stern settlers crowd a cabin to try an accused horse thief *(standing, center)* in this 1877 depiction of the improvisatory justice that ruled many frontier communities.

its proud and prickly citizens brooked little authority of any sort, judicial or otherwise. But they were not all that different from people everywhere on the frontier; disdain and disrespect for the man on the bench were evident throughout the West. Many a judge was cursed out to his face, pointedly subjected by spectators to a display of their pistols and bowie knives, or openly threatened with mayhem. The courtroom itself suffered varying degrees of indignity, from fist fights and brawls to barrages of rubbish. The irreverence of Dodge City's residents moved a police court judge to announce: "Any person caught throwing turnips, cigar stumps, beets, or old quids of tobacco at this court will be immediately arraigned before this bar of justice."

Firmness, resoluteness and iron nerve were a judge's best weapons of counterattack, and the man who refused to be intimidated usually prevailed. One memorable confrontation between an angry populace and a man who could not be buffaloed took place in the same Shelby County that later routed Judge Hansford. The

man was District Judge Robert M. Williamson, better known as "Three-Legged Willie" because he walked on a peg leg attached at one knee, with his own extremity, withered by a childhood illness, bent behind him. But it quickly became clear that there was nothing wrong with Willie's backbone.

The judge had been sent to the town of Shelbyville to set up a court. As a gaggle of resentful ruffians looked on, he improvised a courtroom in a general store, using a dry-goods case as his bench. He had no sooner sat down than the local spokesman informed him that no court was needed in those parts. By way of emphasis, the speaker tossed his bowie knife on the bench and announced contemptuously, "This, sir, is the law in Shelby County." Whereupon Three-Legged Willie whipped out his pistol, whacked it down beside the knife, and roared: "This is the constitution that overrules your law!"

For his show of raw courage, Willie might have met with Hansford's end. He did not. Neither did he go on to tame Shelby County's feuding factions. What Willie accomplished was subtler and longer-lasting. The men he faced down must have felt, perhaps for the first time, a grudging respect for Willie's law.

The same feeling began slowly to insinuate itself into other frontier communities beset by lawlessness. Some citizens continued to resist any rein on their freedom, but more thoughtful elements in the community came to see that courts were an essential aid to local peace-keeping efforts. It was all well and good for a marshal or sheriff to hunt down an evildoer at high risk; but, unless the man was tried and punished, the risk was likely to recur. Peace officers on their own could do little more than fight violence with violence. If the cycle was to be broken anywhere, it had to be done in orderly courts, presided over by capable judges, with the full and unqualified support of the citizenry.

A long time was to elapse before the West had anything approaching this ideal. The system of courts envisaged by the Founding Fathers worked well enough in the East, but on the sparsely populated frontier it proved to be a ramshackle structure, in constant need of propping up and reinforcement. When a territory was organized, the U.S. government would appoint a few district judges, gradually increasing the number as the territory began to fill up. These men shouldered an enormous burden. They tried not only specific federal crimes — train holdups, obstruction of the mails, counterfeiting, selling whiskey to Indians — but also all major crimes later left to the state courts, such as murder, rape and armed robbery. The only cases they did not handle were minor offenses — misdemeanors and breaches of local ordinances — within the purview of locally elected or appointed justices of the peace or police court judges.

Geography alone made the task of the district judge a formidable proposition. Often he had to take long, toilsome, circuit-riding trips to try accused malefactors being detained in various communities within his sprawling jurisdiction; or he might send out his marshals to convoy the accused to the district court for trial. Distances on the frontier could slow justice in other ways as well. A judge in Arizona, on looking over a group of potential jurors, noticed that one of them wore no coat; viewing the casual dress as an affront to the dignity of the court, he ordered the man to go home and get the missing garment. It was three days before the culprit returned, properly clad — belatedly explaining to the irate judge that home was 80 miles away.

Every defendant had a right to trial by jury, but rounding up enough citizens to form a jury was difficult in thinly settled areas. The results were not always encouraging; Mark Twain recalled one Virginia City juror who "thought that incest and arson were the same thing." Even when frontier jurors were of a higher caliber, there was no guarantee that the merits of a case would guide their deliberations. Often, when the defendant was known locally, they would find for him simply to express their distaste for outside authority. In several districts where the payment of jury fees was exasperatingly slow, jurors refused to reveal their findings until they got cash on the barrelhead.

In the best of circumstances, with a conscientious jury and well-intentioned lawyers, a district judge still had his frustrations. Because many lawyers were abysmally ignorant of the law — only a relative few had been formally schooled in it before hanging out their shingles — a judge could expend a good deal of effort in prompting and guiding both prosecutor and defense. Nor was he himself necessarily versed in procedures and precedents. Though judges who presided over jury trials were expected to have some formal education in the law, those appointed to the Western bench often were men left over after others had picked off preferred judicial plums back East.

But for all the failings of the district court, it was there that the Western criminal first met the cutting edge of lawbook law, with a long prison term or a death sentence as a likely penalty if he was adjudged guilty.

At the local level the administration of justice was at best haphazard, sometimes bordering on the farcical. The justice of the peace or police court judge in charge often had nothing to recommend him for the post but his availability. His job was not complex or arduous; by territorial or state law he dealt only with minor offenses such as disorderly conduct or petty theft. About 90 per cent of the cases began with a plea of guilty and ended moments later with the imposition of a small fine.

Working conditions for local judges usually left much to be desired. In the new frontier towns, civic buildings were as scarce as honest gamblers. For the lack of a courthouse, justices held their hearings in pool halls, saloons or wherever they happened to be when a case came up. Overloaded dockets soon forced many towns to erect a courthouse, but it was no easy matter to keep the brand-new building intact. A favorite tactic of outlaws in Texas and Kansas was to burn the place down — either out of plain cussedness or to destroy damaging evidence in the judicial files.

Still, local justice suffered more from the ill-equipped men who administered it than from a dearth of facilities. Many of them could barely read or write. And because the post had no minimal standards of performance, it attracted a disproportionate number of bumblers, drunkards and flamboyant eccentrics like Roy Bean of Vinegaroon, Texas (page 156).

Yet these were relatively acceptable flaws in the judicial character. A man who pared his toenails while hearing a case, or who called a recess so that he and the participants could slake their thirst at the nearest saloon, could be tolerated by an indulgent community. But too many justices took or solicited bribes, or used their authority to impose and pocket exorbitant fines. One Texas justice disguised his venality with a disarming foible. He kept a mail-order catalogue on his bench and, opening it at random, would quote the price of some article listed in it as the fine to be paid by the defendant before him. When one defendant protested the odd fine of $4.88 for some trifling misdemeanor, his lawyer quietly advised: "Be thankful he opened it at pants instead of at pianos."

Honest justices who did not yield to temptation, impartial justices who did not penalize strangers harshly and excuse the transgressions of friends, even learned justices—such men did exist. Probably there were more of them than eyewitness accounts suggest. Even so, the West was patently lucky that its lower courts had only a limited say over the lives of its citizens.

No part of the West was more of a legal and jurisdictional nightmare—and a criminals' paradise—than Indian Territory. This immense wilderness of prairies and mountains was bounded by Arkansas on the east, Kansas on the north, a strip of no man's land on the northwest, and Texas on the west and south. Without doubt the territory offered outlaws their safest refuge and their richest field for uninhibited plunder. At one time or another, the worst scoundrels in the West accepted the open invitation to visit Indian Territory. The James gang vacationed there between holdups, and the Dalton brothers roamed there without challenge, robbing and killing at will.

In Indian Territory, nothing worked in favor of firm and uniform law. Around 1870, the only authorized permanent residents of the territory were some 50,000 Indians — principally the large groups known as the Five Civilized Tribes. The territory had no white man's towns at all. The five tribes—Cherokee, Choctaw, Chickasaw, Creek and Seminole—were recognized by the U.S. government as self-governing nations within their own allotted lands, and each tribe had its laws, courts and police force (called the "Lighthorse" for the ponies that were used on patrol). But the Indian courts had no jurisdiction over white invaders, no power to exert even minimal restraints on fugitives from other parts. Moreover, they lost jurisdiction over every Indian who committed any crime against — or in company with — a white. Such Indians, and every white who committed any crime whatsoever within the territory, fell under the jurisdiction of the United States Court for the Western District of Arkansas, whose sole judge and handful of marshals were expected somehow to enforce law and order over some 70,000 square miles of outlaw-haunted terrain.

Nobody had planned these ludicrous arrangements; they just evolved over the years. Back in the 1830s, Indian Territory was a vaguely defined vastness of undesirable land on which the Five Civilized Tribes were being resettled by the U.S. government after being forced to vacate more desirable eastern lands in the pathway of white progress. Having launched this compulsory and bitterly resisted exodus — the so-called Indian Removal—Congress then proceeded to attempt amends. In an effort to protect all Indians by severely limiting white contacts with them, the federal legislators in 1834 passed what they grandly titled "An Act to Regulate Trade and Intercourse with the Indian Tribes and Preserve Peace on the Frontiers," more familiarly called the Intercourse Act. Among other features, it rigidly excluded white settlers from Indian Territory and permitted the presence of white traders only under federal license. But from the first, whites generally ignored the act's myriad prohibitions, penalties and punishments.

The transplanted Indians accepted their sorry lot and made do; soon, however, white progress again caught

up with them. By the early 1850s, Texas cattle herds bound for Kansas were crossing the territory in the thousands, and prospectors were streaming through on their way to the California gold fields. A few years later, the routing of the east-west overland mail through the territory threatened to turn it into a gigantic thoroughfare.

The Civil War slowed the white incursions but added to the turmoil nonetheless. Wealthy Indians among the Five Civilized Tribes owned a large number of black slaves and therefore sided with the Confederacy. For punishment, or under the subterfuge of punishment, the postwar U.S. government forced the five tribes to cede back a large chunk of their supposedly inalienable Western domains, including an empty section later to be a bone of contention known as the Unassigned Lands. To further complicate matters, emancipated slaves in Indian Territory passed from the jurisdiction of Indian law and became the responsibility of the remote federal court in Arkansas. Some of the freed blacks set up their own towns and businesses, others settled down to farming, and others wandered about the territory getting into trouble.

In the years after the Civil War, the pressures on Indian Territory built up terrifically. The streams of voracious cattle and unruly cowboys swelled to torrents, cutting broad swaths through the territory on their way to railheads in Kansas. The steady influx of white settlers into Kansas and Texas pushed groups of squatters across the borders into the territory. The overland mail service required the establishment of stage stations here and there. Two railroad companies — the Missouri, Kansas & Texas and the Atlantic & Pacific — poked fingers of steel across the region, and flung up depots along the right of way. By the mid-1870s the map of Indian Territory was dotted with American place names.

The presence there of stagecoach stations and of railroad depots and personnel was entirely legal, representing legitimate commerce under the terms of the Intercourse Act. But in the classic pattern of the frontier these installations and the legitimate transients who

143

A sharpshooting lawyer's courtroom theatrics

Lawyers were an essential link in the chain of frontier justice, and none was more able—or more flamboyant—than Temple Houston, son of Texas patriot Sam Houston. Tall and long-haired, he cultivated a dandy's look, favoring long Prince Albert coats, embroidered slippers and white sombreros. But appearances were deceptive: Houston was a crack marksman who once bested Bat Masterson in a pistol match. He was no less formidable in criminal trials across the Southwest, mesmerizing jurors with his oratory. Defending one Millie Stacey against a charge of prostitution in 1899, he declared that "Where the star of purity once glittered on her girlish brow, burning shame has set its seal forever," and asked the all-male jury to let her "go in peace." They did.

At another trial, Houston whipped out a pair of Colt .45s, pointed them

Temple Houston in the 1890s

at the jury box and blazed away—neglecting to inform the jurors that the guns were loaded with blanks. He was trying to prove that his client, who was charged with the murder of a skilled gunfighter, had acted in self-defense by shooting first. "I only wanted to show what speed the dead man possessed," Houston said in apologizing to the court. However, the ploy misfired and the defendant was found guilty. Undaunted, Houston demanded a new trial on the grounds that the jurors, while scattering before his fusillade, had "separated and mingled with the crowd" and therefore had not been sequestered. He won his point, and the case.

Houston could also be deadly serious with a gun. After a courtroom argument with another lawyer, the two men met in a saloon. Houston killed his adversary—and entered a successful plea of self-defense.

When he died of a stroke in 1905, a newspaper described him as "a mingling of nettles and flowers," adding that the Southwest "probably will never see his counterpart."

A collector of frontier memorabilia, Houston filled his Oklahoma home with guns, Indian artifacts and pictures of chiefs—and George Washington.

passed through them attracted countless other individuals whose business was strictly illegal, and whose rush into the territory was greatly accelerated by the total absence of local law-enforcement agencies. With the arrival of such people—gamblers, prostitutes, whiskey peddlers and drifters who lived by the gun—criminal violence took a drastic leap upward.

By the early 1870s cries of alarm and indignation were rising from Indians in the territory and from bordering communities. The *Western Independent* of Fort Smith, Arkansas, prophesied that "if crime continues to increase there so fast, a regiment of deputy marshals cannot arrest all the murderers." An Indian Territory newspaper, the *Indian Progress* of Muskogee, published "a calendar of the operations of the knife and pistol," listing 15 murders, most of them unsolved and some of them uninvestigated, that had been committed in a "peaceful" 30-mile radius in just two years.

These reports, and vociferous complaints from terrorized travelers, did not escape the notice of the men charged with administering justice and enforcing law in Indian Territory. But those authorities—the federal judge and the federal marshal for the Western District of Arkansas—were also responsible for 30 Arkansas counties; that alone was a crushing task for their meager staff of prosecutors and deputy marshals. In 1871, one small step was taken to meet the deepening crisis: the judge, the marshal and the district attorney moved their headquarters southwestward from the town of Van Buren to the town of Fort Smith on the Arkansas River, only 100 yards from the eastern edge of Indian Territory. But at the same time the judicial work load in Arkansas itself increased as more settlers flowed in and business boomed. To add to the problem, in 1872 a corrupt incompetent named William Story was appointed to the federal judgeship. In little more than a year—during which time more than 100 murders were committed in Indian Territory—Story had to resign to avoid impeachment for bribery.

By 1875 the federal court of western Arkansas was in such scandalous disarray that Congress might have abolished it altogether—except for two factors. In the first place, there was no better alternative available and no time to devise one. In the second place, a thoroughly viable nominee for the vacant and unwanted judgeship was suddenly put forward. He was not only honest, capable and vigorous but actually distinguished. To make this paragon even more incredible, he had volunteered for the $3,500-a-year post.

His name, already well known in government circles, was Isaac Charles Parker, but he was soon to win greater fame as the "Hanging Judge" of Fort Smith.

Parker was only 36 in 1875, but he had behind him a long and varied career. He had served as city attorney in his hometown of St. Joseph, Missouri; as a Presidential elector for Abraham Lincoln; as a judge for a backwoods district of Missouri; and as a two-term Representative to the U.S. Congress. But when he applied for the Fort Smith judgeship in a letter to President Grant, more was involved than dedication to the law. As a member of the House Committee on Indian Affairs, he had become deeply concerned with the Indians' plight; his sponsorship of measures to give them economic aid moved his Congressional colleagues to dub him "the Indians' best friend."

Parker was also a stern Methodist. His upbringing had taught him that life is a constant battle between good and evil, and that the punishment of evildoers was an imperative of divine justice. A position on the bench at Fort Smith would bring him plenty of evildoers in need of punishment, at the same time providing him with a first-hand opportunity to rid the Indians of their ruthless exploiters. In short, Parker and the vacant post were a perfect match. He wanted the job as much as it needed him.

President Grant made the appointment, and Congress confirmed it with unusual haste—as if to prevent Parker from changing his mind. He and his wife and their two sons left their home in St. Joe and at Little Rock took a boat up the Arkansas River to Fort Smith. They arrived on Sunday morning, May 2, 1875.

A small group of townspeople turned out at the dock to take a look at the new judge. They liked what they saw. Parker was an imposing figure—a straight-backed six-footer who weighed about 200 pounds, and whose severely handsome face was dignified by a tawny mustache and a thick goatee. His manner was unmistakably authoritative, and it was easy to believe the deputy marshal who observed, "When an attorney started to argue with him, he just pointed his finger at him. The attorney didn't *sit* down, he *fell* down." All the same, Fort Smith people doubted that Parker could do

A double hanging of murderers in Leadville, Colorado, in 1881, draws 10,000 spectators. While most frontier executions were well attended, this event attracted an unusual turnout not only because of its dual nature but because, as a Denver paper noted, it was the town's "first legal hanging."

A disbeliever in tempering justice with mercy, "Hanging Judge" Isaac Charles Parker sentenced a total of 160 men to the gallows during two controversy-ridden decades of keeping rein on Indian Territory.

much to improve conditions in the Indian country.

Parker, for his part, was just as skeptical about Fort Smith. The town, named for a military post built there in 1817, was a dusty jumble of unpaved streets and low wooden buildings. It had a population of about 2,500, and 30 saloons that catered to railroad and riverboat men, to transients on their way west, and to Texas cowboys homeward bound after their long cattle drives to Kansas. The fort itself was a large squat structure enclosed by heavy stone walls with cannon bastions on top; but the soldiers had left, and nothing but drabness remained.

As Mrs. Parker looked around, she reportedly said, "We have made a great mistake, Isaac." But her husband replied, "No, Mary. We are faced with a great task. These people need us. We must not fail them."

Parker emphasized his resolve with prompt action. Just eight days after his arrival in Fort Smith, the judge opened his court for business. The courtroom was housed on the first floor of a two-story former barracks in the fort; it reeked of the jail cells in the basement below. Each day as the clerk called the court to order, Judge Parker climbed to his seat behind a huge cherrywood desk on a platform. Prisoners brought before him could take little comfort from his stern face, and even less from the dispatch with which he proceeded.

A total of 91 defendants were tried by Parker in the first session of his court, which lasted eight weeks. Of the accused, 18 were charged with murder and 15 were convicted. Eight received long prison terms, one was killed trying to escape and the remaining six were condemned to the gallows. In pronouncing their death sentences, Judge Parker bowed his head. "I do not desire to hang you men," he said in a low voice. "It is the law." Then, unaccountably, he wept.

The crimes these six men had committed were fairly typical of those that Parker would try in his 21 years on the bench at Fort Smith. One man had murdered a young cowboy to get his fancy boots and saddle. Another had clubbed and knifed an old friend to death to get his pocket money. A third had borrowed a Winchester from a friend, then used it to kill him on a whim. These defendants were not big-time gunfighters but anonymous men moved by small, sordid motives. For every murder or holdup by a celebrated outlaw, there were scores perpetrated by such lesser men, har-

rying the frontier by sheer numbers far more than the criminal acts that won national notoriety. The spectators who saw Judge Parker weep had good reason to think that the condemned six before him were not worth his tears. They heartily approved the death penalty for men of this sort, firmly believing that it alone could discourage capital crimes. And as a means of insuring the maximum discouragement, they fully endorsed the ritual of the public hanging.

On the day of execution, more than 5,000 citizens jammed the fort compound to watch the six men die. An immense gallows, built at Parker's orders, stood in the courtyard. The posts and crossbeam were 12-inch-thick oak timbers, and a narrow trap door ran the length of the platform. It was a thoroughly awesome instrument, designed to hang as many as 12 men at one time.

Wagonloads of settlers from 40 or 50 miles around had begun rolling into town at daybreak in order to make the 9:30 a.m. deadline. Townsmen and countrymen alike brought their entire families, and the youngsters climbed the walls surrounding the fort to get a better view of the spectacle. The best vantage points were occupied by reporters, many of whom had journeyed from St. Louis, Kansas City and even all the way from the Eastern Seaboard.

At 9:30 sharp, the six doomed men were escorted to the gallows by a dozen armed guards and four local ministers. After the death sentences were read, the six were allowed to speak their last words. One killer told the crowd, "I am as anxious to get out of this world as you are to see me go."

After prayers by the clergy and a little hymn singing by the throng, the six men were blindfolded with sack-like black hoods and led into position over the long trap door. Then the thin, bearded executioner, George Maledon (page 161), adjusted nooses of hand-woven, well-oiled Kentucky hemp rope around the men's necks. Maledon took somber pride in his hangings: only an expert could guarantee that the victim's fall would break his neck, thus sparing him slow strangulation. As Maledon drily remarked years later, "I never hanged a man who came back to have the job done over."

Suddenly Maledon sprang his trap. The six men dropped to quick deaths, and the crowd dispersed. The execution was played up by newspapers from coast to coast. The simultaneous public hanging of half a dozen men horrified many readers, especially in the East, though they might have accepted six separate and well-concealed hangings. The charge was voiced—and would grow steadily in volume—that the judge was inhuman and possessed of an insatiable appetite for hangings. In rebutting the charge for the first but not the last time, Parker went to the heart of the matter: "If criticism is due, it should be [for] the system, not the man whose duty lies under it."

But duty kept Parker too busy for philosophical disputation. Since arriving at Fort Smith he had labored tirelessly, not only trying the 91 cases that awaited him, but also organizing ways and means of bringing in more lawbreakers to stand trial. Congress and the President had invested Parker with unique powers to cope with the unique problems of Indian Territory. His marshal, also a Presidential appointee, was authorized to hire a small army of 200 deputy marshals, many more than the complement of any other state or territory. Of far greater importance, Parker was given exclusive jurisdiction and final authority over all crimes committed in Indian Territory. This meant that his decisions could not be appealed to any higher court; the only hope for a man he condemned to death was a pardon or commutation by the President. Moreover, Parker could conduct his trials virtually without regard to precedents established elsewhere by federal law. Very few of these precedents applied to crimes committed in Indian Territory, because it constituted a kind of special legal limbo whose principal inhabitants were members of sovereign Indian nations. And even if a precedent did apply, Parker could choose to flout it, and a defendant's lawyer was powerless to appeal the matter.

Parker, in sum, was the law—the absolute law—for Indian Territory. And so the battle lines were drawn for the West's climactic clash over the issue of law and order: the West's strongest judge against the West's worst concentration of badmen.

In recruiting his force of deputy marshals, Parker looked reality square in the eye. He hated gunfighters, but he knew that it took one to catch one. He also knew that some of the men who applied for the job were attracted less by its fees and capture rewards—no salaries were paid—than by the opportunities their badge would provide for graft and extortion. Parker tried to screen out the crooks, but if a man was good

Atop a barn fortified against intruders, Cherokee ranchers in Indian Territory watch for roving brigands in the 1880s. Lacking the authority to prosecute rapacious whites, the Indians found their domain, in one newspaper's words, "the rendezvous of the vile and wicked from everywhere."

with a gun, the judge was willing to overlook blank spots in his background. He hired some convincing candidates who later turned to crime, among them two of the Dalton brothers, who caught a number of outlaws and made good witnesses for the prosecution at several of Parker's trials; he also took on some suspicious characters who remained honest and died in combat for the law. Altogether, 65 of his deputies would die in this manner during Parker's two decades at Fort Smith. To all of his men, the judge's orders were simple: "Bring them in, alive—or dead."

Parker's men fanned out through Indian Territory on the greatest mass manhunt in history. Usually the deputies rode in teams of four or five for self-protection, and a team brought with it a movable headquarters—a van or wagon equipped to serve as office, arsenal, dormitory, kitchen and jail. While some teams were sent out as posses on special missions, most were not assigned a definite destination; they were, in their idiom, "on the scout"—poking and prying, searching shacks for stills or contraband whiskey, prowling in canyons and ravines for stolen horses, investigating suspicious wayfarers—trying to flush criminals of any kind.

The deputies never shot to kill if they could possibly avoid it; every man they brought back to stand trial was worth an arrest fee of two dollars, and they got nothing at all for a corpse unless, by a rare stroke of luck, a dead-or-alive reward for the victim had been posted by the railroads or stage companies or some civil authority. A wounded prisoner was permitted to ride in the wagon, chained to its sideboards; the healthy ones were marched alongside at the point of a gun.

As the haul of captives mounted, a team frequently exceeded its allowance of a dollar a day for feeding all prisoners, and the deputies were forced to make up the difference. However, they did have a steady source of funds; they were authorized to collect fines for minor offenses and to keep the money as extra income. This incentive plan inevitably encouraged some deputies to become lawbreakers themselves. Dipping into their collection of evidence, they would plant confiscated booze or stolen goods in someone's wagon, then fine the owner for all the traffic would bear.

The felonious practices of some deputies made a hard job more difficult for all of them. Almost everywhere they met with suspicion, since the territory now

U. S. Marshal's Office,
Western District of Arkansas,
Fort Smith, Arkansas.

LAWS

GOVERNING U. S. MARSHAL

......AND......

His Deputies.

U. S. Deputy Marshals for the Western District of Arkansas may make arrests for

MURDER, MANSLAUGHTER,
ASSAULT, WITH INTENT TO KILL OR TO MAIM,
ATTEMPTS TO MURDER,
ARSON, ROBBERY, RAPE, BURGLARY,
LARCENY, INCEST, ADULTERY,
WILFULLY AND MALICIOUSLY PLACING OBSTRUCTIONS
ON A RAILROAD TRACK.

These arrests may be made with or without warrant first issued and in the hands of the Deputy or the Chief Marshal. It is always better for the Deputy to have a warrant before making an arrest, yet if he knows of any one of the above crimes having been committed and has good reason to believe a particular party guilty of the crime, his duty is to make the arrest.

For violations of the revenue law and for introducing ardent spirits into the Indian Country, the Deputy can not make an arrest without warrant, unless the offender is caught in the act, when he can arrest for these offenses without a warrant. The Deputy can arrest for violations of the revenue law, the intercourse law and the laws of the United States against counterfeiting, and for violations of the postal laws, or for larceny of the property of the United States, when any of these offenses are committed by an Indian. Also when an assault with intent to kill or maim, a murder, or manslaughter has been committed by an Indian upon an Indian Agent, Indian Policeman, Indian United States Deputy Marshal or guard or any person at any time while in the discharge of duty or at any time held plenty of people with reason to be leery of them. Besides those shady characters hanging around railroad depots and other legitimate installations, there were thousands of others who had circumvented the law prohibiting white men from purchasing Indian land; they had married Indian women or signed long leases with Indian landowners, and settled down to farming and ranching. All together, Indian Territory in 1878 had about 20,000 white inhabitants, and many of them translated their wariness of outside authority into hostility toward Parker's deputies, and even into aid and comfort for lawbreakers.

Some whites gave shelter to outlaws or provided them with supplies or even ammunition. They also warned outlaws of the approach of deputies, who left telltale signs of their presence. As an old-timer later explained, "In those days [our] horses were barefooted. If we discovered a horse's tracks which showed that the horse was shod we knew a United States Marshal was in the neighborhood."

Local hostility presented the deputies with still another problem. To expedite trials at Fort Smith, they usually picked up witnesses at the scene and took them back with them. The witnesses were reluctant both to make the long trip and to run the risk of reprisals. As a trip wore on, the deputies might find it slow going if two dozen or more witnesses chose to balk. Even when they came along willingly, it was no easy matter to get them out of harm's way if a gunfight erupted.

The deputies often were involved in short, brisk shoot-outs, and occasionally in lengthy gun battles, with cornered desperadoes. One of their fiercest clashes took place at Rabbit Trap Canyon near Tahlequah, in the Cherokees' northeastern domain. Their quarry was an elusive Cherokee outlaw named Ned Christie, who roved the territory as a train robber, horse thief and whiskey peddler. Christie had built himself a log fort high on the rim of the cliff-sided canyon, and when a 16-man posse tracked him there, he showed no inclination to surrender.

At sunrise the day after they trapped the outlaw, the deputies opened fire on his fort. Christie and another Indian outlaw, Archie Wolf, returned the fire. Unable to find a safe way to scale the canyon to the fort, the deputies devoted the rest of the day to turning a flat-bed wagon into a movable barricade. Under cover of dark-

ness they rolled it up as close to the fort as they could; then, just before dawn, they lobbed a half-dozen sticks of dynamite at Christie's stronghold. The fort exploded and burst into flame, and the deputies started shooting. In the confusion Archie Wolf escaped, but the fire silhouetted Christie as he raced from the blazing ruins, and the storm of bullets felled him.

On more routine tours of duty a four- or five-man team of deputies averaged a haul of perhaps 20 captives. The influx of prisoners and witnesses taxed every facility at Fort Smith. At times, hundreds of witnesses milled around the compound and choked the corridors outside Judge Parker's courtroom, waiting impatiently for their chance to testify.

In turn, the tremendous backlog of prisoners and witnesses kept Parker's staff working frantically to round up enough citizens to form juries; the jurors had to be drawn from the district of western Arkansas, and they were none too eager to leave home just to sit in judgment on "foreigners" from Indian Territory. If the jurors and witnesses were kept waiting too long, some would head for home, jeopardizing a case when it was finally called. And those who stayed to the bitter end, but could not afford better lodgings, had to endure the discomfort of bed and board in the fetid, jam-packed basement jail below Parker's courtroom.

At the head of this clamorous production line, unshaken by its mounting pressures and by rising criticism from distant court-watchers, worked the inexhaustible judge himself. Yet somehow he also managed to take an active hand in Fort Smith's growing civic concerns. He served on its board of education, championing the establishment of a school for black children. He gave liberally of his counsel and money to local charities. People who met him outside the confines of his courtroom found him, to their surprise, to be a thoroughly congenial man; he was an excellent host at parties in his home and a "walking candy bag" to children he passed on the streets.

But the court remained the core of Parker's life. He kept it open from 8:30 a.m. to nightfall six days a week, and sometimes held night sessions as well; with utter disregard for his personal safety, he would walk the mile to his home after dark, alone and unarmed.

Parker conducted his trials with as much dispatch as he could—too swiftly, some said, for a defense attorney

to prepare his case properly. The judge set a speed record of sorts in his handling of two trials, one for rape and one for murder, both involving the same five prisoners, among them a ferocious Indian outlaw named Rufus Buck *(page 164)*. According to a contemporary account, "As soon as the verdict convicting them of rape was read, Judge Parker excused the jury and at once another panel was drawn, a new jury selected, and, without being allowed to leave their seats, the prisoners were placed on trial for murder. The case continued until the next day, resulting in a verdict of guilty." The five defendants, each sentenced to hang twice, swung in unison from George Maledon's nooses and, as usual, once was enough.

During his first 14 years on the Fort Smith bench, Judge Parker sent 46 men to the gallows for murder or rape, and each hanging resulted in new attacks not only on his methods of dispensing justice but on his personal character. None of these attacks seemed to bother him. Nor did any case involving capital punishment cause Parker as much sheer exasperation as the recurrent appearances before him of a leather-faced miscreant named Belle Starr. Because Belle was female, flamboyant and frustrating to the Hanging Judge, the press disregarded inconvenient facts, invented plenty of fictional exploits for her and made her everybody's favorite criminal.

Belle's antisocial career grew out of her consuming passion for cutthroats and robbers. Born Myra Belle Shirley, a native of Missouri whose family moved to Texas, she had barely become nubile when she began to hobnob with the James brothers and bore their confederate, Cole Younger, a daughter. Then she married a horse thief named Jim Reed and bore him a son. When Reed was killed, Belle took up with a gang and moved into the Indian Territory, where she met and married a handsome Cherokee bandit named Sam Starr. From their hideout on the Canadian River, about 75 miles west of Fort Smith, she acted as organizer, planner and fence for rustlers, horse thieves and bootleggers who distilled and sold whiskey to the Indians. Her managerial skills rewarded her well, and when her friends were captured, she spent her money generously to buy their freedom. If bribery failed, Belle would try another approach: she would employ her powers of seduction to persuade a deputy to return empty-handed to Fort Smith.

Repeatedly thwarted by these tactics, Judge Parker was ready to use almost any pretext to jail her. But whenever his deputies brought her in to face a charge of bootlegging or rustling, he was obliged to free her for lack of evidence. Finally, in 1882, Belle was caught in the act of stealing a neighbor's horses, and the evidence stuck for once. After a short trial, Parker sentenced Belle to two six-month terms in prison. She served nine months before being let off for good behavior, but the time she spent behind bars did nothing to dampen her ardor for criminals and the lawless life. As she boasted to one reporter, "I am a friend to any brave and gallant outlaw. There are three or four jolly good fellows on the dodge now in my section, and when they come to my house they are welcome, for they are my friends."

Belle's skirmishes with Judge Parker continued. In 1886—the same year her Cherokee husband was fatally shot at a party—a lover she had taken got into deep trouble with the law; the man, a desperado who flourished under the alias Blue Duck, had gotten drunk and murdered a farmer. Parker sentenced him to hang, but Belle hired the best lawyers she could find and sent them to Washington, to appeal to the White House. President Grover Cleveland commuted the sentence to life in prison. Two years later Belle finessed Parker again. Her son by Jim Reed was caught stealing horses, and Parker sentenced him to seven years in prison. Once more Belle dispatched her lawyers to see the President; he found reason to oblige with a full pardon.

To Parker's relief, and to the sorrow of romantic newspaper readers from coast to coast, Belle Starr came to a bad end in 1889. She was shot from ambush on a lonely road, and she was laid to rest at Younger's Bend, her hideout on the Canadian River. Her murderer's identity was never proved, but it was probably her newest husband, a young Creek named Jim July. After a quarrel with Belle, he had reportedly offered another man $200 to kill her, and on being turned down had shouted, "Hell—I'll kill the old hag myself and spend the money for whiskey!"

By 1889, it was obvious to almost everyone but Judge Parker himself that the case load at Fort Smith was simply too heavy for any one court. As early as 1883, Congress had made the first of several moves designed to lighten the burden: the western half of Indian

Roy Bean: rough-hewn Solomon of the Southwest

The most unorthodox jurist ever to sit in judgment in the U.S. was, bar none, Roy Bean of Texas. A corpulent, bull-voiced saloonkeeper and gambler, Bean tried cases between deals of poker, and regularly recessed trials to sell liquor to counsel, jury and defendant. He read haltingly, knew only a smattering of law and ignored any statutes he personally disliked. While he never held a higher position than justice of the peace in a desert hamlet, he bannered himself, with some accuracy, as the "law west of the Pecos"—the river that ran 20 miles east of his stronghold.

Bean, a native Kentuckian with a checkered past as a trader, bartender and sometime smuggler, began his 20-year-long magisterial reign at the age of 56, shortly after setting up a saloon at a railway construction camp in the west Texas wilds in 1882. Since he ranked as the area's nearest thing to a solid citizen, and since the closest court was some 200 miles away, the Texas Rangers began bringing their prisoners to him for judgment

Roy Bean, judge extraordinary

—even before the state appointed him a justice of the peace.

From the outset, pragmatism was Bean's hallmark. When an Irish railroad hand killed a Chinese worker, 200 Irish roustabouts turned up in Bean's court to see that their countryman got fair treatment. The judge surveyed the tough crowd, thumbed idly through his lawbook and finally

announced that, although there were many prohibitions against homicide, there was no specific ban against killing a Chinese. Case dismissed.

In another memorable example of improvisation, the judge doubled as a coroner. A worker had fallen from a viaduct to rocks 300 feet below. Having pronounced him dead, Bean had to bury the man—but he did not think his five-dollar coroner's fee adequate pay for the job. He reverted to his role as justice of the peace, searched the body and discovered $40 and a revolver. "I find this corpse guilty of carrying a concealed weapon," he intoned, "and I fine it $40."

Virtually all fines stayed in his pockets, and when higher authorities asked for an accounting, he responded, "My court is self sustaining." Nor was he daunted when a federal judge told him that, while he could perform marriages, his practice of granting divorces was beyond the power of a justice of the peace. Bean retorted, "Well, I married 'em, so I figure I've got the right to rectify my errors."

Beer and law receive equal billing at Roy Bean's saloon-courthouse in Langtry, a crossroads that he named in honor of the actress Lily Langtry.

Territory had been removed from Parker's jurisdiction and divided between the two nearest federal district courts in Kansas and Texas. Parker had protested only mildly, even though he saw the move as yet another personal attack—which it was, to some extent.

In 1889 Congress made a more direct attack on the Hanging Judge, empowering the U.S. Supreme Court to hear appeals from prisoners whom Parker had sentenced to hang. Men condemned in other jurisdictions had had this recourse; but up to this point, under the unusual authority originally vested in Parker, his decisions could not be challenged. The move by Congress was a stunning blow to his pride, and he felt it deprived him of the power he needed to administer effective justice. Parker said: "I have no objection to appeal. I even favor abolition of the death penalty, provided that there is a certainty of punishment, whatever that punishment may be, for in the uncertainty of punishment following crime lies the weakness of our halting justice."

Parker suffered still another great disappointment in 1889: he lost his long struggle to protect the Indians from white exploitation. The flimsy, oft-punctured wall of laws that guarded the borders of Indian Territory finally crumbled under the pent-up pressures of the "Boomers" and other large groups of land-hungry whites who demanded that the Unassigned Lands in the territory be opened for homesteading. On April 22, amid wild celebration and wilder melees, 50,000 whites poured into this 1.8-million-acre tract, staked out their claims, founded the towns of Guthrie and Oklahoma City overnight, and looked around for more land to conquer. The tribes were destined to be crowded into ever smaller corners of the territory.

Parker was one of the few white men to challenge the assertion that this turn of events had come about because treating the Indians as independent nations had proved to be a "farce." Perhaps, he noted, "things would have been different had the government given them the protection it promised in 1828. 'Not only will we give you farms and homes in fee simple,' it said, 'but we will protect you in your rights. We will give you every protection against lawlessness; we will see that every refugee, every bandit, every murderer that comes into your country is put out.'" But, Parker went on, "Not one of these pledges has ever been kept, except for the work that has been done by the United

Soon to be high on the most wanted list of felons in Indian Territory, Ned Christie was a law-abiding gunsmith when he stood for this portrait with the weapons he would use to shoot up banks, trains and lawmen.

States courts having jurisdiction over this country."

White opinion, however, was not with the judge on this score. In 1890 all of Indian Territory, except for lands owned by the Five Civilized Tribes, was established as the Oklahoma Territory with its own government and court system, with full jurisdiction over all crimes committed there. Parker, like his Indian friends, was presiding over an ever-dwindling jurisdiction, and wielding ever-dwindling powers within it.

He still drove himself, for there was no less work to do. With so many more whites to prey upon, outlaws increased in number and improved in organization throughout the so-called twin territories—Oklahoma Territory and Indian Territory. In this final decade of the 19th Century, crime in that region was to reach a sensational peak, then start a slow decline. More than

157

any other event, what brought the turning point was the death of one outlaw, Bill Doolin, at the hands of Deputy U.S. Marshal Heck Thomas, whom Judge Parker had brought in from Texas in 1886.

Bill Doolin was far and away the prize catch for any lawman lucky enough, and tough enough, to trap him. The region in which he operated had never known quite his like. His accuracy with a rifle and his readiness to kill were attributes many other gunfighters shared, but Doolin had something else: a cool, shrewd head. He had no zest for the outlaw's life; he was in it not for the thrill but for the money—a commodity that was in lamentably short supply during his days as a hardscrabbling farm boy in Arkansas. And carefully planned robberies, staged at the lowest possible risk, struck him as the way to achieve his goal.

He began his career as a promising young protégé of the Dalton brothers, after they had forsaken the lawman's life to pursue a more lucrative calling in crime. To Doolin's good fortune, the Daltons failed to include him in their featherbrained scheme to stage two simultaneous bank holdups in Coffeyville, Kansas, in the course of which they got shot to pieces (*pages 84-85*). Doolin did not tarry to mourn his mentors. Returning to Oklahoma Territory, he hand-picked his own gang of 10 seasoned holdup men and set up a cave hideout on the Cimarron River, not far from Guthrie. Then, between 1892 and the end of 1894, he planned and executed a series of brisk forays on banks and trains in Arkansas, Kansas, Missouri and Oklahoma Territory.

From 1893 onward, deputy marshals from several jurisdictions were in full cry after Doolin and his gang. Because of the outlaws' base in Oklahoma Territory, the efforts of the lawmen were coordinated by the U.S. marshal for the territory, Evett Nix. Like Judge Parker, Nix had a flair for recruiting talent. One first-rate aide he enlisted was Deputy U.S. Marshal Heck Thomas. A native Georgian, Thomas was only 12 when he served as a Confederate Army courier; after the War, while working as a private detective in Texas, he pulled off the singlehanded capture of two desperadoes, and won renown among outlaws as a man to be shunned. He took the reputation with him to Judge Parker's jurisdiction, where he quickly impressed admirers with his distinctive garb—knee-high boots, corduroy trousers and flannel shirt—set off with two ivory-handled six-

A posse led by Deputy U.S. Marshal Paden Tolbert (*far right*) assembles in 1892 at a sawmill near the Cherokee town of Tahlequah to plot the capture of the robber and killer Ned Christie. It took dynamite to blast him from a makeshift log fort and a hail of gunfire to mow him down.

A jury's verdict, written out by the foreman in line with standard 19th Century practice, contains bad news for a killer known as Cherokee Bill. The jurors took only 20 minutes to reach their verdict.

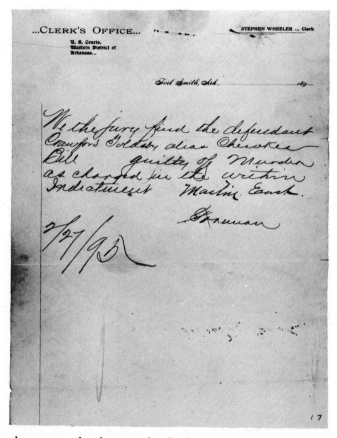

...CLERK'S OFFICE...
STEPHEN WHEELER ... Clerk
U. S. Courts,
Western District of
Arkansas...

Fort Smith, Ark., 189

We the jury find the defendant Crawford Goldsby alias Cherokee Bill guilty of Murder as charged in the within Indictment Martin Each. Foreman

2/27/95

shooters and a shotgun that had been mellowed by hard use and tender care.

With Heck Thomas now at his disposal, Marshal Nix recruited two more supersleuths for the campaign against Bill Doolin. The second man was also from Judge Parker's roster of rugged aides: a red-haired soldier of fortune named Chris Madsen, a Dane who had fought for the Italian rebel Garibaldi and for the French Foreign Legion in Africa before being lured to America in 1870 by tales of gold strikes and Indian wars. Joining the U.S. Cavalry, he fought his lusty way across most of the West in campaigns against the Sioux, Cheyennes, Nez Percé, Bannocks and Utes before he pinned on a nickel-plated deputy-marshal's badge.

The third man Marshal Nix enlisted—Bill Tilghman —had never worked for Judge Parker, but he had chalked up a distinguished gunfighting record as marshal of Dodge City before moving to Oklahoma Territory. The badge he had worn in Dodge was a highly individualistic work of art hammered out of two $20 gold pieces—an insignia famous throughout the frontier. Such

showmanship was characteristic of Tilghman; nobody was much surprised when he later entered politics and was swept in as an Oklahoma state senator.

Tilghman, Thomas and Madsen, soon dubbed the "Oklahoma Guardsmen," formed a triumvirate that in itself marked a kind of milestone on the road to better law and order in the West: teamwork improved the chances of bringing a clever criminal to book. Each of the Guardsmen was assigned to a different slice of Bill Doolin's various stamping grounds, but each lawman knew what the other was doing; Marshal Nix, from his headquarters in Guthrie, directed the joint effort.

For a while it seemed as if Doolin was more than a match for his pursuers. Whenever they got too close for comfort, he would suspend work long enough to let his trail cool. But in December of 1895, Tilghman tracked Doolin to a health spa at Eureka Springs, Arkansas, where the outlaw had gone to soak his rheumatic bones. Doolin was reading a newspaper in a bathhouse when Tilghman strolled in dressed as a minister. Doolin failed to recognize him, but he did recognize the six-shooter the visitor had drawn. Doolin started to reach for his own pistol, then thought better of it. Tilghman wired Nix, "I have him. Will be home tomorrow." There was no need to explain who "him" was.

Next day, a crowd of 5,000 mobbed the Guthrie railroad station to see the famous lawman and his infamous prisoner. Tilghman signed autographs and photographers took pictures. Doolin, who looked too slight and ordinary to deserve his label "King of Oklahoma Outlaws," was given dinner at the best hotel in town, the Royal, but the treat ended there. His lodgings were less regal—Guthrie's jail. For the first time in his busy career, Doolin spent a flea-bitten night behind bars, consigned to await trial and certain conviction.

As it turned out, Doolin refused to wait for the courts in Oklahoma Territory to clear their crowded calendars. In July of 1896, some six months after his capture, he escaped and vanished. The following month Heck Thomas learned from an informer that Doolin was holed up with his wife and small son in a farmhouse at Lawson, Oklahoma Territory, and that he was planning to take them out of the country, perhaps to Canada or to Mexico. Thomas sped to Lawson one moonlit night with a small posse. Near the farmhouse the lawmen found what seemed to confirm the getaway

160

rumor: a well-stocked wagon with a team hitched to it, and a riding horse, saddled and tethered to one of the wagon's front wheels. As Thomas and his deputies took up concealed positions nearby, the door opened and Doolin came out, carrying a Winchester and followed by his wife with their child in her arms. He helped them into the wagon and walked ahead, leading his horse in the bright moonlight. Suddenly Thomas emerged from the bushes that had hidden him. "Drop your gun and put up your hands!" he called. Doolin wheeled, raised his rifle, fired—and missed. Thomas, with his own mellow shotgun, took better aim. Doolin's suddenly lifeless body slumped to the ground.

The death of this seemingly invincible outlaw was sobering news to criminals riding the twin territories. It did not stop their robberies and murders, but it did give them food for thought. The manhunt that put Bill Doolin out of business for good had demonstrated that the forces of the law were no longer scattered, but increasingly well organized and—just as important—more certain than ever before of local support.

Back in Fort Smith, Judge Parker must have felt deeply satisfied at the news of the personal triumph of Heck Thomas, whose gunfighting skills he had recognized a decade before. Certainly there was little else, by now, to give the judge any satisfaction. On March 1, 1895, Congress had delivered the final blow to his court. It removed the last vestiges of Indian Territory from his jurisdiction, establishing three judicial districts there and leaving Parker only a few counties of western Arkansas to preside over. The change was to take effect in September of 1896.

Devastating as this blow was, it could not match the torment Parker had endured for the past seven years as a result of the Congressional move to allow his decisions in capital cases to be appealed to the Supreme Court. During that time the entire tenor and style of Parker's trials had undergone radical change. Parker's high-handed trial practices, once the hallmark of his unlimited powers, became exactly what defense attorneys were looking for—"technicalities" on which to base an appeal to the high tribunal in Washington for review of the death sentence.

The assault on Parker's old-fashioned methods of rule was led by an ambitious lawyer named J. Warren

A busy virtuoso of the rope

Mothers shuddered and pulled their children close whenever George Maledon (*below*) walked past them on the streets of Fort Smith, Arkansas. And small wonder—for Maledon, an immigrant from Bavaria, operated the busiest gallows on the frontier. In his 20 years as chief executioner for the Western District of Arkansas, he carried out 60 death sentences. But despite his chilling reputation as the "prince of hangmen"—as the local press dubbed him—Maledon could be affable enough. Once, when asked if he was haunted by the ghosts of his victims, he cheerily replied: "No, because I reckon I hanged them too."

Bandit queen Belle Starr stands by to lend moral support to her manacled lover, Blue Duck, after his arrest for the murder of a farmer.

Reed. He was a far cry from the frontier lawyers who pitched their tent offices in the early cattle towns and mining camps and set about drumming up clients. Reed habitually dressed in a tail coat and a stovepipe hat and flourished a silver-headed cane. His reputation was as stylish as his getup. He had practiced law in West Virginia and Ohio, becoming known as a man who always won his cases. As the first lawyer to appeal a Parker decision to the Supreme Court, he gained nationwide celebrity.

In that case, Reed's client was a horse trader, William Alexander, who had been convicted in 1889 of murdering his partner for some choice animals. The main evidence against Alexander was that he had consulted a lawyer after the crime, claiming his partner was missing and asking whether it was legal for him to sell the horses. Reed objected that Alexander's conversation with his lawyer was inadmissible evidence, but Parker brushed aside the lawyer-client privilege, ruling it inapplicable when statements in such conversations "tend to prove the guilt or innocence of the person accused." On this ground, Reed appealed, and when the case reached the Supreme Court in 1891 he won his point. Parker was reversed and the case remanded to him for a new trial.

Parker tried Alexander again; the jury was deadlocked. A third trial also ended in a hung jury, and at this juncture the prosecution gave up its attempts to send Alexander to the gallows.

With the tide running in his favor, Reed returned to the Supreme Court time and again on various Parker decisions, and so did a flock of other defense attorneys armed with bills of exception and writs of error. In all, during Parker's seven-year joust with the Supreme Court from 1889 to 1896, 50 of his 78 death sentences were appealed. The Supreme Court reversed and remanded 37 of those cases. Some were thrown out. Some ended in acquittals after several trials. In oth-

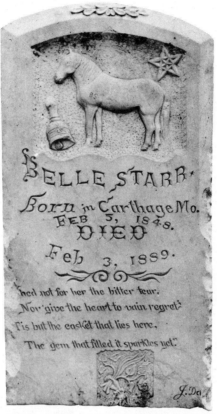

A bell, a star, a pet horse and a brief ode mark the grave of a good girl gone wrong.

ers, the charges were reduced, and several resulted in commutations or pardons by the President. At one point, the Supreme Court reminded Judge Parker that, regardless of the clear need for rigorous law enforcement in his particular section of the country, the rules for administering justice were identical everywhere.

Parker fought back as best he could. He told the *St. Louis Globe-Democrat:* "During the twenty years that I have engaged in administering the law here, the contest has been one between civilization and savagery, the savagery being represented by the intruding criminal class." The fault, he declared, lay with "the laxity of the courts"—and the Supreme Court's tendency to concern itself with the "flimsiest technicalities."

But Parker was a fading frontier voice, raised in vain against the sophisticated judicial hierarchy in the East. The judge had become a tragic figure, always fighting the same lost battles, incapable of adjusting to change. Defendants no longer feared him as they had in the past. One of them even had the temerity to talk back. One day in 1895 Parker was about to impose a death sentence on a bandit named Henry Starr *(page 178),* Belle's nephew by marriage. As Parker launched into his usual stern peroration, Starr broke in.

"Don't try to stare me down, old Nero," he shouted. "I've looked many a better man than you in the eye. Cut out the rot and save your wind for your next victim. If I am a monster, you are a fiend, for I have put only one man to death, while almost as many men have been slaughtered by your jawbone as Samson slew with the jawbone of that other historic ass." For a moment Parker sat speechless at this unexpected onslaught. Then, tersely, he sentenced Starr to be hanged by the neck until he was dead—another judgment that was later to be reversed by the Supreme Court.

In July of 1896, two months before Indian Territory was to be formally removed from Parker's jurisdiction

Shackled hand and foot after a 13-day spree of rape, robbery and murder in 1895, Rufus Buck *(center)* and his confederates await trial. They were among the last men to be condemned by Judge Parker.

by Congressional decree, the Judge took to his bed. Though few people outside his own family were aware of it, he had long been a diabetic. Now, in addition, he was suffering from exhaustion. It was well understandable. In 21 years on the Fort Smith bench, he had tried an incredible total of 13,490 cases. At the age of 57 he looked like a man in his seventies. But if he was old and tired, he took pride in his record: of his total cases, 9,454 resulted in guilty pleas or convictions.

Parker was still confined to his sickroom when, on September 1, his clerk solemnly arose in his courtroom to call out: "Oyez! Oyez! The Honorable District and Circuit Courts of the United States for the Western District of Arkansas, having criminal jurisdiction of the Indian Territory, are now adjourned, forever.

God bless the United States and the honorable courts!"

Parker never returned to preside over his dismembered and moribund jurisdiction. He died two months later. Predictably, the news evoked mixed reactions. Parker's nemesis, J. Warren Reed, said politely, "Our beloved Judge has fallen asleep." There were no polite murmurs from the prisoners in the Fort Smith jail. One of them said, "Is he dead? Whoopee!"

Then the tributes rolled in for Parker's funeral. Many distinguished men said straight out that he was the greatest judge in the history of the West. Various Indian tribes sent moving testimonials to the judge who had been "good enough for any law-abiding people, and too good for some." A chief of the Creeks attended the rites in person, and brought a garland of wild flowers.

164

Languishing in jail, Rufus Buck penned
this poetic farewell to his wife, mother and
sisters on the back of a family photograph.
The heavenly journey he expected to make
was launched from Fort Smith's gallows.

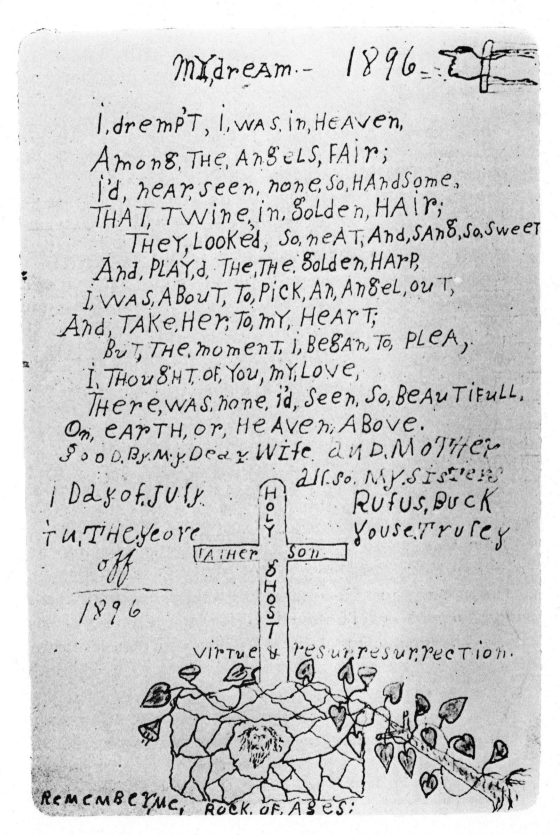

MY dreAm.- 1896

I, dremPT, I, WAS, in, HeAven,
AmonG, THe, AnGeLS, FAir;
i'd, neAr, seen, none, So, HAndSome,
THAT, Twine, in, Golden, HAir;
    THey, Looked, So, neAT, And, SAnG, So, Sweet
And, PLAY,d, THe, THe, Golden, HARP,
I, WAS, ABouT, To, PiCK, An, AnGeL, ouT,
And, TAKe, Her, To, mY, HEART;
    BuT, THe, moment, i, BeGAn, To, PLEA,
i, THouGHT, of, You, mY, LOVE,
THere, WAS, none, i'd, Seen, So, BeAuTiFuLL,
On, eARTH, or, HEAVen, ABove.
GooD, By, M,y, DeAr, WiFe, And, MoTHer
                                       ALso, mY, SiSTers
i, DAy, of, JuLy .   RuFuS, BuCK
tu, THe, yeore   YouSe, TruLey
off

1896

HOLY
FATHER SON
&
HOST
VirTue & resurresurrecTion.

RemeMBer me, ROCK. Of. AGes;

5 | Sinister masters of murder

The chaos that followed on the heels of the Civil War spawned a gunfighting subspecies that seemed to be the very embodiment of anarchy—emotionally maimed and socially alienated killers who, for the most part, took up the gun while they were still in their teens, murdered men with profligate ease and then met an early demise by either the bullet or the noose.

Occasionally the fights of these lone-hand gunmen were fair, as in the anonymous duel below, which took place in 1904 in Quartzite, Arizona, after a saloon argument. But more often the loners bloodied the frontier with assaults that were utterly vicious and capricious. A Texas badman named John King Fisher once shot a man in the head because he wanted to see if a bullet would bounce off his bald pate. Clay Allison prowled New Mexico saloons, where the effects of drink, said a contemporary, transformed him into "hell turned loose," ready to kill at the slightest provocation. Most of the victims of Billy the Kid were either unarmed or plugged from ambush.

The kill tally of the loners was staggering. John Wesley Hardin dispatched 44 men in 10 years, and others of his ilk may have surpassed his total, if not his callousness. The public scarcely knew how to judge individuals who were capable of such senseless slaughter, and in the end the loners came to be regarded with a kind of amazed awe —which was as much as most of them ever wanted from their doomed lives.

In a rare photograph of a frontier showdown, a gunman stalks a foe *(at fence)* while a witness *(far right)* stands mesmerized. The prey fired once before running away.

"I see many enemies around and mighty few friends"

Well, I do not propose to boast of being brave at all, but I have had no help in my meanness when it came to killing a man. I have done such things on my own account and always alone." From a Texas jail where he was being held for murder in 1877, a young desperado named Bill Longley wrote these words to the sheriff who had captured him. Longley's statement, made more by way of explanation than expiation, also served to identify him in a special sort of way. He was a loner—one of a particularly vicious type of gunfighter that roamed the West in the tumultuous years after the Civil War.

Solitary killers of Longley's stripe were among the most renowned figures on the frontier. A few of them attracted national attention in their brief lifetimes and became enduring legends from the moment of their own violent deaths. One frontier editor fumed at the celebrity that was accorded such gunmen. "There is a class of persons," he wrote, "who cannot restrain a sort of admiration for a stupendous criminal. One who has murdered many, and shown no mercy—who has hesitated at no deed of darkness and inhumanity—is sure to be admired as a sort of remarkable character who approaches the measure of a genuine hero."

Still, there was warrant for the fascination that the loners aroused. Each was his own kind of enigma, yet certain generalizations are possible. In a later age the loners would have been labeled psychopathic killers—and indeed there seemed no sense, except in their own dark minds, to most of the deaths they dealt out. Killings were a common enough phenomenon in frontier America, but by and large the reasons for them

could be understood if not commended. The loners frequently murdered out of sudden impulse. They appeared to lack any semblance of self-control, any means of cooling the passion to wipe other men off the face of the earth, any inner check that told them when to stop. They tended to regard their victims less as human beings than as mere impediments in their paths, to be outdrawn or—when stealth proved more expedient—to be gunned down from behind.

Nor did the loners suffer any evident remorse in the wake of their monstrous victories. Their egos swelled in direct proportion to their mounting credits, and they seemed to derive intense satisfaction from being given a wide berth by mortals who did not have their deadly skills. Yet they knew moments of crisis and exhaustion, and on such occasions they often did something that seemed totally out of character for them. They turned to their sworn enemies, the officers of the law, for protection—or simply for somebody to talk to.

For all the cruelty of their deeds, the loners possessed something of the aura of tragedy—of lives gone terribly wrong. Most of them embarked on their homicidal careers before they had emerged from adolescence. But, as a rule, they did not come from squalid homes: more often they were the strays of upright and hard-working families. And although their schooling was largely outside the classroom, they were quick-minded and remarkably literate.

Certain circumstances of time and place contributed to the appearance of the breed. Most of them were Southerners, and the bitterness of the lost Confederate cause apparently had a lot to do with shaping them into predators upon society. The still-raw West offered them an arena where their private furies could be acted out with a lack of constraint that was possible nowhere else. Although perhaps no more than a score or so of loners ever roved the frontier, their records belied their

Storied even in his own time, Billy the Kid smirks into the camera near the end of a trail of killings that began when he was 17 and ended with his own death at 21.

numbers. Just four of them—Bill Longley, Clay Allison, John Wesley Hardin and Billy the Kid—won infamy enough for a small army of villains.

Bill Longley came to his career by a typical route. He was a 15-year-old in Austin County, Texas, in 1866, when he killed his first man. At the time Texas was dominated by carpetbaggers—Northerners who had moved into the Southern power vacuum that followed the Civil War—and Governor E. J. Davis' state police force was manned largely by ex-slaves enjoying their first taste of freedom. One day young Longley observed a black lawman riding through the streets of the village of Old Evergreen, brandishing a rifle and cursing at whites in his path—including Bill Longley's own father. The boy ordered the former slave to stop waving his gun around. When he proved too slow about it, Longley raised his own gun—which he regularly carried, despite his tender years—and shot the man dead. Whites hid the corpse and Longley was never prosecuted for his crime; indeed he was, for a time, something of a local hero.

But he turned into a drifter, earning a haphazard living as a cowboy, a gambler and a field hand chopping cotton. His aimless travels took him to Indian Territory, Arkansas, Kansas, Wyoming and Dakota Territory. For a brief period he ran a small saloon in the gold camps of the Black Hills—a milieu he found attractively lawless. "There was no law at all," he said later. "It was simply the rule of claw and tooth and fang and the weakest went to the wall. When the majority of people got down on a man, they simply took him out and strung him up on a limb, and they had a big spree on the strength of it."

Longley carried violence with him wherever he went, killing men sometimes in blazing bursts of temper, sometimes in ritualized, stand-up gunfights, sometimes from ambush. Finally, back in Texas in 1877, he was brought to book for the murder of a man who had shot a Longley cousin. He was then 27 years old, and by his own count he had killed 32 men in all.

Feeling some terminal need for human companionship the night before he was hanged in the town of Giddings, Longley confided to a guard what amounted to his last testament. "He said that he didn't regret killing but one man," the guard later recalled. "They were in

Evincing a true loner's nerve, Jim Miller *(in the white hat, at table)* forgoes the relative security of a back-to-the-wall seat for a game of faro in Pecos, Texas. Miller boasted a total of 51 killings, beginning at the age of eight when he did in his grandparents. He was finally strung up by a mob.

camp together and Bill said it seemed like the feller was watching him. He said he had had a hard day and he was sleepy, but he wasn't going to sleep with the feller watching him. Well, he said, that kept up until midnight, when he got plumb tuckered out, so he got up and shot the feller in the head and went to sleep. The next day he found out that the feller was on the dodge just like him, so he always felt sorry about killing him."

That same evening the guard asked Longley, "How come you weren't ever caught or killed in all those years on the road?"

"Because," Longley replied, "I never had any confidence in nobody."

He made one final observation from the gallows. Surveying a crowd of 4,000 that had assembled to witness his drop through the trap, he said, "I see a good many enemies around, and mighty few friends."

Even in his most vicious moments, Longley never matched the volcanic and deranged deeds of Clay Allison of Tennessee. In two key respects, Allison was a deviant from the pattern of the loner. He was older than most when he launched his criminal activities, somewhere in his middle twenties. And, unlike Longley and other notorious killers, he may have derived his homicidal bent from physical as well as emotional damage in his youth. When the Civil War began, Allison left the family farm near Waynesboro and enlisted in the Tennessee Light Artillery. Three months later he was given a medical discharge by Confederate Army doctors; they described him as "incapable of performing the duties of a soldier because of a blow received many years ago. Emotional or physical excitement produces paroxysmals of a mixed character, partly epileptic and partly maniacal." Whatever the true nature of his aberration, Allison was a capriciously violent man, and the record of his progress through life sufficiently justified the almost superstitious dread in which he was held on the frontier.

After the war Allison, like many another young Southerner, could not abide the unrelenting reminders of defeat around his home. In the autumn of 1865 he migrated with relatives to the Brazos River country of Texas, where he became a cowpuncher and trail hand driving cattle into New Mexico. Five years later he acquired his own ranch in Colfax County, New Mexico.

Fettered and flanked by lawmen, Bill Longley faces the prospect of a Texas noose for one of his 32 murders. He went with one final bit of bravado, writing to a girl, "Hanging is my favorite way of dying."

Already he had come to be feared—particularly when in his cups—and people around him believed that he had killed many men, although nobody alive could vouch for the details. In any event Allison, when sober, resented his sinister reputation. When he learned that a Missouri newspaper had accused him of 15 killings, he wrote an indignant letter to the editor: "I have at all times tried to use my influence toward protecting the property holders and substantial men of the country from thieves, outlaws and murderers, among whom I do not care to be classed."

This missive begged the question of how many men had actually fallen before Allison's wrath, or in what circumstances. But his neighbors were soon to get first-hand evidence of his primal savagery when aroused. One night in 1870, while drinking in a saloon in the tiny mining camp of Elizabethtown, he was approached by a distraught ranch wife with a tale of horror. She told him that her husband, a rancher named Kennedy, had gone berserk and killed a number of strangers in their cabin, then capped the bloody rampage by murdering their own infant daughter. Rounding up his drinking mates, Allison descended on the Kennedy ranch and found its owner soddenly drunk. No corpses were in evidence, but a few days later when a collection of bones was dug up in a search of the ranch property, Allison reached his own verdict on Kennedy's guilt — and proper punishment.

While medical experts were still debating whether or not the bones were of human origin — and they were by no means certain what their findings would be — Allison and a few companions broke into the Elizabethtown jail where Kennedy had been detained, seized him, dragged him to a nearby slaughterhouse and lynched him. Then, not yet content that justice had been fully served, Allison cut off the head of the corpse, impaled it on a pike, and rode with it 29 miles to the town of Cimarron, where he carried it in gruesome triumph into his favorite drinking haunt, Henri Lambert's saloon.

It was almost inevitable that Allison would someday find himself confronted by a foe whose regard for human life was as slight as his own. The challenger was an outlaw named Chunk Colbert, who claimed seven kills. For no apparent reason other than the desire to burnish his reputation for gunslinging superiority, Colbert felt that Allison would make a suitable eighth. He invited his proposed target to dine with him at a Colfax County inn. Allison accepted with every appearance of amiable good fellowship, and the two men enjoyed a leisurely meal. The charade ended just as the coffee cups arrived at the table. Colbert reached for his cup with his left hand; but his right was slowly bringing his gun up from below the table. Allison went for his own weapon. Colbert fired in desperate haste, but his gun had not quite cleared the table top and the bullet went through the wood and was harmlessly deflected. Allison then calmly plugged his host just above the right eye. Later, asked why he had consented to dine with a man he knew intended to kill him, he said, "Because I didn't want to send a man to hell on an empty stomach."

Another meeting with a professional colleague had an outcome that was less lethal but equally bizarre. A formidable gunman named Mace Bowman sought Allison out, evidently toying with the thought of killing him. But instead of trying to destroy each other, the two men got drunk together and decided to practice fast draws. Allison could not match Bowman's speed at getting his gun out of his holster, and he suggested a new test of prowess. Both men pulled off their boots, stripped to their underwear, and took turns shooting at each other's bare feet to determine which of them performed the livelier dance under fire. When the contest — rated a standoff — was finally called on account of exhaustion, both terpsichoreans were miraculously unscathed.

Allison's flair for harrowing improvisations was even more vividly displayed when he felt wronged. Once, arriving in Cheyenne with a trail herd of cattle and a raging toothache, he repaired to one of the two dentists then practicing in the town. By an unfortunate professional error, the dentist began drilling on the wrong tooth. Allison left, went to the other dentist and paid $25 to have the damage corrected. He then returned to the first dentist, pinned the man to his own chair, seized a forceps, pried open his victim's mouth and wrenched a tooth from it. He was at work on a second extraction, with a section of the dentist's lip inadvertently gripped in the instrument, when the man's screams brought help and interrupted the operation.

Closer to home, in Colfax County, Allison fell into dispute with a neighboring rancher. They hit upon a novel way to resolve their differences. Together they dug a grave and carried an unmarked tombstone to its edge. Then they negotiated an agreement whereby they would both descend naked into the grave pit, each armed with a bowie knife; whoever was able to climb out at the conclusion of the encounter would have the tombstone suitably engraved for the other. They set a date, but before the bout could be staged, Allison came to an inglorious end. On July 1, 1887, he was hauling a load of supplies home from Pecos, Texas, when a sack of grain fell off the pile; as it did so he tried to grab it and toppled from the wagon. One of the wagon wheels rolled across his neck, breaking it and killing him. In this oddly inappropriate fate Allison once again differed from his fellow loners who, for the most part, died by the gun or by the rope.

Summing up after his demise, a Kansas newspaper expressed puzzlement about his dual roles as a successful rancher and an explosive killer. Whether Allison "was in truth a villain or a gentleman," the editor of the paper observed, "is a question that many never

Occasionally a menace to himself as well as to society, Clay Allison recuperates in 1870 after shooting himself in the foot in a mule stampede. That same year, he helped lynch a suspected killer, then beheaded him.

A 19th Century depiction details Allison's after-dinner shoot-out with another killer, Chunk Colbert. The barrel of Colbert's pistol hit the table top as he tried to get the drop on Allison, who instantly drilled him.

settled to their own satisfaction. Certain it is that many of his stern deeds were for the right as he understood that right to be."

No such quandary of judgment confronted those who observed the career of another loner, John Wesley Hardin. In the history of the West, Hardin ranks as one of the most profligate killers of all. By the time he went to prison in 1878, he claimed to have slain 44 men—and his reckoning was probably not far off.

Hardin was born in Bonham, Texas, in 1853. His father, a Methodist minister, named him for the founder of the faith. He grew up to be an attractive lad—blue-eyed ("mild blue," a contemporary recalled), handsome in a square-jawed way and rather slight of build. But even in early adolescence, he revealed a capacity for stark, murderous fury. He was about 14 when a bigger boy taunted him as the author of some graffiti on the schoolhouse wall, a puppy-love paean to a girl in his

class. John Wesley went for the boy with a knife; before they could be separated, he stabbed his tormenter twice, obviously ready to kill him.

Within a year, Hardin did kill. Like Bill Longley, he was spurred by the hatred that seethed between newly freed blacks and defeated Southern whites. Visiting relatives near Moscow, Texas, in 1868, he was egged into a wrestling match with an ex-slave named Mage. In the rough-and-tumble bout, Mage's nose was bloodied. By Hardin's version, the black man then declared that "no white boy could draw his blood and live." The next day, Mage caught up with him as he was riding home and dared him to fight again. Hardin was armed. When Mage seized the bridle of his horse, he later recounted, "I shot him loose. He kept coming back and every time we would start, I would shoot him again and again until I shot him down."

Hardin's father, "distracted" by the killing, urged his son to go into hiding. The elder Hardin believed, in the

175

John Wesley Hardin had this tintype made in 1871 in Abilene, where Marshal Wild Bill Hickok briefly befriended him — until Hardin shot a snoring hotel guest for disturbing his rest and had to flee town.

son's words, that to be tried "at that time for killing a Negro meant certain death at the hands of a court backed by Northern bayonets." The boy fled, and for the next 10 years he stayed on the run, eluding pursuers who sought to bring him to justice for one crime or another.

But he seldom wandered far from his native ground. Central Texas abounded with John Wesley's kinfolk. All of them — and most of their neighbors — were happy to shelter any fugitive from carpetbagger justice. At one point, while he was in hiding, he received word from his older brother Joseph that Union soldiers were looking for him. Knowing the byways through the back country, John Wesley bushwhacked three of the pursuing Yankees — two whites and a black man — at a creek crossing. "Parties in the neighborhood took the soldiers' horses and as we burned all their effects everything was kept quiet," he noted in the remarkable autobiography that he composed in the last year of his life. "Thus by the fall of 1868 I had killed four men." He was then only 15 years old.

By ironic chance, Hardin was arrested late in 1870 for a murder in Waco that he had not committed. Unable to persuade a judge of his innocence, he was held temporarily in a log jail in the town of Marshall, awaiting transfer to Waco. In the privacy of this crude lockup, he bought two useful items from a fellow prisoner: an overcoat against the winter cold — and a Colt .45. Thus he was ready when a Captain Stokes of the state police and a guard named Jim Smolly came to convey him to Waco for trial. Hardin was wearing the overcoat when they arrived. Under it, tied to his shoulder with twine, was the Colt.

One night while the three men were camping en route, Stokes went to rustle up some fodder for the horses, and Hardin was left alone with Smolly, a loud, overbearing man. Smolly began to revile his 17-year-old

charge. Hardin, who had a canny sense of the uses to which callow youth could be put, burst into tears and huddled against his pony's flank while Smolly watched in amusement. Behind the pony, Hardin slipped his hand into his coat and untied the string that held his gun. He shot Smolly dead and ran.

A few days later, several of Hardin's relatives were gathering at Gonzales in southern Texas for a drive up the Chisholm Trail to Abilene, Kansas. They persuaded a rancher to hire John Wesley as trail boss for his herd. Toward the end of the drive, a Mexican herd crowded in behind Hardin's, and there was some trouble keeping the animals apart. Hardin got into a verbal battle with the Mexican in charge of the other herd. Both men were on horseback. The Mexican fired, putting a hole through John Wesley's hat. Swift to retaliate, Hardin found that his own weapon, a worn-out cap-and-ball pistol with a loose cylinder, would not fire; he dismounted, managed to discharge the gun by steadying the cylinder with one hand and pulling the trigger with the other, and hit the Mexican in the thigh. A truce was then declared, but John Wesley was not content with merely winging his opponent. He borrowed a pistol from a friend, went after the Mexican again, and this time shot him through the heart. A general fire fight between the rival camps ensued. The Mexicans suffered all the casualties. Six vaqueros died in the exchanges — five of them felled by the six-shooter in John Wesley Hardin's hand.

In Abilene, Hardin met Wild Bill Hickok, at the time the cattle town's reigning peace officer. Hickok took an indulgently paternal attitude toward the young killer. He drank with Hardin, whored with him and gave him advice, and at one point, when a gang of Hardin's Texas pals and relatives got into trouble, disarmed them but left Hardin his weapon, presumably to allow

After 15 years in prison for one of his 44 murders, Hardin received this pardon. Having boned up on law while incarcerated, he launched himself as an attorney in El Paso in 1895 but was gunned down soon after.

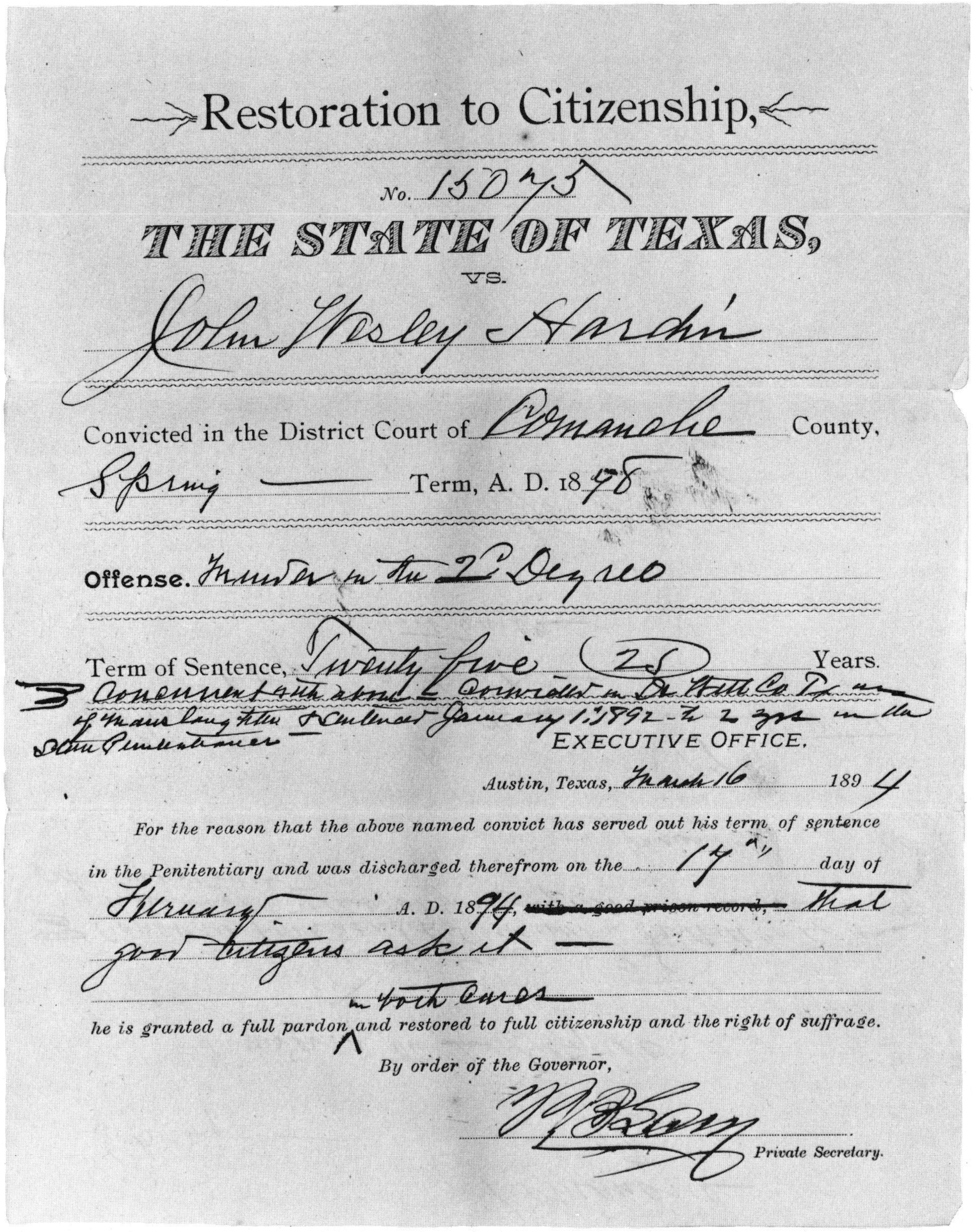

Restoration to Citizenship,

No. *15075*

THE STATE OF TEXAS,

VS.

John Wesley Hardin

Convicted in the District Court of *Comanche* County,

Spring ———— Term, A. D. 18*78*

Offense. *Murder in the 2ᵈ Degree*

Term of Sentence, *Twenty five* (*25*) Years.

Concurrent with above — Convicted in De Witt Co Tx of Manslaughter & Sentenced January 1, 1892 to 2 yrs in the State Penitentiary —

EXECUTIVE OFFICE.

Austin, Texas, *March 16* 189*4*

For the reason that the above named convict has served out his term of sentence in the Penitentiary and was discharged therefrom on the *17ᵗʰ* day of *February* A. D. 189*4, ~~with a good prison record,~~* that *good citizens ask it — in both cases*

he is granted a full pardon and restored to full citizenship and the right of suffrage.

By order of the Governor,

[signature]

Private Secretary.

A shooting gallery of solitary rogues

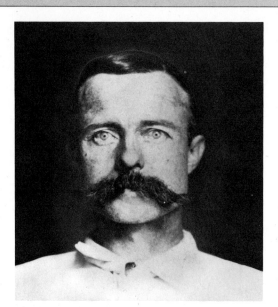

BUCKSKIN FRANK LESLIE strode the streets of Tombstone with his pistol at the ready in a fast-draw belt rig *(page 43)*. He was rumored to use his wife for target practice, tracing her outline with bullets as she stood against a wall in their home.

BILL MOORE had one bad eye, but with the other he took fatal aim in turn at a relative, a black cowboy and two New Mexico neighbors. Later he lit out for Alaska, became a trapper under an assumed name and was never trapped himself.

HENRY STARR insisted he didn't get a fair shake when he was arrested in Indian Territory at 17 with a stolen suitcase, and at 18 on a stolen horse. Then he killed a lawman and became a model prisoner. Out on parole, he met his end on a bank job.

THE APACHE KID killed an Arizona man to avenge the murder of his father. President Cleveland pardoned him, but local authorities did not. He took to the hills as a renegade, swooped down to rape and rob from time to time, and eluded all pursuers.

JOHN SELMAN dabbled in rustling when he was not working for the law in Texas. His prize victim was John Wesley Hardin, whom he shot from behind in a saloon, saying later that Hardin had a fair chance to see him reflected in the mirror over the bar.

JOHN KING FISHER served a brief prison term for a robbery at 16, then went on to become the premier rustler along the Texas-Mexico border in the 1870s. A crack shot, he admitted to killing seven men but explained, "I don't count Mexicans."

AUGUSTINE CHACON, a Mexican *bandito,* had a system: after each raid on the U.S. side of the border, he would retreat to a blameless life back home. Arizona Rangers finally hauled him to justice — but not before he toted up as many as 29 killings.

BILLY THOMPSON, the kid brother of gunman Ben Thompson, yearned to be no good in his own right. "For God's sake, Billy," Ben reproached him after one shoot-out, "you've shot our best friend." Billy retorted, "I'd of shot him if he'd been Jesus Christ."

him either to protect his friends or to keep them in line.

For his part, Hardin was fascinated by Wild Bill and glowed at being seen on intimate terms with so celebrated a gunfighter. But all the while, down deep, he realized that Wild Bill would kill him without qualm if circumstance suggested the need — perhaps not out of ill will, but certainly for self-protection.

The climax of their association came with one of Hardin's most callous crimes, so ignoble that even he showed some faint sign of shame and attempted to pass it off as the justifiable shooting of a man who was trying to steal his pants. Actually, he had less excuse than that. At the American House Hotel, where Hardin had put up for his stay in Abilene, he began firing bullets through a bedroom wall simply to stop the snoring of a stranger in the next room. The first bullet merely woke the man; the second killed him. In the silence Hardin realized that he was about to plunge into deep trouble with Wild Bill Hickok. Still in his undershirt, he exited through a window and ran onto the roof of the hotel portico — just in time to see Hickok arriving with four policemen, alerted by other guests. "I believed," Hardin said later, "that if Wild Bill found me in a defenseless condition, he would take no explanation, but would kill me to add to his reputation."

Not waiting to determine Hickok's disposition in the matter, Hardin leaped from the roof into the street and hid in a haystack for the rest of the night. Toward dawn he stole a horse and made his way back to the cow camp outside of town. The next day he left for Texas, never to return to Abilene. Years later Hardin made a casual reference to the episode. "They tell lots of lies about me," he complained. "They say I killed six or seven men for snoring. Well, it ain't true, I only killed one man for snoring."

Surrounded by a hovering shadow-army of kinsmen, Hardin enjoyed occasional interludes of restful security. During one of them, in 1871, he bethought himself of his longtime sweetheart, Jane Bowen, and married her. Jane's father was an upstanding citizen, owner of a store in Hardin's home county in Texas, and the two families were well acquainted. The marriage was a strange alliance, interrupted by John Wesley's long, unexplained absences. Jane could only guess at the reasons for her husband's extended absences from home, but she bore him two children and evidently remained totally loyal and uncomplaining. "She was as true to me as the magnet of steel," Hardin later said of her.

Now and then on his travels, suffering an attack of desperate loneliness, John Wesley would contrive to return for a spell of domesticity and wifely affection. He described one such compulsive visit in which he rode a favorite mount to death in order to get to Jane. He was at Banquetto, Texas, feeling relatively safe. "There I got to thinking that I had one of the prettiest and sweetest girls in the country as my wife," he wrote in his autobiography. "The more I thought of her the more I wanted to see her. So one night about ten o'clock I started from Banquetto for Gonzales County a hundred miles away. I got home about four a.m. but forever ruined a good horse worth $50 doing so. The sight of my wife recompensed me for the loss of old Bob."

The killing for which Hardin was finally sent to prison occurred in the town of Comanche, 130 miles north of Austin, on the night of his 21st birthday — May 26, 1874. Apparently the gunfight was as near to justified as any he ever had; this fact may have induced the court to let him off with a 25-year sentence instead of ordering him summarily hanged. A race meeting took place that day in Comanche, and Hardin had three good horses running. All three won, and bets earned their owner $3,000 in cash, 50 head of cattle, a wagon and 15 saddle broncs. Understandably elated, Hardin embarked on a round of the local saloons. The pleasure of the evening was only slightly dimmed by his awareness that Deputy Sheriff Charles Webb of nearby Brown County was in town. Hardin had been given to understand that Webb intended to kill him. Webb had no one complaint in mind; he simply felt that Hardin had been getting away with murder and that the State of Texas would be a better place without him.

Webb caught up with Hardin at Jack Wright's saloon. As he approached, Hardin politely invited him to have a drink, and Webb no less politely assented. As they moved toward the bar, Hardin leading the way, somebody yelled, "Look out!" Hardin wheeled, saw that Webb had pulled his gun, and jumped aside — just as the lawman fired. The shot grazed Hardin, but by then he had his own gun out. A bullet hit Webb in the face, and the sheriff fell, mortally wounded — the 39th statistic in Hardin's tally of kills to date. Hardin departed town without interference, but the law was bay-

The singlehanded crusade of a cowboy detective

Charles Angelo Siringo was a rarity — a loner who served on the side of the law. Employed by the Pinkerton agency for two decades, he scoured much of the North American continent for fugitives, operating on his own most of the time and revealing an insatiable appetite for the excitement of the chase.

Slight and gray-eyed, Siringo was the Texas-born son of immigrants — an Italian father and an Irish mother. He got his first taste of man-hunting at the age of 22, while working as a cowboy. His prey, Billy the Kid, was five years younger, but already an object of dread. Siringo tracked the adolescent killer across New Mexico, but he had to give up the pursuit when he was separated from his traveling money at a gaming table.

After 15 years as a cowhand in the Southwest and two dull years as a grocer in Kansas, Siringo journeyed to Chicago in search of bigger money. There he met a blind phrenologist who fingered his skull and concluded that he was "cut out to be a detective." Siringo became a Pinkerton man in 1886 and soon proved to be an almost unshakable bloodhound. He trailed desperadoes through blizzards on the northern plains and through scorching days in the desert. Once he paddled an Indian dugout canoe in stormy Alaskan waters to catch up with two gold thieves.

Siringo's self-reliance was tested even more sharply when he turned to another facet of law enforcement, the infiltration of gangs. On one audacious mission, he rode into a bandit hideout at Powder Springs, Colorado, and identified himself as Charles Carter, freelance gunman. Within a few days he had ingratiated himself with his hosts — Butch Cassidy's Wild Bunch (pages 90-93). Every time the new gang member got wind of a

Retired to a full-time writing career, Charles Siringo at 62 savors a moment back in the saddle.

plan to rob a Union Pacific train, he notified railroad officials, who would change the train schedule and foil the holdup. When Cassidy caught on and went gunning for him, "Carter" vanished. He then surfaced in his lawman's role and began chasing Cassidy in turn. For four saddle-sore years, he dogged the gang leader from Wyoming to Arkansas and back again, covering some 25,000 miles in all. Siringo gave up the hunt only after

the outlaw fled to South America.

Such exploits paid off handsomely in an indirect way, for this anomalous loner wrote almost as hard as he rode. He churned out seven books about his Western adventures, four of them dealing with Billy the Kid. But with pen in hand, Siringo sometimes lost perspective on his subjects, most notably when he recalled the murderous Kid as "a prince of a human being, who got off on the wrong foot."

ing close behind—so close that he soon decided to leave Texas altogether, taking his wife with him.

He first hid out in Florida, under the alias of J. H. Swain. The pseudonym worked so well that he was even invited to help a local police officer round up some suspected criminals. In the course of that hunt Hardin shot and killed one of the suspects—his 40th man.

After two years in Florida, Hardin was unmasked; his identity was discovered by Pinkerton detectives. Again he took flight, this time hoping to get to Mexico, but lawmen intercepted him near the Florida line. In the ensuing gun battle he killed two more men, and made his escape. He and his wife then took up residence in Alabama. His final two victims, so far as is known, were slain after a poker game in Mobile during which he had piled up winnings of $3,500.

Hardin remained at large in Alabama for 10 more months, until the Texas Rangers learned of his whereabouts; they intercepted a letter sent to Hardin's relatives in Texas by his brother-in-law, who was visiting him. On July 23, 1877, Hardin was cornered in the smoking car of a train at Pensacola Junction, Florida, en route back to his Alabama home from a gambling foray. As Ranger John Armstrong and local deputies rushed him from both ends of the car, Hardin's pistol caught in his suspenders. When the rangers had him subdued and bound to a chair, one of the officers told him, "John Wesley Hardin, you are the worst man in the country"—then tempered this critique by presenting him with a cigar.

Hardin was tried in Austin for the killing of Deputy Sheriff Webb. The jury found him guilty of second-degree murder and, at the age of 25, he was sentenced to spend his next quarter-century in Huntsville prison. Between abortive escape attempts thereafter, he studied algebra, theology and the law. In 1894, after he had served 15 years of his term—and shortly after his wife died—the Governor of Texas pardoned him.

Hardin opened a law office in El Paso but passed more time arguing in saloons than in court. His last clash with the law came at the age of 42. When his lady love of the moment was arrested for carrying a pistol, Hardin was overheard making threats against the arresting officer, a policeman named John Selman. Some days later, on August 19, 1895, Selman stepped into the Acme saloon, spotted Hardin at the bar shaking

dice with a friend, walked up behind him and shot him dead. A jury acquitted Selman, apparently in gratitude for his having rid Texas of a major menace.

Considering the sheer number and callousness of his killings, Hardin should have well outranked Billy the Kid in the Old West's annals of infamy. But somehow —such being the intangible qualities of notoriety and charisma—Billy in the end came off with a far more lurid and lasting reputation. Newspapers the country over reported his exploits while he lived, and within 10 months of his death, no fewer than eight novels were published romanticizing his career. They sold more than a million copies.

The attention riveted on Billy is hard to explain. His lifetime score of men killed was much lower than Hardin's. Even his fierceness was patently of an inferior order—at the start, anyway. Perhaps the odd turnabout that made him more celebrated than Hardin resulted from the absurdity of the good-humored, obliging and generally polite Billy being a killer at all. For the fact was that, at the worst of his deadly career, he was a downy-cheeked, blue-eyed orphan lad whose engaging and guileless grin enlisted the motherly concern of women and made men want to help him however they could.

But a killer he was, and that smiling young countenance made this truth all the more grotesque. The number of men who fell to his guns is not known for sure to this day. Billy himself, as he got the hang of casual murder and came to regard himself as an important personage, reportedly once claimed a toll of 21—"one for every year of my life." Some contemporary authorities believed the total was more likely nine.

Billy the Kid was as good a name as any for the boy gunman. Nobody, perhaps not even Billy, was certain of his surname. At one time or another he called himself McCarty, Bonney or Antrim. He was born, probably in New York, around 1860, the second son of a woman known variously as Catherine McCarty and Katherine McCarty Bonney. Billy's father—either Patrick Henry McCarty or William Bonney—apparently died young, and around the end of the Civil War Catherine took her two boys to Indiana. In 1873 she married one William Antrim, and the family moved to Silver City, New Mexico. Billy, who had been baptized Henry, took his stepfather's first name—but that

Orphaned and adrift, Billy the Kid was a teen-age ranch hand working in Arizona when this tintype was made. Soon afterward, in August 1877, he killed his first victim — a man who had idly insulted him.

then escaped by worming his way up the chimney. He fled across the territorial line.

Scrawny, striving to be reckoned a man among men, Billy the Kid became a teen-age saddle tramp, an itinerant ranch hand and sheepherder in southeastern Arizona. Sometime in 1877 he appeared at the Camp Grant Army Post and was taken on as a civilian teamster, hauling logs from a timber camp to a sawmill.

The civilian blacksmith at Camp Grant, a burly fellow named Frank "Windy" Cahill, enjoyed making fun of the rootless youngster. One day in August 1877, he called the Kid the unlikely epithet of "pimp." The Kid, in turn, called the smith a "sonofabitch." Cahill jumped on him and threw him to the ground. Like everybody else who made a claim — no matter how slender — to manhood, the Kid wore a gun. He pulled it and fired. "He had no choice; he had to use his equalizer," a witness said. Cahill died the next day, and the Kid was locked in the Camp Grant guardhouse. A few nights later he broke out and got away.

He next turned up in the Pecos valley of New Mexico, at the ranch house of Heiskell Jones. Apaches had stolen Billy's horse while he was getting water at a spring, and when he arrived at the ranch after a walk of many miles he was in a pathetic state. He was bootless, with swollen and bleeding feet, half-starved and perishing of thirst. Mrs. Jones took him in, fed him and nursed his ailments. The Kid stayed with the family, helping around the ranch. He formed a strong attachment to them, and they to him. They lent him a horse when he left to look for work a few weeks later.

His trait of ready and almost desperately clinging loyalty probably goes a long way toward explaining how Billy the Kid came to be a terror. For he was soon swept up in what became known as the Lincoln County War and witnessed the murder of his newest benefactor, John Tunstall, a cattleman, banker and merchant who had employed the Kid as a cattle guard.

Tunstall, a wealthy 24-year-old English emigrant, had aligned himself with Alexander McSween, a lawyer, and John Chisum, a cattleman with huge herds in the Pecos valley, against a powerful Lincoln County faction led by two Irishmen, J. J. Dolan and Lawrence Murphy. Dolan and Murphy owned a big general store, called The House, in the town of Lincoln, the county seat. This enterprise had long held a virtual

was almost all Antrim gave him. By trade a part-time carpenter and bartender, Billy's stepfather was at heart a prospector, and in his restless search for fortune he was seldom at home.

To support her sons in Silver City, Catherine took in boarders. She impressed her neighbors as "a jolly Irish lady, full of life and mischief," although she was by then afflicted with tuberculosis. In 1874, when Billy was 14, she died. After that, he worked for his board in a hotel and earned a sort of accolade from the owner as "the only kid who ever worked here who never stole anything." To his teacher he was "no more of a problem than any other boy, always quite willing to help with chores around the schoolhouse."

Billy's first brush with the law was trivial, yet it had a profound effect, turning him into a lifelong fugitive at age 15. An older man, playing a joke on a Chinese laundryman, stole a bundle of clothes and got the ever-obliging Billy to hide it. A Silver City peace officer clapped the boy in jail just to teach him a lesson. Terrified by confinement, Billy stood it for two days and

monopoly of the county's trade. The proprietors —
who had close ties to influential territorial officials in
the capital at Santa Fe — also controlled most government contracts for supplying beef to Army posts and
Indian reservations. The contracts brought juicy profits
and, with them, formidable financial power in a region
whose economic mainstay was cattle. And so Dolan
and Murphy more or less called the tune in Lincoln
County and the surrounding Pecos valley. Dominant
in its economic affairs, they had corresponding political
clout, with law enforcers at their beck and call.

The Tunstall-Chisum-McSween faction saw no reason why mere merchants, with little or no experience in
cattle-raising, should have a corner on the government
contracts, or why men who owned vast herds should
not deal directly with the government as beef suppliers.
A number of small ranchers, who detested Chisum for
preempting public grazing lands for his great herds, sided with the proprietors of The House; other small
ranchers and farmers with whom The House had dealt
harshly on credit matters lined up on the other side.
Tunstall further infuriated the foe by setting up a general merchandise store in the town of Lincoln in com-
petition with The House.

When Billy the Kid signed on with Tunstall in the
fall of 1877, the power struggle was already teetering
on the brink of violence. Through political connivance,
the proprietors of The House obtained a court order at-
taching some of Tunstall's horses as payment of an outstanding debt. When Tunstall refused to give them up,
the sheriff of Lincoln County, William Brady — who
was in the pocket of the House faction — sent a posse to
seize the animals, deputizing a friend named William
Morton as the posse's leader. Billy and some other Tunstall hands fled as the posse approached; but they were
only a short distance away when Tunstall rode up to
the lawmen and protested their presence. He was immediately shot in the head by Morton.

The killing of his new boss seemed to trip the trigger
on some fatal quirk in Billy the Kid. Although he had
not known Tunstall long, his wrath was unbounded,
and he promptly dealt himself into the war against The
House and its allies. His first foray, however, was an
embarrassment. After he tried to help a policeman who
had been enlisted by Tunstall's friends to serve warrants on members of Morton's posse, Billy was jailed

A sketch by Charles Russell re-creates one of Billy the Kid's most dastardly deeds in New Mexico. Riding with an unofficial posse that captured two deputies involved in the murder of his rancher-employer, Billy gunned them down after they had been promised safe conduct back to town.

for three days and suffered the humiliation of having his rifle confiscated by Sheriff Brady.

Shortly after Brady released him, the Kid joined his late employer's foreman, Dick Brewer, and a posse, whose members called themselves the Regulators, in a hunt for Tunstall's killer. Somewhere in the countryside near the Rio Peñasco, they flushed William Morton and another deputy sheriff, Frank Baker. After a five-mile, running gun battle, Morton and Baker surrendered on Brewer's pledge to return them, alive, to the town of Lincoln. From a ranch along the way, Morton was permitted to mail a letter to a relative in Virginia. It said in part, "There was one man who wanted to kill me after I had surrendered and was restrained with the greatest difficulty by others." That man—or boy—was not to be restrained forever. On the third day of the journey to Lincoln, when the party was strung out in rough country, the Kid and another hired hand killed both prisoners, plus a member of the posse who apparently tried to protect the captives.

Billy's vendetta was just beginning. Three weeks later, when Sheriff Brady sought to arrest him for killing the prisoners, the Kid holed up with other members of his faction inside Tunstall's store in Lincoln. Sometime during the night, Billy cut a groove rest for a rifle in the top of an adobe wall around a corral next to the store. On the morning of April Fool's Day, 1878, Sheriff Brady, a deputy named Hindman and a third man, Billy Matthews—all carrying rifles—emerged from the courthouse and began walking toward Tunstall's store. The Kid and his cohorts loosed a volley of shots, killing Brady instantly, mortally wounding Hindman and sending Matthews scurrying for shelter. Then the Kid broke from cover to grab the sheriff's weapon—the very rifle Brady had confiscated from him weeks before. Just as he picked it up, a bullet from Matthews ripped a gash inside the Kid's thigh. For the moment, the fight was over and the hunt for Billy began. He might have fled, but with the new bravado he had acquired he decided to hide in town until his wound healed. Townspeople later reported that at one point he concealed himself inside a closed barrel on the top of which a Mexican housewife mixed tortillas even as her house was being searched.

With Tunstall dead, the Kid transferred his allegiance to Tunstall's ally, lawyer McSween, and took part in the only pitched battle of the Lincoln County War. It erupted when a force of gunfighters fortified themselves in McSween's adobe home in the center of Lincoln. The opposing forces of the House faction, under a new sheriff, George Peppin, and a stockman named Marion Turner, positioned themselves in nearby buildings. For three days, in a desultory exchange of sniper fire, the only casualties were a horse and a mule. The besiegers suffered a psychological setback at one point when they heard Mrs. McSween gaily playing the piano inside the barricaded home, while a black servant accompanied her on the violin. But these festivities soon ceased.

On the fifth day of the siege, July 19, 1878, stockman Turner and some of his men gained the outside wall of McSween's house. When their demand for surrender was refused, they piled kindling against doors and window frames and set the place afire. The flames slowly worked through the wooden parts of the adobe building and began to consume floors and furniture inside, forcing the defenders from room to room.

As the battle wore on, the exhausted McSween grew dispirited and increasingly indifferent to the outcome. He had spurned the use of a gun himself, on the odd but lawyer-like ground that active participation in a fight would invalidate his $10,000 life insurance. The Kid, lacking a leader, became one. He persuaded Mrs. McSween to leave the house, knowing she would not be harmed. But he threatened to kill one of his cohorts, a Mexican gunslinger, who was wounded and wanted to give up. And he did kill a besieger who got as far as the door with another surrender demand.

At dark on the fifth day, with the smoldering house no longer tenable, the Kid led two of his men in a sprint for the river a few hundred yards away. He had instructed McSween and some others to try to get away under cover of the break. McSween waited a moment too long. He made an easy target as he appeared outside the kitchen doorway in his white shirt, and a burst of gunfire cut him down.

With Tunstall and McSween both dead, the Lincoln County War was over. And with no cause to serve as a backwoods knight-errant, Billy the Kid became in fact what some of his detractors believed he had been at bottom all along—"just a little, small-sized cow and horse thief," according to a man who knew

Former Union general and future author of *Ben Hur,* Governor Lew Wallace of New Mexico agreed to pardon the Kid if he turned state's evidence on Lincoln County killings, but a prosecutor foiled the plan.

him. Temporarily abandoning his role as loner and assembling a ragtag band of relicts from the war, Billy began stealing stock indiscriminately from white ranchers and from Apaches on the Mescalero reservation. He also developed a streak of mean avarice. When one band of stolen cattle fetched $800 from a Colorado beef buyer, he reportedly gave $30 to one confederate "because he had a family," paid off another rustler with new boots because the pair he had on was worn out —and kept the rest of the money himself.

All the while, he was a fugitive from enough murder warrants to ensure a trip to the gallows the moment he was caught. It might have been the better part of valor to depart for safer pastures. But Billy's reluctance to abandon his adopted region revealed a peculiar facet of his character: somehow he found a measure of security in the familiar, even at the cost of daily peril. Many other loners felt the same way.

However, there were also signs that Billy longed for a clean slate, if that could somehow be attained. For a time it seemed possible. In the autumn of 1878, a new territorial governor—retired Union General Lew Wallace—arrived in New Mexico. Lincoln County's war was over, but unrest persisted. Determined to restore order in the county, Wallace issued an amnesty proclamation. Although the amnesty did not apply to anyone under indictment, the Governor was intrigued by rumors that Billy the Kid might be ready to give up and testify against other participants in the Lincoln County War. And so General Wallace, although by then absorbed in writing the final chapters of his classic novel *Ben Hur,* took the time to get word to the Kid that his status was at least open to discussion.

Soon the Governor was handed a letter that read in part: "I have heard that you will give one thousand dollars for my body which as I can understand it means alive as a witness, but I have indictments against me for things that happened. I am afraid to give up because my enemies would kill me. If it is in your power to annul these indictments I hope you will do so, so as to give me a chance to explain. I have no wish to fight any more. Your obedient Servant W. H. Bonney."

A secret meeting was arranged through intermediaries, and at 9 o'clock one night in March 1879 Wallace answered a knock at the door of a house where he was waiting. In the doorway stood the Kid, with a Winchester in one hand and a revolver in the other. The Governor and the gunman sat down to negotiate. Wallace promised that if the Kid would agree to supply evidence against other killers, "I will let you go scot free with a pardon in your pocket for all your misdeeds." The Kid said he would consider it. In five days he replied by letter: "General Wallace, Sir, I will keep the appointment I made, but be sure and have men come that you can depend on. I am not afraid to die like a man fighting but I would not like to die like a dog unarmed."

And so Billy laid down his arms. By prearrangement with Wallace he agreed to submit to a false arrest, spend a short time in jail, give his evidence against the Lincoln County killers—and then go scot free, as Governor Wallace had guaranteed. Billy's testimony helped indict one of the proprietors of The House, John Dolan, for complicity in one Lincoln County murder. Then the district attorney defied Wallace's orders. He pointed out that there were various indictments still outstanding against the Kid, refused to quash them and remanded him to jail. Billy simply slipped off his handcuffs—something he could do easily because his hands

Jailed for murder, Billy bombarded Wallace with letters — signed with his family name, Bonney — seeking the freedom he had been promised. When his pleas went unheeded, he killed two guards and made his escape.

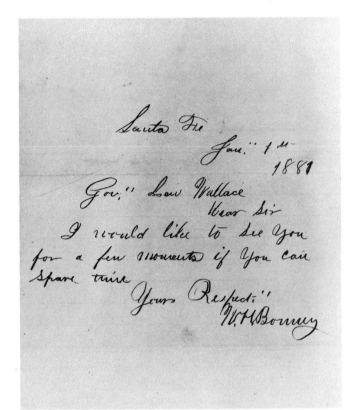

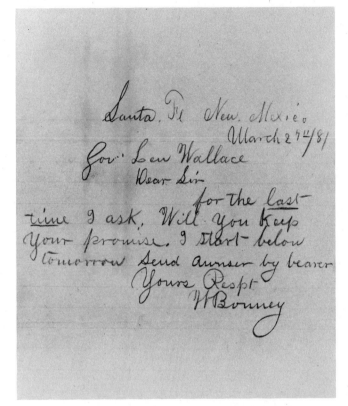

were small and his wrists large — and took his leave.

The Kid remained at large for another year, stealing as before. He hung around Fort Sumner on the Pecos River, where he developed a fateful friendship with one Pat Garrett, the bartender in Beaver Smith's saloon at the fort. In the fall of 1880, Garrett was elected sheriff of Lincoln County. One of the first duties laid upon his shoulders was the apprehension of Billy the Kid.

Up and down the Pecos valley, Garrett laid trap after unavailing trap for his erstwhile drinking customer and friend. He almost caught Billy in mid-December in an ambush he set up outside Fort Sumner, but some animal instinct warned the Kid away at the last moment. By then Billy again was riding at the head of a band of outlaws. Just before the trap was to be sprung he sent one of his cohorts, Tom O'Folliard, ahead of him, saying he wanted to go back down the line to borrow a chew of tobacco. As O'Folliard approached the ambush point, Garrett and his posse opened fire. O'Folliard was hit immediately; the Kid and his friends got away.

Garrett got Billy a few days later. Trailing the Kid and his band to an abandoned stone building in a re-

mote spot called Stinking Springs, the sheriff's posse surrounded the house in the dark. At dawn, a man wearing a hat like the Kid's came to the door carrying a feed bag for a horse tethered just outside. Seven rifle shots killed him in his tracks; the victim turned out to be Charles Bowdre, a 47-year-old cattleman who had branched out into rustling.

Somebody inside the house reached through the door and grabbed the horse's halter rope, but Garrett killed the animal. That finished the Kid's hope of escape. He had planned to bolt from the house but, as he later told the sheriff, he was afraid his own mount — which he had kept with him inside — would balk at the dead animal lying by the door. Later in the day, while the posse broiled a meal outside, delectable cooking odors reached the trapped outlaws, and they abruptly gave up. The men inside were famished, the Kid explained to Garrett, and since they had no wood for cooking a meal of their own, it seemed as good a time as any to surrender.

The Kid was held in jail in the town of Mesilla until his trial in April 1881. The court took exactly one day to convict him of murdering Lincoln County Sheriff

Brady, and sentenced him to hang. Sheriff Garrett began to gather technical information on the building of gallows and the procedures of hanging. Then, on April 28, the Kid stunned all of New Mexico by escaping once again. While one guard, Robert Olinger, was escorting the jail's other inmates across the street to a restaurant for supper, the Kid persuaded his other guard, J. W. Bell, to lead him to the privy in the jail yard. As he was being returned to his cell, he practiced his old trick of slipping his handcuffs; he slugged Bell by swinging the released shackles like a flail, then shot him dead—either with Bell's own gun or, as some theorized, with a weapon a sympathizer had cached for Billy in the privy. Next, the Kid seized a double-barreled shotgun in Sheriff Garrett's office and waited in a window on the balcony of the jail until Olinger, aroused by the shot, came running across the street. "Hello, Bob," Billy called with a grin, and fired when Olinger looked up. As Olinger fell, a bystander shouted that the Kid had killed Bell. "And me too," Olinger gasped, and died.

Standing on the balcony, laughing, the Kid smashed the shotgun and threw the pieces down at the corpse. "Take it, damn you," he told the dead deputy. "You won't follow me any more with that gun." He then ducked inside to Garrett's office and came out to the balcony with two revolvers. Garrett, who was away on business, later got a report of what followed. "The Kid was all over the building, on the porch, watching from the windows. He danced about the balcony, laughed and shouted as though he had not a care on earth. He remained for nearly an hour after the killing."

Apparently onlookers were paralyzed, for Billy left at his leisure. But he did not go very far. Still unable to tear himself from familiar ground, he made fleeting appearances in the vicinity for the next two and a half months. He was now again a loner, as he had always been in spirit. During one of his brief sojourns behind bars, he had expressed his essential preference for solitude to a newspaper reporter: "I wasn't the leader of any gang. I was for Billy all the time."

But his time was running out. On July 13, 1881, Sheriff Garrett rode to Fort Sumner to check on a report that the Kid was hiding nearby. He decided to call

BILLY THE KID.

$500 REWARD.

I will pay $500 reward to any person or persons who will capture William Bonny, alias The Kid, and deliver him to any sheriff of New Mexico. Satisfactory proofs of identity will be required.

LEW. WALLACE,
Governor of New Mexico.

on an old friend, a rancher named Pete Maxwell, who, he thought, would be likely to know if the Kid had been seen anywhere in the area. After midnight, he arrived at Maxwell's cabin, posted two deputies outside and went in to wake the rancher. At the moment, the Kid was in another building on Maxwell's property in Fort Sumner that was occupied by some of the rancher's employees. He had just returned from a dance and he was hungry. One of the ranch hands told him that there was a fresh-killed quarter of beef hanging on the porch of the main house, and Billy decided to help himself to some of it. He took a butcher knife and walked across the yard, barefoot and hatless. When he detected the stirrings of strangers out front, he drew his gun, slipped around the side of the house and ducked through a door. It led into Maxwell's bedroom.

In the dark, Garrett did not recognize the man who had entered, and the Kid did not see Garrett sitting on the edge of Maxwell's bed. The sheriff described the next few moments: "The intruder came close to me, leaned both hands on the bed, his right hand almost touching my knee, and asked in a low tone, 'Who are they, Pete?' At the same instant Maxwell whispered to me. 'That's him!' Simultaneously the Kid must have seen or felt the presence of a third person at the head of the bed. He raised quickly his pistol, a self-cocker, within a foot of my breast. Retreating rapidly across the room he cried 'Quién es? Quién es?' [Who's that? Who's that?] All this occurred in a moment. Quickly as possible I drew my revolver and fired, threw my body aside and fired again. The second shot was useless; the Kid fell dead. He never spoke. A struggle or two, a little strangling sound as he gasped for breath, and the Kid was with his many victims."

Later, Garrett found himself musing on the nature of the baffling young man he had killed—this most complex of all loners. What he said did not clear up the mystery of Billy the Kid, but his observation served as well as any for an epitaph. "Those who knew him best will tell you that in his most savage and dangerous moods his face always wore a smile. He ate and laughed, drank and laughed, rode and laughed, talked and laughed, fought and laughed—and killed and laughed."

Six feet four and fast on the trigger, Sheriff Pat Garrett dispatched the Kid with the proverbial shot in the dark.

Pat Garrett's fanciful farewell to the Kid

The original cover of the Garrett opus

The legend that grew up around Billy the Kid had many promoters, but none more unlikely than Sheriff Pat Garrett, the man who did him in. Soon after shooting the young killer in July 1881, Garrett teamed up with an itinerant journalist, Ashmun Upson, to produce *An Authentic Life of Billy the Kid.* The preface declared loftily: "I am incited to this labor by an impulse to correct the thousand false statements which have appeared in the public newspapers and in yellow-covered cheap novels."

In fact, the book, while accurately illustrated, was as careless with the truth as the dime novels Garrett purported to despise. For example, Billy did not, at the age of 12, kill a loafer because the man insulted his mother — or for any other reason. Nor did he rescue a wagon train by routing Indian attackers with an ax, or ride 81 miles in six hours to spring a friend from a Texas jail. Yet, since such tales were printed under the byline of the Kid's nemesis, many readers came to accept them as gospel.

Garrett's own reputation suffered no harm from these fictional touches. Already famed throughout the Southwest, he went on to serve as a captain in the Texas Rangers and win an appointment as a customs collector from President Teddy Roosevelt — whom he had met at a luncheon in San Antonio. But when a New Mexico ranch he had purchased began to fail, Garrett became a morose fixture in saloons. Finally, in 1908, he was killed by a neighbor after a protracted feud — an ironic end for a man who, in his book, had claimed responsibility for bringing New Mexico "a season of peace and prosperity to which she has ever, heretofore, been a stranger."

Trapped in a cabin, the Kid and his rustler cohorts signal surrender after one outlaw and a horse are killed by Sheriff Garrett's possemen.

Billy fells a deputy with a shotgun blast from the balcony of the Lincoln County jail prior to his final escape from the clutches of the law.

Entering a friend's darkened bedroom, Billy is surprised by Garrett and brought down with a bullet to the heart without returning fire.

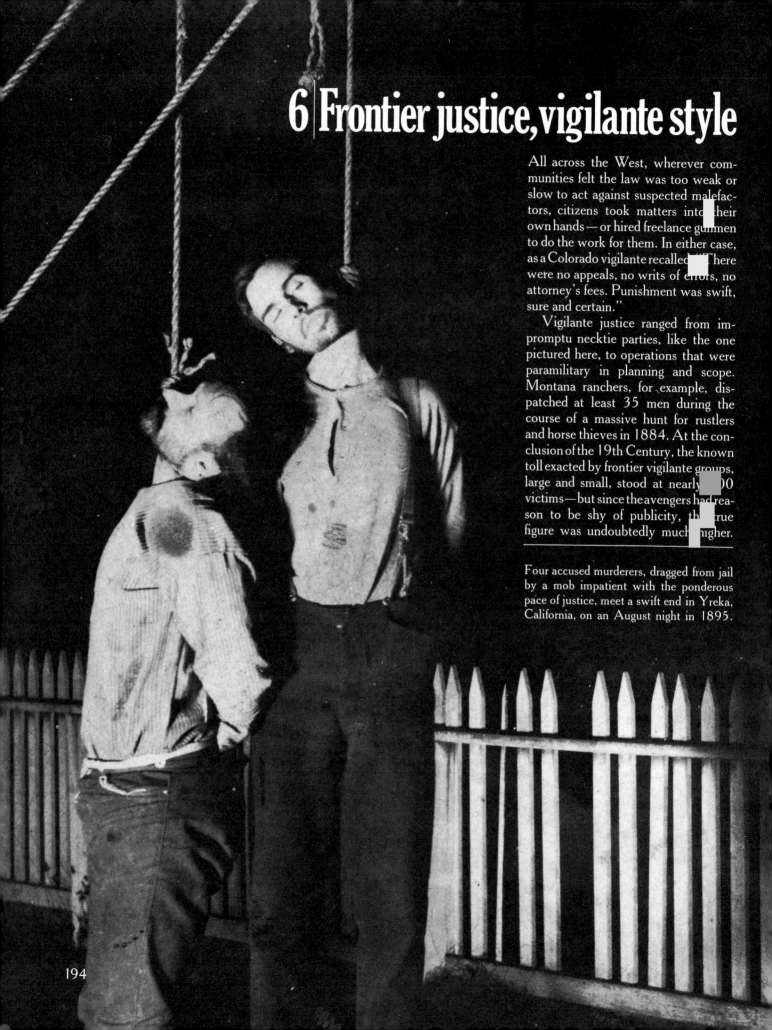

6 | Frontier justice, vigilante style

All across the West, wherever communities felt the law was too weak or slow to act against suspected malefactors, citizens took matters into their own hands — or hired freelance gunmen to do the work for them. In either case, as a Colorado vigilante recalled: "There were no appeals, no writs of errors, no attorney's fees. Punishment was swift, sure and certain."

Vigilante justice ranged from impromptu necktie parties, like the one pictured here, to operations that were paramilitary in planning and scope. Montana ranchers, for example, dispatched at least 35 men during the course of a massive hunt for rustlers and horse thieves in 1884. At the conclusion of the 19th Century, the known toll exacted by frontier vigilante groups, large and small, stood at nearly 600 victims—but since the avengers had reason to be shy of publicity, the true figure was undoubtedly much higher.

Four accused murderers, dragged from jail by a mob impatient with the ponderous pace of justice, meet a swift end in Yreka, California, on an August night in 1895.

WARNING!

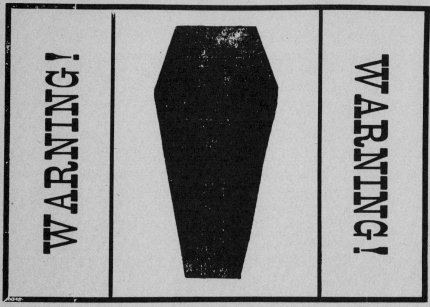

WARNING!

WARNING!

FOOT-PADS, THIEVES AND DANCE-HOUSE LOUNGERS MUST GET OUT OF LAKE CITY AND STAY---OTHERWISE HANG.

The Foot-pads who are known to be in this city are hereby warned to leave immediately and

SAVE THEIR NECKS!

The proprietors of the Dance Houses are notified to close them immediately, and saloon keepers are notified that they will be held accountable for any injuries that may occur to persons or property. Miners are requested to go to their respective places of work and remain there. Parents are enjoined to keep their children off the streets at night.

By order of THE VIGILANTES.

Clandestine wars at the edge of the law

Few men in the history of the Old West ever met a death as emphatic as that visited by Montana vigilantes in 1864 upon a bandit named Joe Pizanthia. Implicated in a number of murders and stage robberies, Pizanthia was cornered in a cabin on a wooded hillside near the town of Bannack. When two members of the vigilante party tried to force their way in, Pizanthia killed one and wounded the other in the hip. At this point, the besiegers' rage "rose nearly to madness," as one participant later recalled. They procured a small howitzer from the town, blew several holes in the cabin walls and followed the cannonade with a storm of small-arms fire. Then they rushed the place. Inside, they found their quarry badly wounded—but that was not enough to appease them. The man who had been shot in the hip proceeded to empty his revolver into the outlaw. Still not wholly satisfied, the vigilantes strung him up with a clothesline and fired more than 100 bullets into the swaying corpse. Then they set the shattered cabin ablaze and tossed what remained of Joe Pizanthia onto the flames.

While the penalty inflicted on Pizanthia was unusual, the savage impulse behind it was not. On a frontier where every advance toward prosperity and security was hard won, citizens would go to any lengths to protect what they had gained. Criminal elements—known or merely suspected—posed a threat to the stability that communities cherished, and if constituted authority appeared powerless to deal with the problem, determined individuals had to step in. And so, from the parched plains of Texas to the wooded valleys of the Black Hills, ordinary men took on the role of vigilantes, banding together in secret committees, unauthorized posses or impromptu mobs to eradicate the criminal menace. Some objects of their fury were hanged, shot or burned, with or without pretense of a trial; others were beaten, flogged and, in a grim application of eye-for-an-eye retribution, branded like the cattle they had tried to rustle. In one notorious instance, a vigilante force of wealthy cattlemen and their hired gunmen declared war on an entire Wyoming county, in an attempt to root out rustlers and simultaneously discourage the spread of small ranching interests; the invaders lost the Johnson County War, as it became known, but only after a three-day pitched battle with several hundred defending settlers.

Such episodes clearly demonstrated that vigilante action contained the seeds of a lawlessness greater than the crimes it curbed. Yet a Montana schoolmaster who was present at Joe Pizanthia's brutal demise expressed the dilemma of his contemporaries when he wrote: "The question of the propriety of establishing a Vigilance Committee depends upon the answers to the following queries: Is it lawful for citizens to slay robbers and murderers when they catch them; or ought they to wait for policemen, where there are none, or put them in penitentiaries not yet erected?"

At the fringes of the frontier, vigilantes had a ready answer to such questions: they acted on their own because there was virtually no other law. But vigilantism also flourished in settled parts of the West, wherever peace officers and magistrates seemed overly concerned with the statutory niceties of due process, or wherever they simply proved ineffectual against wrongdoers. Indeed, some authorities welcomed vigilantes, even incorporating them into the law-enforcement apparatus.

These alliances might be tacit and informal, signalized only by a lawman standing idly by while vigilantes

A vigilante edict of the 1880s, adorned with a coffin, serves an eviction notice on ruffians in Lake City, Colorado. Special emphasis was placed on footpads—sneak thieves who skulked about on padded soles and relieved miners of gold and silver.

In this *Harper's Weekly* illustration of 1874, vigilantes on the Texas-Oklahoma border await the rigging of a telegraph-pole gallows, while a man with a six-shooter *(left)* guards three captured horse thieves.

did their work. That happened, for example, at Aurora, Nevada, in 1864. After some 30 settlers in the area had been murdered by horse thieves and desperadoes, a vigilance committee rounded up several bandit leaders. As its members set about building a gallows in front of the town armory, one dissenting citizen dashed off a telegram of protest to the Territorial Governor in Carson City, informing him of the situation. The Governor in turn wired an inquiry to U.S. Marshal Bob Howland, who was in Aurora at the time. The marshal's reply was terse but crystal-clear: "Everything quiet in Aurora. Four men to be hanged in 15 minutes."

In 1861 the Colorado Territory actually conferred official status upon district vigilance committees, providing by law that each committee should be empowered to "examine and report all criminal violations of the law." And throughout the West, state or territorial charters were granted to vigilante groups formally or-

ganized as range associations, stock growers' associations and homesteaders' protective associations. Many of them held annual meetings, issued reports—and quietly went about hanging and shooting outlaws.

While most vigilantes were well-intentioned citizens whose aim was to protect the commonweal, some were impelled by less exalted motives. Men of wealth, seeking to insure their private interests, had little trouble finding hired guns to serve them. Of all the gunfighters, these mercenaries were the hardest to classify. As a group, they were neither outlaws nor lawmen, though many had pursued both careers in the past. In their role as vigilantes, they usually operated not so much in defiance of the law as simply beyond its reach.

For the most part, these hirelings were nameless, faceless individuals who sought no notoriety and left little trace as they went about their lethal labors. Once they received their blood money, they just rode over

the horizon, never to be seen again. They regarded their trade as a way of earning a day's pay — and they found no lack of employers. In the early 1860s, the Overland Stage Line called upon freelance gunmen to help guard a newly opened route through the Rockies against harassment by road agents and horse thieves. After a few shootings and lynchings of the miscreants, all paid for by the Overland, the stages went through unmolested. Railroads everywhere in the West recruited professional gunslingers as private detectives to combat train robberies, thereby extending the extraordinary police powers granted to the companies by state and territorial governments. Wyoming, for example, authorized railroad conductors to make arrests, and North Dakota designated all trainmen as peace officers; still, the railroads chose to maintain their private armies as well.

On the great public grazing lands from Texas to Montana, cattlemen who monopolized the lands relied on hired guns to beat back challenges from sheepherders and homesteaders or, more commonly, to protect their herds from rustlers. One reason large ranches brought in gunmen was the fact that ordinary cowboys would not always use their six-shooters against rustlers. The foreman of a big Wyoming ranch complained: "The men working for the cattle outfits seemed to have an understanding among themselves that they were being paid so much a month for working, not fighting, and it was up to the owner or manager to do his own fighting." Naturally, owners or managers preferred to delegate such work to professionals.

Often, range-roaming gunfighters were recruited by stockmen's associations and given such bland titles as "cattle detectives" or "stock inspectors." When rustlers were spotted making off with cattle, the gunmen would arrive in a body, suddenly pounce on and dispose of the culprits, then as suddenly disperse. In most

Lashed to a windmill by a Nebraska mob that dragged him from court, a murderer faces an exotic death. The sheriff halted the rite—depicted in the *Police News* in 1884—and the man got a life term instead.

cases, they went unidentified, and even when caught they could usually depend on the protection of their employers to elude the law's grasp.

Respectable and influential, these employers were also well-heeled—so well that the cattle detectives who worked for them ranked among the best-paid guns in the West. Their wages averaged between $100 and $150 a month—roughly three times as much as the remuneration of a typical deputy U.S. marshal. In some places the pay scale rose to $250 a month, plus bounties for obtaining the conviction of a horse thief or cattle rustler. That kind of money bought some men of impressive records and reputations—men whose names still gleam in contrast to the gray anonymity of the average hired gun. In the 1880s, when two big west Texas spreads, the LS and the XIT, sought to wipe out outlaws and small ranchers suspected of rustling, the ranch owners were able to attract top gunfighter talent. The LS forces were led by Pat Garrett, the ex-sheriff from New Mexico who had killed Billy the Kid. One of the XIT gunmen was former Texas Ranger John Armstrong, the man who finally brought John Wesley Hardin to book.

But the most celebrated of all the hired guns, the one who probably was paid the most money and the only one to win national fame for his freelance deeds, was Tom Horn. He was also one of the few who wound up on the gallows for practicing his trade.

A swaggering, broad-shouldered six-foot-two cowboy out of Arizona, Tom Horn proved his gun hand as a deputy sheriff in Colorado. Then he worked as a roving gunman for the Pinkerton Detective Agency for four years (his reputed score of victims for that period was 17), and finally went off on his own as a cattle detective. He turned up in Wyoming in 1894, denying he had killed anyone for the Pinkertons and simultaneously offering the same lethal services to Wyoming cattlemen. His price varied, but he often charged $500 for each rustler he shot. "Killing men is my specialty," he once said. "I look at it as a business proposition, and I think I have a corner on the market."

Though the corner he held was not quite a monopoly, he did pretty well. One rancher described him in these glowing terms: "Tom Horn had the honorable trait never to peach on accomplices or employers. He classed cattle thieves with wolves and coyotes, and looked upon himself as a benefactor of society in destroying them, killing without feeling or compunction when certain he was after a guilty man."

Horn was admired—and hired—by the most reputable stockmen in the state. On one occasion his services as a range detective were even sought out by the governor of Wyoming, W. A. Richards, who owned a large ranch in the Big Horn Mountains. The Governor was too prudent to invite Horn to his own office at the state capitol; instead, he arranged to meet the gunman in an adjoining office that was, conveniently enough, occupied by the state Board of Livestock Commissioners, an agency under the thumb of the Wyoming Stock Growers Association. A prominent stockman, William Irvine, was present at the encounter and later recalled: "The governor was quite nervous, so was I, Horn perfectly cool. He talked generally, was careful of his ground; told the governor he would either drive every rustler out of the Big Horn County, or take no pay other than $350 advanced to buy two horses and a pack outfit; that when he had finished the job to the Governor's satisfaction he should receive $5,000 because, he said in conclusion, 'Whenever everything else fails, I have a system which never does.' He placed no limit on the number of men to be gotten rid of."

According to Irvine, the Governor got cold feet just as Horn began to lay out his plan, and the gunman shrewdly sensed that there was no business to be done, at least on this occasion. Tactfully, he rose from his chair to leave. "I presume that is about all you wanted to know, Sir," he said. "I shall be glad to hear from you at any time I can be of service."

Despite widespread knowledge of his death-dealing activities, Tom Horn remained at large until 1901, when he was accused of shooting a 14-year-old boy from ambush. The victim was the son of a small rancher who had committed the heresy of introducing sheep onto an accustomed cattle range. Horn may have killed the boy by mistake: he was big for his age, he was wearing his father's hat and coat and riding his father's horse, and the killing took place in the dim light of dawn.

Soon after his arrest, Horn made a second mistake that proved fatal to himself. Although no one had witnessed the shooting of the rancher's son, a deputy U.S. marshal got Horn drunk and then drew him into making a confession—which a concealed stenographer took

Furious residents of Guthrie, Oklahoma Territory, besiege the jail to demand the release of a fellow citizen. The prisoner, arrested for defiance of a ruling by the town's corrupt land-claim board, was freed and the board member replaced.

down. After Horn sobered up, he swore that he had just been bragging, and charged the stenographer with falsely embellishing the incriminating document. But he was convicted on the strength of his own evidence, and he went to the gallows. A Wyoming cattleman reported: "He died without 'squealing,' to the great relief of many very respectable citizens of the West." Typically, this cattleman offered not a single word of regret for the death of the 14-year-old.

The taking of innocent lives was a frequent price of vigilante action, and the likelihood increased whenever cattle barons went after small ranchers or homesteaders who were trying to claim a piece of the range. Not all the victims were above reproach; sometimes they had succumbed to temptation and snitched a few of the big operators' cattle to start their own herds. A leading Montana stockman, Granville Stuart, wryly described such a case. He had been missing some calves from his herds. "Near our home ranch," he said, "we discovered one rancher whose cows invariably had twin calves and frequently triplets, while the range cows in that vicinity were nearly all barren, and would persist in hanging around this man's corral, envying his cows their numerous children and bawling and lamenting their own childless fate. This state of affairs continued until we were obliged to call around that way and threaten to hang the man if his cows had any more twins."

Stuart was not always so restrained. In 1884, when he was serving as secretary of the Montana Stock Growers Association, 429 stockmen met at Miles City, determined to put a stop once and for all to rustling in Montana. "The Montana cattlemen were as peaceable and law-abiding a body of men as could be found anywhere," Stuart said later, "but they had $35,000,000 worth of property scattered over seventy-five thousand square miles of practically uninhabited country and it had to be protected from thieves. The only way to do it was to make the penalty

Four bullet-riddled corpses lie strewn about a hayfield, casualties of an 1888 war between two southwestern Kansas towns vying to become

for stealing so severe that it would lose its attractions." At the Miles City meeting, a proposal was made to raise an army of gunmen and subdue the countryside by sheer force of numbers. Stuart helped dissuade the stockmen from such an action: it could lead to the loss of too many lives, he argued, and the law would take a dim view of it. He thought the matter could better be handled quietly by the stockmen themselves, with forces drawn from their own ranch employees.

So Granville Stuart led his neighbors and their hired hands in a series of raids on suspected rustlers and horse thieves in the area. The vigilante stockmen soon became known as the Stranglers for their willingness to resort to the rope — though generally a noose was brought out only when the evidence of misdeeds was strong. In one case, the Stranglers descended on a cabin occupied by two suspected horse thieves. The men fervently denied stealing any horses, except from Indians. They went on denying it as the vigilantes counted 26 horses in the corral with well-known brands. They were still denying their guilt as the rope went around their necks.

Stuart's Stranglers occasionally added sadistic touches to their triumphs. Once they seized a half-breed boy accused of rustling — on little or no evidence — and condemned him to death. But they took their time about it, forcing the youth to entertain them with merry airs on his violin through a long night of drinking and rollicking. At dawn, they hanged him.

Even that sort of gratuitous brutality failed to make a powerful enough impression on Montana rustlers and eventually the stockmen decided to import gunfighters after all. They laid their plans in such secrecy that, when they finally and swiftly struck, it was impossible for Montanans to reconstruct accurately the full story. Rumors flew, but the facts were hard to confirm.

The mystery was penetrated at least in part by a young newspaperman named Owen Wister, who was later to write the classic Western novel, *The Virgin-*

the county seat. Because the killings took place in a jurisdictional no man's land across the border in Indian Territory, the culprits went free.

ian. Visiting the West in the early 1890s, Wister heard and assembled the details of the clandestine war. "It happened like a visit from the Destroying Angel," he wrote. "The ringleaders among the cattle thieves suddenly died, as it were, in one night. There may have been twenty, there may have been fifty, who met their deaths in this way. I am not certain of the number, but I know that the stroke was the result of long and elaborate preparation, that when it fell it was a single stroke and a clean one, and that those physically concerned with the killings were never known in Montana. Their names did not come to light; they were brought into the state for this purpose and they left it shut invisible in a freight car on the Northern Pacific Railway."

Wister never went to Montana himself, but he did spend time in Wyoming, and probably got his story from stockmen who entertained him there. Though he did not know it at the time, a far more spectacular story was under way in Wyoming itself.

Like their counterparts in Montana, the wealthy stockmen of Wyoming detested rustlers; but they also found considerable cause for irritation in the rising expectations of small ranchers—upstarts, they felt, who somehow posed a threat to their control over the state's cattle economy. The hotbed of many small independents was remote Johnson County, in the northern part of the state, hundreds of miles from the capital of Cheyenne, where the cattle barons liked to take their ease. But distance was no deterrent in the campaign that they contemplated in 1892. Well able to afford the transport and other expenses of an army of hired gunmen, they envisioned no more, no less, than an all-out war on Johnson County — planned and executed on military lines.

Later, this venture would come to be known variously as the invasion of Johnson County, the Johnson County War and the War on Powder River—but by any name it proved an utter fiasco for the cattlemen. From the start, they made blunders that all but assured total failure, and they finally extricated themselves only through the timely aid of the U.S. Cavalry and the President of the United States.

The cattlemen who planned this grim comedy of errors were a curious lot of vigilantes to begin with. Among them were Hubert Teschemacher, a stylish young Bostonian, and Frederic O. de Billier, a New York blue blood; they had been classmates at Harvard before heading West with a half million dollars to invest. William Irvine managed a large ranch backed by Omaha millionaires, and served as a director of the Cheyenne and Northern Railroad and other corporations. Fred Hesse, an Englishman, had worked (swindled, some said) his way up from foreman to manager of a ranching system that grazed tens of thousands of cattle on far-flung Wyoming ranges. The most determined cattleman of all was Major Frank Wolcott; a former Army officer from Kentucky, he still wore his puttees and maintained his military bearing despite a twisted neck — acquired in a tussle with a Laramie cowboy — that left his head permanently cocked to one side. Wolcott's jaw, a friend observed, "closed with a snap after every sentence he uttered." Eventually the cattlemen chose Wolcott to command their forces.

Most of the plutocrats in the group had spent less time in the saddle than in the state capital, amid the plush and exclusive surroundings of the Cheyenne Club. Built in 1881 as an alternative to barbarous frontier hotels or remote ranch houses, the Club was aptly described in its charter as a "pleasure resort and place of amusement." Here in the early 1890s, its members plotted their little war while waiting a turn at the billiard table or nibbling at pickled eels and French hors d'oeuvre prior to a table d'hôte dinner sent up by dumbwaiter from the kitchen below. From time to time they laid aside their cares for some especially grand wingding; at one Club banquet the 41 attending members washed down their dinner with 20 bottles of red wine and 66 bottles of champagne. But at more sober intervals they returned to their problems, and at last their plan of attack materialized.

Though the scheme was hatched in private, its authors' aims were no secret; in one way or another, they had long since signaled their intentions. They certainly wanted to end the rustling, but in so doing they also proposed to keep Wyoming's cattle wealth concentrated in the hands of the big ranchers.

For years, the cattlemen had been blaming rustlers for almost all their losses of livestock. Actually, most losses were due to poor management practices such as overstocking the range; to unpredictable whims of nature in the form of prairie fires and plagues of feed-

destroying grasshoppers; and to sieges of bad weather: But whenever lean dividends had to be explained to far-off investors, rustlers provided the best excuse. After a while, the Wyoming cattle barons began to use this excuse to justify any actions they took.

First the cattlemen had thought up the idea of a cowboy black list, agreeing not to hire cowboys who owned cattle on the assumption that any mere cowboy who managed to acquire stock must have rustled it. The black list not only antagonized the cowboys, but by denying them employment spurred many of them to strike out on their own as small ranchers.

Next, the cattlemen had enraged all small ranchers by persuading the state legislature to pass a "maverick law," making every unbranded stray calf on the range the property of the Wyoming Stock Growers Association, which then sold the calves to the highest bidder. Theoretically the law was aimed at rustlers; actually it meant that struggling ranchers could not claim their own strays; in many cases they could not even afford to buy them back from the W.S.G.A.

Further aggravating matters, the cattlemen had used the proceeds of the maverick sales to pay their own detectives, who were regarded by the populace as bounty hunters at best (they received $250 for every conviction of a rustler) and as hired assassins at worst. Several lynchings and mysterious shootings of suspected rustlers and small ranchers helped build a climate of fear and hatred of the detectives' employers.

The most infamous of the lynchings occurred on the Sweetwater range in 1889. Its victims were two homesteaders who had dared to settle on a huge tract of land claimed by a wealthy and arrogant cattleman, Albert Bothwell, and used for grazing his vast herds. One of the homesteaders was Jim Averell, who had turned his place into a small store, saloon and post office. The other was Ella Watson, a robust prostitute from Kansas who, it was rumored, was sometimes paid in rustled cattle for her dalliances with local cowboys.

Ella and Jim were taken from their cabins one summer morning by Bothwell and five other men and hanged from the same tree, side by side. When the lynchings caused an unexpected outcry from citizens in the area, Bothwell's stockmen friends hastily drummed up a post-mortem justification for the action. They planted newspaper stories with the friendly press in Cheyenne in which 28-year-old Ella Watson was transformed into "Cattle Kate," a gun-toting rustler queen. In death, Ella even made it onto the pages of the *Police Gazette*. But to those who had known them, Ella Watson was merely an enterprising whore, while Jim Averell, who apparently owned no cattle at all, was an innocent businessman wantonly killed.

Many small ranchers laid the Sweetwater lynchings at the door of the W.S.G.A., and in 1891 suspicion of the organization turned to fury when two other settlers were shot from ambush on the Powder River in Johnson County. The prime suspect in the murders was Frank Canton *(page 215),* chief cattle detective for the stock association. And behind Canton, of course, loomed the blithe barons of the Cheyenne Club.

The killings aroused Johnson County to the point of open rebellion. Although state law gave the W.S.G.A. authority over all roundups, the small ranchers of Johnson County formed a rival organization called the Northern Wyoming Farmers' and Stock Growers' Association; the group announced plans to hold a roundup independent of the W.S.G.A. and, moreover, to treat as their own any stray cattle they found. In a grim mood, honest men took to calling themselves rustlers as a term of defiance, and their children invented a game called rustlers and white caps, in which the white caps were the big cattlemen and the rustlers always won.

It was at this point that the members of the Cheyenne Club fashioned their plot. Over their Cuban cigars and Rum St. Cruz, they determined to wipe out the competing organization and exterminate the "rustlers." Their plan was simple, but drastic. First, recruit a force of gunfighters from outside the state to descend on Johnson County. Next, cut all telegraph wires that linked the county to the rest of the state, thus isolating the citizenry when the invasion got underway. Next, take over the town of Buffalo — the county seat — and assassinate the sheriff, his deputies and the three county commissioners, thereby stripping the populace of leadership. And finally, dispose of all the men on a "dead list" drawn up by the W.S.G.A.'s cattle detectives — a list that, by one estimate, included 70 names.

The cattlemen rushed off in several directions at once to implement their plan. Tom Smith, a stock association detective, led the recruiting drive. Once a deputy U.S. marshal in Texas, he returned there to hunt up old

friends. Smith offered a tempting package: wages of five dollars a day, plus expenses; a bonus of $50 to every man for each rustler killed, no matter who killed him; and, with a bow to prudence, a $3,000 accident policy for each volunteer. Twenty-two gunmen quickly signed on and agreed to rendezvous at Denver.

While the gunfighters were gathering, two stockmen left Cheyenne for Colorado to buy horses for the expedition lest suspicion be aroused by a roundup of too many horses from their own ranches. In Cheyenne, other cattlemen bought three heavy freight wagons and placed orders for tents, bedding, guns, pistols and ammunition. To cover the mounting costs, 100 members of the W.S.G.A. put up $1,000 each. On April 5,

1892, a special Pullman car at Denver, with the Texas gunfighters aboard, started for Cheyenne. The $100,000 invasion was launched.

Charles Penrose, a young doctor from Pennsylvania, was on hand as both a friend of the cattlemen and official surgeon to the expedition, and he described the Texans' arrival at the Denver depot. They were, he said, "a good-looking body of men, who were well able to take care of themselves. Each man carried a rifle and wore a six-shooter in his belt. They were not very warmly clad for April in Wyoming—their clothes were more for the Texas climate." Penrose was especially fascinated by the getup of one particularly noticeable Texan, Jim Dudley, "a big, good-natured-looking party

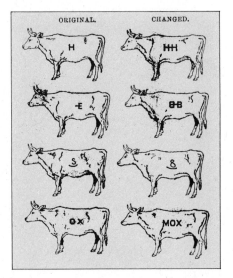

of 225 lbs., who arrived clad in nothing but a summer undershirt, trousers and shoes."

At Cheyenne, the Pullman was shunted into the switching yard and joined to a train that included a baggage car, three stockcars, a flatcar bearing the three big freight wagons the cattlemen had equipped, and a caboose. Of the 100 stockmen who had put up the money for the expedition, 19 chose to go along with the gunfighters. With their cattle detectives and a few guests, they boarded the Pullman for their first look at the Texans. Among the guests were two newspapermen: the city editor of the *Cheyenne Sun,* and a *Chicago Herald* correspondent. They had wangled an invitation to the expedition when the canny Chicago man said exactly the right thing to the cattlemen: "I will see that your side of the story reaches the public."

As a Union Pacific locomotive was readied for a fast run to Casper, a little range town at the foot of the Big Horn Mountains, the expedition's commander, Major Wolcott, issued his first order. "Hurry up," he barked at the railroad superintendent, "put us at Casper and we will do the rest." On the evening of April 5, the train chugged off, due at Casper before dawn.

In the passenger car the Texans were bunched at one end playing cards, the Wyoming stockmen at the other talking over their plans. The cattlemen valued their hired gunfighters but would not dream of admitting them to the society of gentlemen, and the Texans showed no interest in pressing the matter.

In the baggage car Major Wolcott and a few men working under his direction were busy rearranging the supplies to expedite unloading at Casper. Wolcott had barred everyone else from the car, and when Frank Canton, the chief cattle detective, strolled in, the major unwisely ordered him out. Swearing that he would take no further guff from the prickly Wolcott, Canton rejoined his fellow detective Tom Smith and the Texans in the passenger car. The foolish little spat became a full-fledged quarrel: Smith sided with Canton, and Smith had the Texans' backing. At breakfast the next

day, Wolcott grandly resigned his command. Tom Smith took charge of the Texans, and Frank Canton of the expedition as a whole.

En route to Casper, the train stopped at a small junction where the cattlemen checked out a key phase of their strategy. They tried to telegraph the town of Buffalo and were delighted when the telegraph operator reported he could not get through. Their allies in Johnson County had done their job; the wires to the county seat were down.

The wire cutting, however, was about the last thing that went according to plan. As the train was unloaded at Casper and the Texans picked their horses for the 150-mile ride to Buffalo, a minor problem arose. Jim Dudley, the heavyweight, could not find a horse strong enough to carry his bulk. An exasperated Major Wolcott shouted to Dudley's cohorts: "For heaven's sake, isn't there a one of you smaller men who will trade with him?" None of the Texans would even consider helping their comrade-in-arms — but aid came from an unexpected source. One of the cattlemen's guests, an Englishman named W. B. Wallace, offered to trade mounts.

With Jim Dudley finally settled in the saddle and the sun half an hour high, the horsemen and wagons began their ascent into the hills to the north. Now more serious problems arose. The wagons soon bogged down in the turf, left muddy after recent snows. While making camp for breakfast some of the cattlemen carelessly picketed their horses to shallowly rooted clumps of sagebrush. The horses tore loose and it took hours to round them up. Later, a freight wagon broke through the flimsy flooring of a bridge and had to be dragged from the gulch below with ropes tied to saddle horns.

The schedule called for the mini-army to spend the first night at the home of John Tisdale, a W.S.G.A.

A petition from cowboy Jack Cooper — absolved in court after the Wyoming Stock Growers Association accused him of illegal cattle-branding — asks that he be removed from the organization's black list. Without W.S.G.A. say-so, he could not join roundups; his request was grudgingly granted.

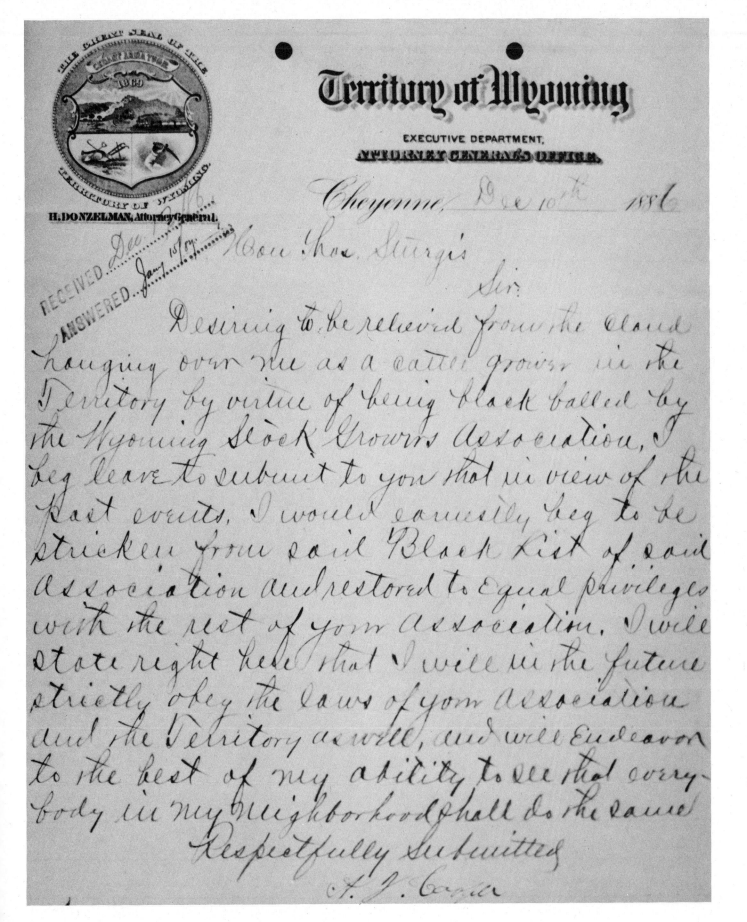

Territory of Wyoming

EXECUTIVE DEPARTMENT,
ATTORNEY GENERALS OFFICE,

H. DONZELMAN, Attorney General.

RECEIVED Dec 11th / 86
ANSWERED Jany 10th / 87

Cheyenne, Dec 10th 1886

Hon Thos. Sturgis

Sir:

Desiring to be relieved from the cloud hanging over me as a cattle grower in the Territory by virtue of being black balled by the Wyoming Stock Growers Association, I beg leave to submit to you that in view of the past events, I would earnestly beg to be stricken from said Black List of said Association and restored to equal privileges with the rest of your Association. I will state right here that I will in the future strictly obey the laws of your Association and the Territory as well, and will endeavor to the best of my ability to see that everybody in my neighborhood shall do the same

Respectfully Submitted

A. J. Cap___

Storekeeper Jim Averell, who made the mistake of settling on Wyoming range land coveted by a cattle millionaire, was lynched in July 1889. Three witnesses to the crime vanished and another died mysteriously.

member whose ranch was located 65 miles out of Casper. But a sudden, heavy snowstorm struck and the expedition took almost two days to reach this way stop.

Next day, events took another unforeseen turn. An excited range foreman rode up with the news that a band of rustlers was holed up at the KC ranch, about 15 miles away. He urged an immediate attack, and several stockmen seconded the motion. Frank Canton, reasoning that time was growing dangerously short, argued for sticking to the original plan and moving directly to Buffalo. A noisy debate ensued in the ranch house and, in the end, the majority voted to dispose of the rustlers first.

The vigilante force started off at midnight in a snowstorm so fierce that the horsemen took nearly six hours to cover the 15 miles to the KC ranch. A few miles short of the ranch the men had to stop and build fires to thaw out. But by first light they had surrounded the cabin, concealing themselves in a stable, along a creek bed and in a wooded ravine in back of the house.

The "band of rustlers" turned out to be two cowboys, Nate Champion and Nick Ray, both on the cattlemen's dead list; with them were two fur trappers who had taken refuge from the storm. When the trappers came outside and walked down to the creek to get some water, the invaders took them in hand and quietly led them away. Soon Nick Ray stepped outside to look for them. In the stable loft, Major Wolcott nodded to a young redhead called the Texas Kid, who had his rifle trained on the unsuspecting cowboy. His first shot staggered Ray, and it was followed by a sudden fusillade from the vigilantes hidden in the creek bed. The sound brought Nate Champion to the cabin door, sixshooter in hand. As Ray crawled back toward him, mortally wounded, Champion dragged his friend inside, slammed the door and alone held off the attackers all day. With remarkable poise, he also managed to write a running account of the siege, scribbling in pencil in a battered notebook whenever there was a lull in the shooting. Champion's words make clear that he was writing

to and for Johnson County friends.

"Me and Nick was getting breakfast when the attack took place," Champion began. He described the trappers' disappearance, and two hours later tersely noted that Nick Ray was dead. Still early in the day he wrote: "Boys, there is bullets coming like hail. They are shooting from the stable and river and back of the house." Toward noon, he added: "Boys, I feel pretty lonesome just now. I wish there was someone here with me so we could watch all sides at once." At about three o'clock, he noted that a man in a buckboard and another on a horse went by the ranch and were fired on: "I seen lots of men come out on horses on the other side of river and take after them."

The last entry was made that evening: "Well, they have just got through shelling the house like hail. I heard them splitting wood. I guess they are going to fire the house to-night. I think I will make a break when night comes, if alive. Shooting again. It's not night yet. The house is all fired. Goodbye, boys, if I never see you again." He carefully signed that entry as Nathan D. Champion, then broke from the back door of the flaming house. Four bullets cut him down.

The decision to attack the KC ranch proved the costliest mistake of the cattlemen's venture. The two men Nate Champion saw riding past the ranch managed to elude their pursuers, went on to Buffalo and called the town to arms. After killing Champion, the vigilantes rode hard toward Buffalo, leaving their wagons behind. But it was too late. Sheriff W. E. "Red" Angus and an armed posse were already galloping out to meet them, and night riders were raising reinforcements throughout the country.

The cattlemen knew nothing of all this; as they rode on, they were still confident of success. At 2 a.m. the vigilantes rested their horses at the ranch of one of their Johnson County allies. After swilling hot coffee, everyone remounted — except poor, hefty Jim Dudley. He wanted a fresh horse. The ranch foreman tried hard to please him, but after Dudley tried five horses and was

Ella Watson, a prostitute whose place of business was located near Averell's, shared a hanging tree with him. The lynchers quieted a storm of outrage by asserting that she was really "Cattle Kate," a rustler.

unhappy with all of them, trigger-tempered Major Wolcott erupted. "Cinch up or stay behind," he shouted.

One of the newspapermen with the expedition described this lighter moment: "Dudley drew a rueful face; his last horse was the poorest of the lot — a weak-kneed, ugly brute, utterly unfit to carry a man of Jim's weight. The ragged little sorrel soon tired of trying to throw its rider; 225 pounds is a pretty solid mass to unseat, so the animal turned its attention to a system of dogged meanness that nearly drove Dudley crazy."

As Dudley did his best to keep up, the vigilante force rode on in ragged formation, with two outriders a short distance ahead. Suddenly the outriders came racing back to report the presence of a large body of men camped down the road. The invaders halted in confusion, and Major Wolcott seized the chance to reassert his leadership. Cattleman William Irvine, who was on the expedition, later recalled: "Wolcott and myself got down afoot and walked ahead, and after going a considerable distance and listening intently we had about decided that the boys had run into a bunch of range horses, when a gun was discharged ahead, which gave Sheriff Angus and his party away. Well, when we got back to the bunch we found our men in such a state that Wolcott at once assumed command. Nobody suggested it but we were all glad he did so, recognizing the fact that he was the right man in the right place. He rode out in front of us and gave us a good blowing up, saying, 'I can take ten good men and whip the whole damned bunch of you,' and then lined us up and proceeded to drill us by moonlight."

Irvine did not specify the nature of the drill, but it held up the expedition for a few crucial hours. When Wolcott was finally satisfied, he ordered that a barbed-wire fence be cut, and led his troops across the range in an attempt to outflank the sheriff's posse. A halt was called at the TA ranch, another friendly outpost about 14 miles from Buffalo. While the major took a few men ahead to reconnoiter, Jim Dudley went looking for an easier horse. The foreman found him a big gray that had never been known to buck — but it bucked and threw Jim Dudley. His rifle strap slipped from the saddle horn and the gun went off when it hit the ground, shooting Dudley through the knee as he fell. A spring wagon carried him to nearby Fort McKinney, where gangrene set in. He later died in agony, crying out for the wife he had left in Texas and would never see again.

Meanwhile, the main party of vigilantes hurried from a TA ranch to close ranks with Wolcott's scouts. In the dawn light a lone rider galloped toward them — James Craig, a W.S.G.A. member. "Turn back! Turn back!" he yelled. "Everybody in town is aroused. The rustlers are massing from every direction. Get to cover as soon as you can if you value your lives!"

Wolcott crisply ordered a retreat to the TA ranch. His old adversaries, Frank Canton and Tom Smith, opposed him again: they wanted to go on to Buffalo according to the original plan. In the Sunday morning sunrise the expedition's leaders sat in their saddles arguing as the Texas gunfighters awaited the outcome. The Texans, paid to fight someone else's war, had come too far to quit. At a word from Tom Smith, they would have ridden into Buffalo with guns blazing. But the members of the Cheyenne Club, aghast at the prospect of taking on ready-and-waiting townsmen, decided on retreat. So the vigilantes skulked back to the TA ranch to await attack from their intended victims.

The ranch seemed well situated for defense. Its main buildings, nestled in a bend of Crazy Woman Creek, were surrounded by a log fence seven feet high, with a barbed-wire fence beyond it. The ranch house stood in a windbreak of trees, surrounded by outbuildings — a stable, an icehouse, a small hen house and a dugout for storing potatoes. Within this compound there was also a stack of thick timbers, recently purchased for the construction of a new building. Beyond the barbed-wire fence the terrain stretched away in rolling hills creviced with ravines, making an approach in force difficult.

All day and into the night Major Wolcott barked out orders for the fortification of the ranch. On a knoll about 50 yards from the stable he had his men build a log fort measuring about 12 by 14 feet, with openings through which sharpshooters could cover the approaches to the ranch. Trenches were dug inside the fort and breastworks were raised around the ranch house. By nightfall the formerly fashionable cattlemen of the Cheyenne Club were a sight, their hands blistered and their shoulders bruised from lifting 10-inch-thick timbers. Along with their Texas hirelings, they dined on potatoes — and they made no fuss about etiquette.

At dawn the vigilantes could see their attackers in the distance, digging rifle pits and throwing up breast-

The two lives of a professional gunfighter

When Wyoming's wealthy stockmen persuaded Frank M. Canton, the former sheriff of Johnson County, to become chief detective in their vigilante war on alleged rustlers, local reaction was mixed. The stockmen, of course, rejoiced in their recruit; as a gunfighting lawman, he had already shown his mettle by capturing a number of rustlers and robbers. But the ordinary citizens who had twice elected Canton to office, including the small ranchers who were targets of the stockmen's war, felt that he had sold out to the big interests.

Canton himself felt no compunction about making the switch. As much as any gunfighter in Western history, he epitomized the flexible attitude that stamped such men as a breed. Theirs was a profession in which the opportunity for action, and for gain, tended to outweigh ethical considerations. Crossing the line that separated lawful from lawless acts was a common practice—though not necessarily one that gunfighters were eager to publicize.

Canton's own past held a secret known neither to his cattle-raising employers nor to Johnson County voters. Only after his death at age 78 was it revealed. His name was a pseudonym; he was born Joseph Horner in 1849, the son of a Virginia doctor who moved to Texas after the Civil War. By the age of 26 he was wanted for bank robbery, rustling and assault with intent to kill. His rakehell years reached their climax in 1874 in a saloon brawl with some U.S. cavalrymen in which one soldier was killed. Joe Horner shot his way out of town and soon thereafter disappeared from Texas—later surfacing in Wyoming under his new name.

After his stint as top gun in the Johnson County War, Canton moved to Oklahoma Territory and resumed his career as a lawman. He did triple duty as undersheriff of Pawnee County and as deputy U.S. marshal for both Marshal Evett Nix of Guthrie and "Hanging Judge" Isaac Charles Parker of Fort Smith, Arkansas. In this period Canton helped to wipe out Bill Doolin's gang, and also outdrew and killed the sharpshooting desperado Bill Dunn. When Oklahoma grew too tame for Canton in the late 1890s, he followed the gold rush to the Klondike and served for two years as a deputy U.S. marshal in Alaska.

Years later, in failing health, Canton returned to Texas to make peace with his past. In an interview with the Governor, he secretly confessed that he was Joe Horner and won official forgiveness for his youthful crimes. Close friends then urged him to resume his true identity. But he declined, choosing to be remembered as Frank Canton, gunfighter for the law.

Sheriff Frank M. Canton of Johnson County stands tall and grim in a Wyoming winter scene.

works on every hill and hogback around the ranch. About 50 men had dug in during the night and Sheriff Angus soon brought another 40 recruits from Buffalo. In town one merchant had thrown open his store and was giving away blankets, clothing and ammunition to anyone who would fight. The ladies of Buffalo had set up a kitchen and were preparing wagonloads of food for the men at the front. As armed settlers and small ranchers rode into town, they were organized into companies of 20 men and led to the battlefield on the TA ranch by deputy sheriffs. The mood in the little town was grim —though there was a moment of laughter when a four-year-old boy armed with a toy pistol came strutting down the main street to join the troops.

Shooting started at the TA ranch early in the morning of April 11, a Monday. The attackers' first target was the corral; their rifles picked off the horses until a few of the men inside the compound managed to bring the panicked, jostling survivors into the stable. Cattle provided the next target, and after that "anything that moved." According to one of the beleaguered stockmen: "They were constantly firing on the house, which was considerably shot up. They finally got the range of the doors and it was dangerous to go in or out. There was a boy about sixteen at the ranch when we arrived. He was very keen to be in on the fighting, tried to borrow a gun from several of our party, and finally found an old shotgun in the loft. He had hardly finished cleaning it when a bullet came in one of the windows and creased him across the neck just so the blood would ooze out of the wound. This sure quieted the boy, who went and layed in a corner, and it was the last we heard of him."

The attackers soon had more than 300 men in the field, commanded by a local flour mill manager named Arapahoe Brown, a burly, unkempt figure who had twice been defeated for county sheriff. He simply appeared on the scene and started giving orders. In the absence of Sheriff Angus, who had returned to Buffalo to direct the townsmen's continuing efforts, no one stepped forward to challenge Brown. His plan of battle was simple but sound: close in on the TA ranch by short dashes, then burn the vigilantes out.

Although their situation was hardly promising, the cattlemen believed they could hold out until other big ranchers sent reinforcements. They were counting on

Nate Champion (*second from left*), destined to meet a brutal end in the Johnson County War of 1892, breaks for a meal during a roundup. Death came to the cowboy after 50 vigilantes, convinced he was a rustler, laid seige to his cabin for a full day, finally burning him out and shooting him.

A contemporary diagram of the final battle in the Johnson County War pinpoints the encirclement of vigilante positions by attacking citizens. A force of U.S. cavalrymen *(top right)* arrived in the nick of time to keep the vigilantes from being overrun.

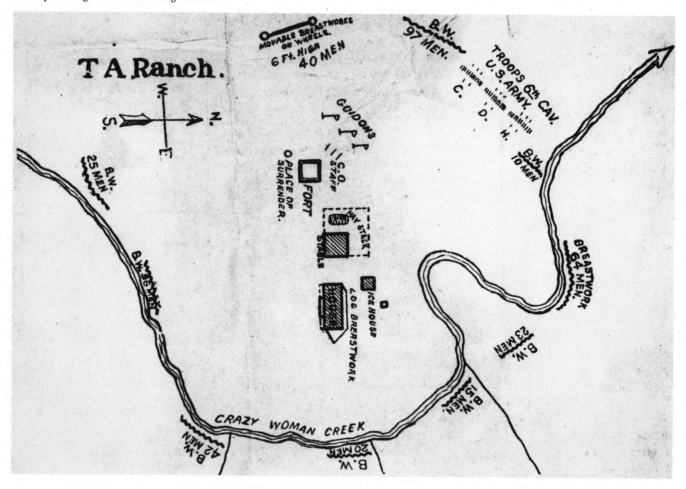

friends in Buffalo to get word to Cheyenne, but to be doubly sure they drafted a telegram to the Governor. A courier carried it through the enemy lines on the first night of the siege. The vigilantes assumed that the telegraph wires, cut almost a week earlier for their own convenience, had by now been repaired. Indeed the chief line repairman for the Wyoming Inland Telegraph Company had been out looking for breaks day and night, riding until his horses gave out in the mud and snow, then going ahead on foot. But each time he fixed a break, the line was severed somewhere else: now the culprits were Johnson County citizens, who wanted to prevent any call by the foe for outside aid.

As additional repairmen got to work, Wyoming Inland did manage to keep the telegraph open for brief periods, though it was touch and go. On Tuesday, the second day of the siege, two Buffalo officials got a telegram through to Governor Amos Barber, informing him

that an illegal armed force had invaded Johnson County, that the invaders had killed two settlers, and that they were now resisting arrest by the sheriff and a posse. The telegram requested the Governor to call in the U.S. troops at Fort McKinney "to assist in putting down the rebellion." In fact, Barber had known of the invasion plans all along and favored the vigilantes: what shocked him was the news of their plight. As more telegrams came from Buffalo, with more appeals for help against the cattlemen, he was in a distinct quandary. The Governor chose to delay answering the appeals, pending word from the cattlemen or their allies.

Barber's dilemma was resolved late on Tuesday night, when the telegram from the cattlemen finally reached him. Their courier had slipped past the attackers at the TA ranch, ridden 100 miles to the next county and sent the message from there. With his worst fears confirmed, Barber immediately wired President

218

Benjamin Harrison, asking for troops to quell an "insurrection." Fortunately for his friends, the Governor also alerted Wyoming's two Senators in Washington. When the telegram for the President arrived, Harrison was asleep. But the Senators from Wyoming rushed to the White House and roused Harrison from bed.

At long last, and just in time, something had gone right for the cattlemen. Now that they were in really deep trouble, some of the highest officials in the land leaped to their rescue. The results were described by a Cheyenne editor: "Military history fails to record another instance where such prompt action and celerity of movement was had as in this case. Barber's telegram to the president left Cheyenne after dark on April 12. Reaching Washington, 2,000 miles away, a consultation between the president, secretary of war and Wyoming's Senators was held, a telegraph order was flashed to Omaha, 1,500 miles, and in turn transferred to Fort

McKinney, another thousand miles, all before 1 o'clock on the morning of April 13th, or inside of six hours. Within another hour three troops of cavalry were on the road, and before sunrise their bugle notes sounded rescue to the waiting barons, 15 miles from the post."

At the TA ranch, the cattlemen had all but given up hope for outside help. Friction was mounting between the gentlemen from Cheyenne and the Texas gunfighters. The Texans muttered among themselves when Frederic de Billier retired to a back room at noon, blandly announcing that he always took a midday nap. There was another bad moment that afternoon when Major Wolcott asked one of the cattlemen to take some of the gunfighters up the hill behind the house to relieve the defenders at the outlying fort. After the cattleman had picked seven men, the eighth refused. Wolcott ordered him to climb the hill. "It's still too light," the gunman protested; "I'll be killed going up." The major explod-

219

In custody after their defeat by Johnson County settlers, Wyoming Stockmen and hired Texas gunslingers retain a self-assured air. Their confidence was borne out when county officials dropped murder charges against them after they won a change of venue to a sympathetic court in Cheyenne.

"THE IN
JOHNSON COUNTY CA
(FRANCIS E. WA

Kirkland
PHOTO
CHEYENNE
1892

NO. 1 TOM SMITH	NO. 8 A.R. POWERS	NO. 15 W.C. IRVINE
" 2 A.B. CLARKE	" 9 A.D. ADAMSON	" 16 BOB TISDALE
" 3 J.N. LESLIE	" 10 C.A. CAMPBELL	" 17 JOE ELLIOTT
" 4 E.W. WHITCOMB	" 11 FRANK LABERTEAUX	" 18 JOHN TISDALE
" 5 D. BROOKE	" 12 PHIL DUFRAN	" 19 SCOTT DAVIS
" 6 W.B. WALLACE	" 13 MAJOR WOLCOTT	" 20 FRED DEBILLIER
" 7 CHAS FORD	" 14 W.E. GUTHRIE	" 21 BEN MORRISON

220

AR. TAKEN AT Ft. D.A. RUSSELL
MAY 4th 1892
22. W.J. CLARKE
23. L.H. PARKER
24. TESCHMACHER
25. B.C. SCHULZE
26. W.H. TABOR
27. J.A. GARRETT
28. W.A. WILSON

NO. 29. J. BARLINGS
" 30. M.A. McNALLY
" 31. MIKE SHONSEY
" 32. DICK ALLEN
" 33. FRED HESSE
" 34. FRANK CANTON
" 35. Wm LITTLE

NO. 36 JEFF MYNETT
" 37. BOB BARLINGS
" 38. S. SUTHERLAND
" 39. BUCK GARRETT
" 40. G.R. TUCKER
" 41. J.M. BENFORD
" 42. WILL ARMSTRONG

No.5174

221

ed: "Which do you prefer, being killed going up the hill or being killed right here? You white-livered son-of-a-bitch, you will either do as ordered or I'll kill you myself!" The reluctant gunman ran up the hill.

At dawn on Wednesday morning the cattlemen looked out and saw an immense ark of heavy timbers and bales of hay slowly moving toward the ranch compound. They recognized the wheels on which this mobile fortress was rolling, for they came from the W.S.G.A.'s own supply wagons, which had been left loaded with spare arms, ammunition and—as the cattlemen recalled with sinking hearts—dynamite. The attackers had the weapons they needed to end the siege: all they had to do, once they got close enough, was to lob sticks of dynamite from behind the ark.

The Texas gunmen were directing a heavy but hopeless fire at the impregnable ark when, in a moment worthy of the most banal blood-and-thunder melodrama, a bugle sounded across the range. Peering through a crack in one of the boarded-up ranch house windows, Hubert Teschemacher spotted cavalry flags and shouted that the troops were coming. The cattlemen gasped with relief, but one Texan still failed to understand what was happening. "What! United States Troops! Have we got to fight United States Troops too? Great God almighty, we are sure done up now!"

The shooting stopped as the troops drew up in formation and their officers conferred with Sheriff Angus behind a hill. The officers had their orders: to save and take charge of the men inside the compound. In response, Angus offered a compromise. The troops could have the besieged men, but on one condition: the vigilantes must later be turned over to civil authorities for trial. The officers agreed. Then, flanked by flag bearers, the officers and the sheriff approached the ranch buildings. As they did so, someone behind the breastworks began waving a soiled white rag.

Major Wolcott greeted Colonel J. J. Van Horn, the commander of the cavalry detachment, with a formal bow, and Van Horn announced he had an order from President Harrison to assist in quelling the disturbance. "Are your people willing to surrender quietly?" asked the colonel. "To the military, yes," the major answered. Then he pointed at Sheriff Angus. "But not to that man." Placed under military arrest, the vigilantes were led away to Fort McKinney, as several hundred armed

citizens of Johnson County looked on from the hills.

"We only figured on fighting rustlers," Wolcott said afterward, "and we were willing to take all chances of a war with them. Their ability to enlist aid amazed and stunned me. The whole country turned out to whip us, and they almost did it." But Sheriff Angus was still far from satisfied. As he watched the departing cavalry and their prisoners, he spoke angrily to a newspaper reporter: "These people came in here with murder and destruction in their hearts and hands. They have murdered and burned and defied the law, and it was my duty to arrest them. They were mine. I had them in my grasp and they were taken from me."

The sheriff's forebodings were justified. Soon after their arrest, the prisoners at Fort McKinney were whisked away to Cheyenne, where their chances of avoiding a lynching or even a trial were much improved. The only ordeal remaining to them was a humiliating six-day horseback trip from Fort McKinney to Douglas, the nearest railroad station. A detachment of troops guarded them along the way, not to prevent their escape but to protect them from furious settlers who lined the route. Adding injury to insult, the men from sub-tropical Texas had to ride through a raging blizzard for the entire distance. But at Douglas the defeated forces boarded a troop train with a private Pullman stocked with champagne and piled with telegrams from the cattlemen's families and friends. When the train pulled into Fort Russell, just outside Cheyenne, it was the Texans who emerged from the train restored—fit as ever, swaggering and as carefree as if they were back on their native terrain. By contrast, the disheveled cattlemen seemed almost humbled; all they wanted was a hot bath and some clean clothes.

For 10 weeks the prisoners were held at Fort Russell, and during that time the cattlemen and the Texans scarcely spoke to one another. They slept in the same dormitory—the fort's bowling alley—with the Texans herded to the rear while the stockmen lived at the front. They were served meals in the same mess hall, but separately, each contingent taking turns at eating first. One cattleman was given free run of the commissary, attending to his associates' needs, and they could all count on the use of the post commander's parlor when their wives visited. Only Frederic de Billier took an interest in the Texans. He spent hours instructing them in the fine points of baseball and football.

All the while, the cattlemen's lawyers were busy arranging for their day in court. The only criminal charges brought against the vigilantes dealt with the murders of Nate Champion and Nick Ray, and the burning of their cabin. These counts were considerably weakened when the key witnesses—the two trappers who were at the ranch when Champion and Ray were killed—were bribed and spirited out of the state. Then the lawyers arranged for the trial to be held at Cheyenne, the cattlemen's headquarters. (The friendly judge who changed the venue from the town of Buffalo ruled that only in Cheyenne could they get an impartial, unprejudiced trial.) The Texans were moved from Fort Russell to a large auditorium in Cheyenne, and the same judge ordered Johnson County to pay for their confinement, at a cost of $100 a day for each man. Within a few weeks, Johnson County's treasury went broke.

When the judge next ordered that the prisoners be turned loose without bond, everyone knew that Johnson County would lose its case in court, and there was a great celebration and farewell party at the Cheyenne Club, with the Texans as guests of honor. William Irvine described the occasion in a letter to a friend:

"If you can for the moment put youself in the place of one of us who had borne the burden of hiring, paying, feeding, and protecting that Texas bunch, you can imagine what pleasure and relief it was to us to be able to see the end. We invited many of our friends to meet them, and we prepared a banquet without regard to expense. It never occurred to any of us, however, that while the average Texan knew what old red eye was, he might not be used to champagne; and as it looked something like water, they drank it as they drank water, and you can imagine the result.

"They soon, or at least many of them, wanted to fight, and as no one but themselves seemed so disposed, they commenced to fight among themselves. It was no easy matter to quiet them; it took hours. Well, we got through with them finally without any accidents, and the other day started them for Texas; and I shall always remember that event with pleasure."

Eventually the Johnson County authorities dropped the charges against the stockmen and their hired guns. By then the Texans, undaunted by their Wyoming misadventure, had gone their separate ways to other gunfights in a still-wild West. Some drifted back to their old haunts around Paris, Texas, where Tom Smith had recruited them. Others headed for the lawless hills of Indian Territory and the wide-open towns of Oklahoma Territory. Those who took this route included G. R. Tucker and Buck Garrett, who were respectively only 19 and 22 years old when they fought in the Johnson County War. In later years their six-guns were to bring the first touch of law to the area around Ardmore, Oklahoma, where Tucker served as deputy U.S. marshal and Garrett as sheriff.

Some of the gunfighters died with their boots on soon after they left Wyoming. Tom Smith, once again a deputy U.S. marshal in Texas, was killed within a few months in a shoot-out with a black desperado. Another casualty was the Texas Kid, who had fired the first shot at Nick Ray at the KC ranch. When the Kid got home, he quarreled with his girl about his work as a hired gun in Wyoming. She hated what he had done there and refused to marry him, so he shot her to death. Just before he was hanged, he declared, not surprisingly, that he wished he had never gone to Wyoming at all.

A grisly score card written in bullets

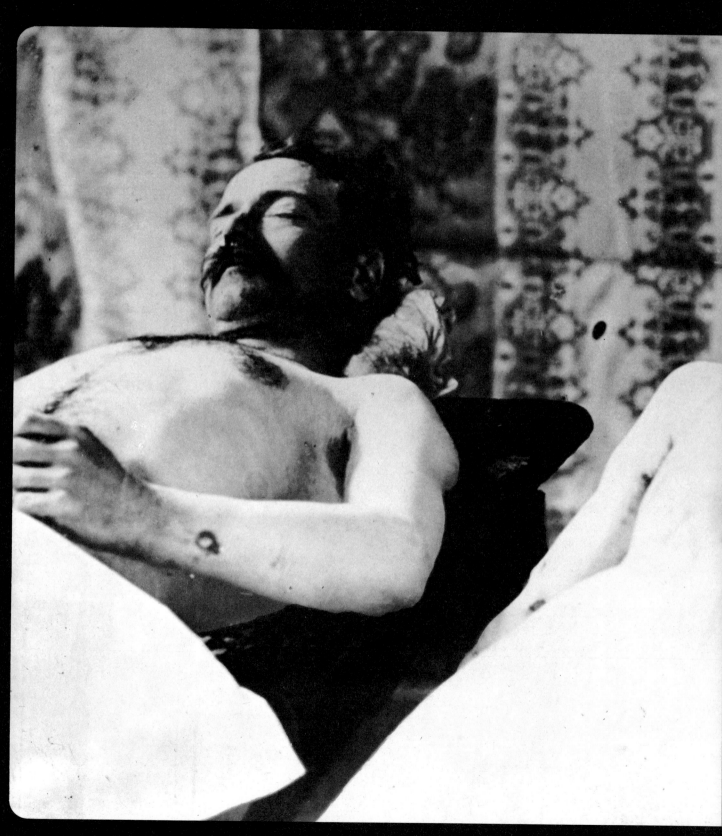

224

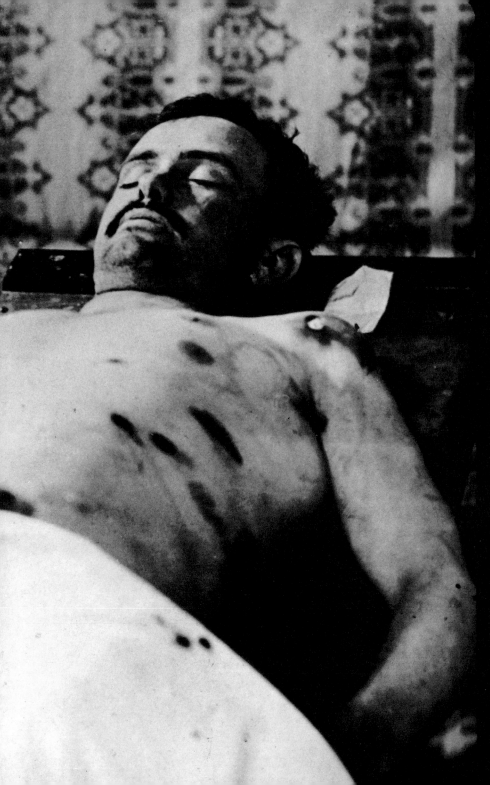

As the 19th Century drew toward a
close, outlaws who could rob a bank or
train and remain at large long enough
to brag about it were becoming as rare
as the buffalo. They had to contend
not only with growing armies of peace
officers but with daunting technological
forces as well. Lawmen used the telegraph and telephone to disseminate descriptions of malefactors and gather
information on their movements. Often
the hunters pursued the quarry on
trains, bringing along horses in boxcars
for use in the final miles of the chase.

In the face of such crime-fighting ad-
vances, ordinary desperadoes like Charlie Pierce and Bitter Creek Newcomb
(*left*) were doomed. Members of the
Doolin gang, they separated from their
companions after a train holdup and
went into hiding in a farmhouse near
Guthrie, Oklahoma Territory, in May
1895. Deputy U.S. marshals, alerted
to their whereabouts by wire, soon surrounded the lair. In moments, according
to the *Guthrie Daily Leader*, Pierce
"was transformed into a lead mine,"
with bullets "planted in his arms, legs
and even the soles of his feet." Newcomb was also riddled.

Lawmen frequently followed up their
triumphs by having the victims photographed — sometimes in lifelike poses
— for identification, as mementoes and
in the case of at least one bandit to record a striking disguise (*page 2*). But
such pictures, shown here and on the
following pages, served still another
purpose: they gave notice warning to
would-be outlaws that while outfight-
ing might pay well for a time, the ultimate wages were likely to be death.

His chest perforated by bullets, Charlie
Pierce (*right*) reposes in a Guthrie funeral
parlor with his pal Bitter Creek Newcomb.

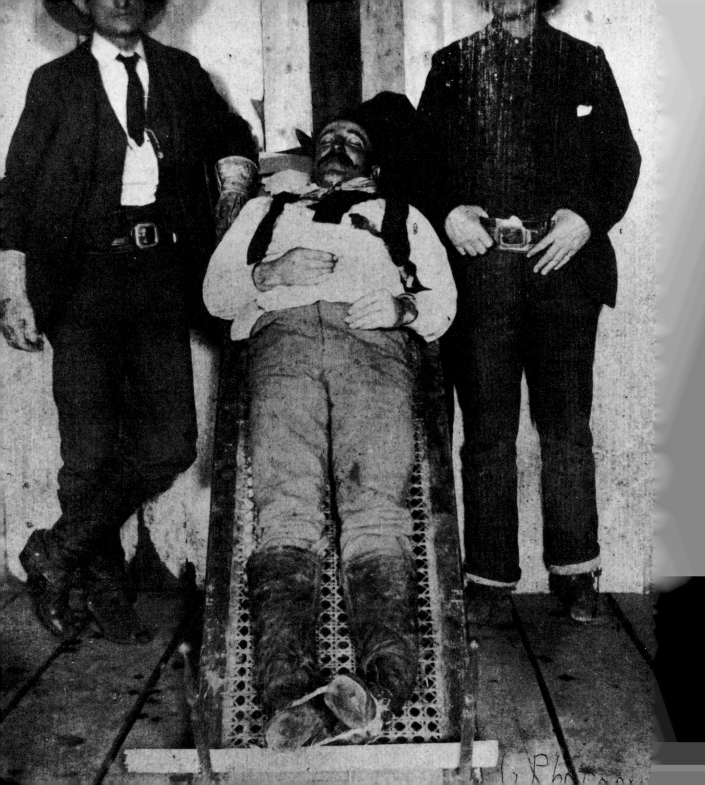

Bandit brothers Sam *(left)* and Billy LeRoy remain teamed after death.

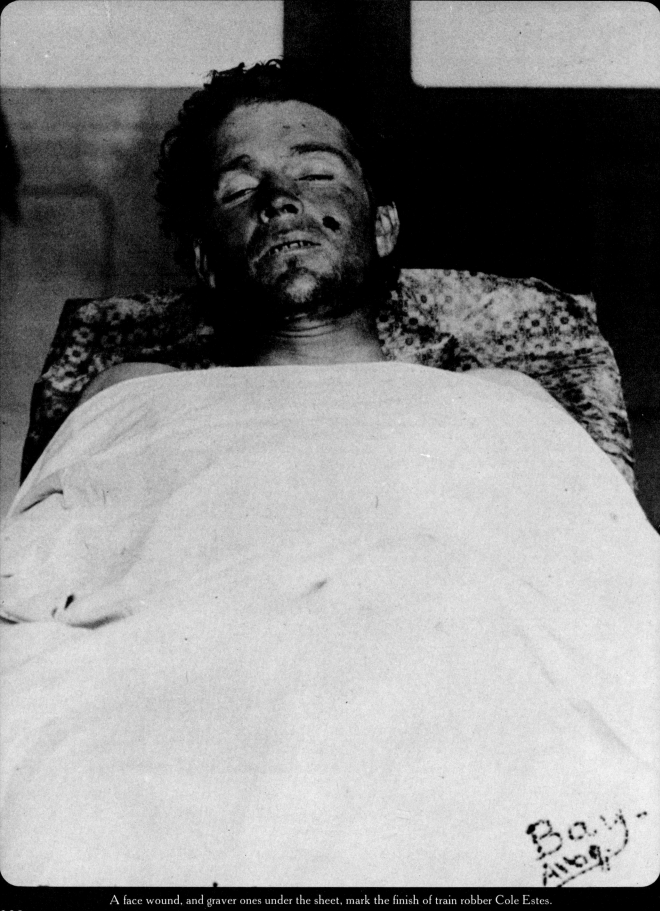

A face wound, and graver ones under the sheet, mark the finish of train robber Cole Estes.

Dick West, dead at the hands of deputy U.S. marshals, was the last of the Doolin gang to go.

The lifeless hands of Cherokee badman Ned Christie hold the rifle he so adroitly wielded.

Slain by a posse, stagecoach robber Bill Brazelton still wears his highwayman's mask.

TEXT CREDITS

For full reference on specific page credits see bibliography.

Chapter 1: Particularly useful sources for information and quotes in this chapter were: Ed Bartholomew, *Wyatt Earp: The Man and the Myth,* Frontier Book Co., 1964; Ed Bartholomew, *Wyatt Earp: The Untold Story,* Frontier Book Co., 1963; *The Daily Nugget,* Tombstone, Arizona, selected issues, Oct. 29, 1881, to Dec. 2, 1881; Douglas D. Martin, *The Earps of Tombstone,* Tombstone Epitaph, 1959; Nyle H. Miller and Joseph W. Snell, *Great Gunfighters of the Kansas Cowtowns, 1867-1886,* University of Nebraska Press, 1963; Joseph G. Rosa, *The Gunfighter: Man or Myth?* copyright 1969 by the University of Oklahoma Press; Dale T. Schoenberger, *The Gunfighters,* The Caxton Printers, Ltd., 1971; 25 — excerpts from 1881 letter, Gosper to Blaine, Nat'l. Archives, Washington, D.C.; 39 — shooting advice quote, Myers, pp. 97-98. Chapter 2: Particularly useful sources for information and quotes: J. W. Buel, *The Border Bandits,* Historical Publishing Co., 1880; J. W. Buel, *The Border Outlaws,* Historical Publishing Co., 1882; H. H. Crittenden, *The Crittenden Memoirs,* G. P. Putnam's Sons, 1936; William A. Settle, *Jesse James Was His Name,* University of Missouri Press, 1966; 67 — news quote, *Daily Times,* St. Louis, Feb. 2, 1874; 69,72 — Youngers in Texas quote, Horan, *Desperate Men,* p. 101; 73 — Pinkerton quote, Horan, *Desperate Men,* p. 89; 87 — James trial quotes, Wellman, p. 126. Chapter 3: Particularly useful sources for information and quotes: Robert R. Dykstra, *The Cattle Towns,* Alfred A. Knopf, Inc., 1968; Nyle H. Miller and Joseph W. Snell, *Great Gunfighters of the Kansas Cowtowns, 1867-1886,* University of Nebraska Press, 1963; Frank R. Prassel, *The Western Peace Officer: A Legacy of Law and Order,* copyright 1972 by the University of Oklahoma Press; Joseph G. Rosa, *They Called Him Wild Bill,* copyright 1964 by the University of Oklahoma Press; Dale T. Schoenberger, *The Gunfighters,* The Caxton Printers, Ltd., 1971; Floyd B. Streeter, *Ben Thompson: Man With A Gun,* Frederick Fell, Inc., 1957; Frederic R. Young, *Dodge City,* Boot Hill Museum, Inc., 1972; 101 — county officials quote, Keleher, p. xi; 103 — rustlers' quote, Wagoner, p. 374; 112

— botched bank robbery quote, Yost, p. 83; 125 — Masterson retirement quote, Breihan, *Great Gunfighters,* p. 102. Chapter 4: Particularly useful sources for information and quotes: Glenn Shirley, *The Law West of Fort Smith,* University of Nebraska Press, 1968, quotes used by permission of the author; 139 — Hansford quote, Gard, p. 25; 140 — Dodge City quote, Gard, p. 258; Three-Legged Willie quote, Gard, p. 261; 145 — marshal quote, Jones, p. 21; 153 — old timer quote, Prassel, p. 233; 155 — Belle Starr quote, Horan, *Desperate Women,* p. 22; 156 — Roy Bean quote, Gard, p. 266; 163 — Henry Starr quote, Drago, p. 126. Chapter 5: Particularly useful sources for information and quotes: Ed Bartholomew, *Bill Longley: A Texas Hardcase,* Frontier Press of Texas, 1953; Maurice G. Fulton, *The Lincoln County War,* Univ. of Arizona Press, 1968; Pat F. Garrett, *The Authentic Life of Billy the Kid,* copyright 1954 by the University of Oklahoma Press; John Wesley Hardin, *The Life of John Wesley Hardin as Written by Himself,* copyright 1961 by the University of Oklahoma Press; Robert N. Mullin, "The Boyhood of Billy the Kid," *Southwestern Studies,* Vol. 5, No. 1, Univ. of Texas, 1967; 169 — celebrity accorded gunmen quote, Crittenden, p. 193; 172 — Allison's medical quote, Schoenberger, p. 1; Allison's letter quoted, Schoenberger, p. 15; 173 — Allison's life quote, Snell, p. 26; 180 — Hardin quote, Koop, p. 26. Chapter 6: Particularly useful sources for information and quotes: Robert B. David, *Malcolm Campbell, Sheriff,* Wyomingana, Inc., 1932; Dr. Charles B. Penrose, *Correspondence & Memoirs,* courtesy of the Western History Research Center, University of Wyoming, Laramie; Dr. Charles B. Penrose, *The Rustler Business,* Douglas Budget, 1959; Helena Huntington Smith, *The War on Powder River,* University of Nebraska Press, 1966, used with permission of McGraw-Hill Book Co.; 197 — propriety quote, Dimsdale, p. 16; 201 — Horn's specialty quote, Prassel, p. 147; 204 — twin calves story, Stuart, p. 195; peaceable cattlemen quote, Stuart, p. 196; 210 — Wolcott quote, Mercer, p. 50; 214 — horse quote, *Cheyenne Daily Leader,* May 11, 1892; 219 — rescue quote, Mercer, p. 76.

PICTURE CREDITS

The sources for the illustrations in this book are shown below. Credits from left to right are separated by semicolons, from top to bottom by dashes.

Cover — Copied by Oliver Willcox, courtesy Thomas Gilcrease Institute of American History and Art, Tulsa, Oklahoma. 2 — Courtesy State Historical Society of Missouri, Columbia. 6,7 — Copied by Oliver Willcox, courtesy Thomas Gilcrease Institute of American History and Art, Tulsa. 8,9 — Copied by Benschneider, courtesy J. Laurence Sheerin. 10 through 13 — Copied by Linda Lorenz, courtesy Amon Carter Museum, Fort Worth, Texas. 14 — Courtesy Photo Collections, Museum of New Mexico, Santa Fe. 16 — Courtesy Arizona Historical Society, Tucson. 18,19 — Courtesy Arizona Historical Foundation, Charles Trumbull Hayden Library, Arizona State University, Tempe. 20,21 — Courtesy Arizona Historical Society. 22 — Benschneider, courtesy Sam and Theda Medigovich, owners, Silver Nugget Museum, Tombstone, Arizona. 23 — Benschneider, courtesy Bird Cage Theatre, Tombstone, Arizona. 24 — Courtesy Arizona Historical Society. 26 — Benschneider, courtesy Sam and Theda Medigovich, owners, Silver Nugget Museum. 27 — Courtesy Library of Congress. 28,29 — Courtesy Arizona Historical Society. 30 — Drawing by Nicholas Fasciano. 31 — Courtesy The Bancroft Library, Berkeley, California. 32 — Courtesy Denver Public Library, Western History Department. 33 — Benschneider, courtesy Bird Cage Theatre. 35 — Courtesy Charles W. Carter Collection, Archives Historical De-

partment, The Church of Jesus Christ of Latter-day Saints, Salt Lake City, Utah. 36,37 — Courtesy Denver Public Library, Western History Department. 40 — Ken Kay, courtesy Private Collection. 41 — Benschneider, courtesy Collection of Donald M. Yena, Western Artist, San Antonio, Texas — Ken Kay, courtesy Colt Firearms Collection, Connecticut State Library Museum, Hartford — Ken Kay, courtesy Winchester Gun Museum, Olin Corporation, New Haven, Connecticut. 42 — Ken Kay, courtesy Private Collection, except bottom, Charles Phillips courtesy The Wallace Beinfeld Collection, Studio City, California. 43,44 — Ken Kay, courtesy Private Collection, except bottom center, S. P. Stevens, courtesy Harry Jersig Collection, Lone Star Brewing Co., San Antonio, Texas. 45 — Ken Kay, courtesy Carlos H. Mason Collection, Bristol, Connecticut — Ken Kay, courtesy Winchester Gun Museum, Olin Corporation. 46,47 — Ken Kay, courtesy Carlos H. Mason Collection (3) — Ken Kay, courtesy Colt Firearms Collection, Connecticut State Library Museum (2), except center, S. P. Stevens, courtesy Donald M. Yena, Western Artist. 48 — Ken Kay, courtesy Colt Firearms Collection, Connecticut State Library Museum, except bottom, Ken Kay, courtesy Winchester Gun Museum, Olin Corporation. 49 — Ken Kay, courtesy Colt Firearms Collection, Connecticut State Library Museum, except bottom, S. P. Stevens, courtesy Donald M. Yena, Western Artist. 50,51 — Ken Kay, courtesy Winchester Gun Museum, Olin Corporation (5) — Benschneider, courtesy Donald M. Yena, Western Artist. 52,53 — Courtesy Collection of S. P. Stevens, San Antonio, Texas. 54 — Courtesy The Jackson County (Missouri) Historical Society Archives, Rogers Collection, Independence. 57 — Courtesy Denver Public Library, Western History Department. 58,59 — Courtesy The New-York Historical Society. 60 — Courtesy State Historical Society of Missouri. 63 — Martin Ismert Collection, courtesy Historical Society of Missouri. 64,65 — Courtesy Wilbur A. Zink Collection, Appleton City, Missouri. 66,67 — Courtesy Denver Public Library, Western History Department. 68 — Courtesy State Historical Society of Missouri. 69 — Courtesy Denver Public Library, Western History Department. 70,71 — Courtesy The Jesse James Bank Museum, Liberty, Missouri. 73 — Courtesy Pinkerton's, Inc., New York. 74 — Courtesy Western History Collections, University of Oklahoma Library, Norman. 76 through 79 — Courtesy Minnesota Historical Society, St. Paul. 81 — Courtesy Sy Seidman, New York. 82 — Courtesy Archives Division, Texas State Library, Austin. 83 — Courtesy St. Joseph Museum, St. Joseph, Missouri. 84,85 — Courtesy Kansas State Historical Society, Topeka. 86 — Courtesy The Jackson County (Missouri) Historical Society Archives, W. W. Welch Collection. 87 — Courtesy State Historical Society of Missouri. 88,89 — Courtesy Culver Pictures. 90 — Courtesy Pinkerton's, Inc. 91 — Courtesy Wyoming State Archives and Historical Department — courtesy Pinkerton's, Inc. 92,93 — Courtesy Pinkerton's, Inc. 94,95 — Courtesy Oklahoma Historical Society, Oklahoma City. 96 — Courtesy Western History Collections, University of Oklahoma Library. 97 — Top left and lower right, courtesy Boot Hill Museum, Inc., Dodge City, Kansas, top right and lower left, courtesy Western History Collections, University of Oklahoma Library. 98,99 — Courtesy Arizona Historical Society, 100 — J. R. Eyerman, courtesy Collection of Ron Donoho, Las Vegas, Nevada, except top center, J. R. Eyerman, courtesy Mrs. Raymond Garrett, loaned in memory of her husband, Raymond Garrett, and his father Buck Garrett, a lawman, and right center, Ken Kay, courtesy Private Collection. 102 — Courtesy Arizona Historical Society. 104, 105 — Courtesy The Cunningham Collection, Stillwater, Oklahoma. 108,109 — Courtesy Western History Collections, University of Oklahoma Library. 110, 111 — Courtesy Arizona Historical Society. 112 — Courtesy Kansas State Historical Society. 113 — Courtesy Montana Historical Society, Helena. 114, 115 — Courtesy Western History Collections, University of Oklahoma Library. 116,117 — Courtesy The Cunningham Collection. 118 — Courtesy Archives Division, Texas State Library. 120 — Courtesy Kansas State Historical Society. 121 — Courtesy Boot Hill Museum, Inc. 122 — Courtesy Kansas State Historical Society. 123 — Copied by Oliver Willcox, courtesy Thomas Gilcrease Institute of American History and Art, Tulsa. 124 — Courtesy Kansas State Historical Society. 126,127 — Courtesy Harry E. Chrisman, *Fifty Years on the Owl Hoot Trail,* Swallow Press, Inc., Chicago. 128, 129 — Courtesy Collection of Fred and Jo Mazzulla, Denver, Colorado. 130 — Courtesy Stimson Collection, Wyoming State Archives and Historical Department, Cheyenne — Benschneider, courtesy Tombstone Courthouse State Historic Park, Arizona State Parks; Benschneider, courtesy Arizona Historical Society (2). 131 — Joseph E. Smith photograph, courtesy David R. Phillips Collection, Chicago — Benschneider, courtesy Sam and Theda Medigovich, owners, Silver Nugget Museum; Benschneider, courtesy Boot Hill Museum, Inc. 132,133 — Al Lucke Collection, courtesy Montana Historical Society. 134 — Benschneider, courtesy Boot Hill Mu-

seum, Inc. — Benschneider, courtesy Bird Cage Theatre. 135 — Benschneider, courtesy Arizona Historical Society. 136,137 — Courtesy Arizona Historical Society. 138, 139 — Courtesy Montana Historical Society. 140 — Courtesy The Bancroft Library. 143 — T. H. Routh photograph, courtesy Denver Public Library, Western History Department. 144 — Courtesy Western History Collections, University of Oklahoma Library — courtesy Oklahoma Historical Society. 146, 147 — Courtesy Denver Public Library, Western History Department. 148 — Courtesy Signal Corps, no. 111-B-3202, Brady Collection in National Archives. 150, 151 — Courtesy Oklahoma Historical Society. 152, 154 — Courtesy Glenn Shirley Western Collection, Stillwater, Oklahoma. 156 — Courtesy Sy Seidman — courtesy Western History Collections, University of Oklahoma Library. 157, 158, 159 — Courtesy Glenn Shirley Western Collection. 160 — Courtesy Cecil Atchison, President, Judge Parker's Historical Society, Fort Smith, Arkansas. 161 — Courtesy Glenn Shirley Western Collection. 162, 163 — Courtesy Oklahoma Historical Society. 164, 165 — Courtesy Glenn Shirley Western Collection. 166, 167 — Roscoe G. Willson Collection, courtesy American Heritage Publishing Co. Inc., New York. 168 — Courtesy *The Cattleman Magazine,* Fort Worth, Texas. 170, 171, 172 — Courtesy Western History Collections, University of Oklahoma Library. 174 — Courtesy Barney Hubbs Collection, Pecos, Texas. 175 — Courtesy Denver Public Library, Western History Department. 176 — Courtesy Bob McNellis, El Paso, Texas. 177 — Courtesy Archives Division, Texas State Library. 178 — Courtesy Western History Collections, University of Oklahoma Library except top left courtesy Arizona Historical Society. 179 — Courtesy Denver Public Library, Western History Department; courtesy Western History Collections, University of Oklahoma Library — courtesy Western History Collections, University of Oklahoma Library; courtesy Kansas State Historical Society. 181 — Courtesy Pinkerton's, Inc. 183 — Courtesy Western History Collections, University of Oklahoma Library. 184, 185 — Courtesy Kennedy Galleries, Inc., New York. 187 — Courtesy Bettmann Archive, New York. 188 — Courtesy Photo Collections, Museum of New Mexico. 189 — Courtesy Indiana Historical Society Library, Indianapolis. 190 — Courtesy The James D. Horan Civil War and Western Americana Collection, Little Falls, New Jersey. 191 — Courtesy Denver Public Library, Western History Department. 192,193 — Courtesy Western Americana Collection, Beinecke Library, Yale University, New Haven, Connecticut. 194, 195 — Courtesy California Historical Society, San Francisco. 196 — Courtesy Library, The State Historical Society of Colorado, Denver. 198 — Courtesy Denver Public Library, Western History Department. 199 — Courtesy Montana Historical Society. 200 — Charles Phillips, from *The Illustrated Police News,* January 28, 1882, courtesy Library of Congress. 202 through 205 — Courtesy The Cunningham Collection. 207 through 212 — Courtesy Western History Research Center, University of Wyoming, Laramie. 213 — Denver Public Library, Western History Department. 215 — Courtesy Western History Collections, University of Oklahoma Library. 216,217 — Courtesy Turk Collection, Buffalo, Wyoming, copied by Pat Hall, Cheyenne. 218 — Courtesy Western History Research Center, University of Wyoming. 219 — Courtesy Anita Webb Deninger, Buffalo, Wyoming. 220,221 — Courtesy Western History Research Center, University of Wyoming. 222 — Courtesy Wyoming State Archives and Historical Department. 224, 225, 226 — Courtesy The Cunningham Collection. 227 — Courtesy Denver Public Library, Western History Department. 228 — Courtesy Wells Fargo Bank History Room, San Francisco. 229,230 — Courtesy Western History Collections, University of Oklahoma Library. 231 — Courtesy Wells Fargo Bank History Room, San Francisco.

ACKNOWLEDGMENTS

The editors give special thanks to the following persons who read and commented on portions of the book: Dr. Frank R. Prassel, San Antonio; Dr. William A. Settle, Professor of History and Political Science, Univ. of Tulsa, Tulsa, Okla.; William B. Shillingberg, Tucson, Ariz.; Glenn Shirley, Stillwater, Okla.; Joseph W. Snell, Curator, Manuscript Div., Kansas State Historical Society, Topeka; R. L. Wilson, Manchester, Conn.

The editors also acknowledge the assistance of Edna May Armold, Librarian, El Reno, Okla.; Manon Atkins, Mary Moran, Oklahoma Historical Society, Oklahoma City; John Bundy, Windham College Library, Putney, Vt.; Lee L. Burtis, California Historical Society, San Francisco; Carol Carefoot, Archivist, Texas State Library and Archives, Austin; Carl Chafin, The Chafin Collection of Western Americana, Tombstone, Ariz.; Pierce Chamberlain, Museum Curator, Loretta Davisson, Ass't. Research Librarian, Margaret Bret Harte, Research Librarian, Tom Peterson, Curator of Collections, Jan van Orden, Ass't. Curator, Arizona Historical Society, Tucson; Robert Cunningham, Stillwater, Okla.; Mary K. Dains, State Historical Society of Missouri, Columbia; James H. Davis, Picture Librarian, Opal Harber, Librarian, Western History Dept., Denver Public Library, Denver; Ron Donoho, Las Vegas; Elaine G. Dowty, Ass't. Director, Wells Fargo Bank History Room, San Francisco; Faye Duncan, Curator, West of the Pecos Museum, Pecos, Texas; Dr. Gardner P. H. Foley, Baltimore; Stella Foote, Billings, Mont.; Pauline S. Fowler, Director of Archives, Jackson County Historical Society, Independence, Mo.; Suzanne Gallup, Reference Librarian, The Bancroft Library, Berkeley, Calif.; Bill Garett, Tombstone; Gene M. Gressley, Director of Rare Books and Special Collections, David Crosson, Research Historian, Western History Research Center, Univ. of Wyoming, Laramie; Frances Gupton, Marjorie Morey, Amon Carter Museum, Fort Worth; Jack D. Haley, Western History Collections, Univ. of Oklahoma, Norman; Charles "Pat" Hall, Wyoming Bicentennial Commission, Cheyenne; Thomas E. Hall, Curator, Winchester Gun Museum, New Haven; Archibald Hanna, Curator, Western Americana Collection, Yale University Library, New Haven; Laura Hayes, Viola A. McNealey, Wyoming State Archives and Hist. Dept., Cheyenne; George Henrichs, Exec. Director, Boot Hill Museum, Inc., Dodge City, Kans.; James D. Horan, Little Falls, N.J.; Bill Hunley Jr., Bird Cage Theatre, Tombstone; Marjorie Kinney, Dept. Head, Peggy Smith, Virginia Wright, Missouri Valley Room, Kansas City Public Library; Waldo Koop, Wichita, Kans.; Cora Land, Fort Scott, Kans.; Allan MacDougall, E. C. Barker Texas History Center, Univ. of Texas, Austin; Bob McNellis, El Paso; Terry Wm. Mangan, Media Librarian, Colorado State Hist. Society, Denver; Theda Medigovich, Silver Nugget Museum, Tombstone; Harriet C. Meloy, Librarian, Montana Historical Society, Helena; Nyle Miller, Exec. Director, Eugene D. Decker, Archivist, Kansas State Historical Society, Topeka; Arthur L. Olivas, Photographic Archivist, Museum of New Mexico, Santa Fe; Charlotte Palmer, Still Picture Archivist, National Archives, Washington, D.C.; David R. Phillips, Chicago; Richard Pintarich, Portland, Ore.; Kate Plourd, Connecticut State Library, Hartford; Don L. Reynolds, Ass't. Director, St. Joseph Museum, St. Joseph, Mo.; Professor Gary Roberts, Dept. of Social Sciences, Abraham Baldwin Agricultural College, Tifton, Ga.; S. P. Stevens, San Antonio; Susan M. Thomas, Valdosta, Ga.; Gladys Thompson, Butterfield Library, Westminster, Vt.; Tom Tisdale, Cheyenne; Mr. and Mrs. Ben Traywick, Tombstone; David Walters, Missoula, Mont.; Fred Walters, Research Ass't., Idaho Historical Society, Boise; John Whitlock Jr., Library, School of Dental Medicine, Univ. of Pennsylvania, Philadelphia; Oliver Willcox, Staff Photographer, Thomas Gilcrease Institute, Tulsa; Bonnie Wilson, Audio Visual Reference Librarian, Minnesota Historical Society, St. Paul; Robert Wing, Supervisor, Tombstone Courthouse State Historic Park; Wayne Winters, Tombstone; Jack B. Wymore, Jesse James Bank Museum, Liberty, Mo.; Frederic R. Young, Dodge City, Kans.; Wilbur A. Zink, Appleton City, Mo.

BIBLIOGRAPHY

Adams, Ramon F., *Six-Guns & Saddle Leather: A Bibliography of Books & Pamphlets on Western Outlaws and Gunmen.* University of Oklahoma Press, 1969.

Appleman, Roy E., "Charlie Siringo, Cow Boy Detective." *The Great Western Series, No. 3.* Potomac Corral, The Westerners, October 1968.

Bartholomew, Ed:
  Bill Longley: A Texas Hardcase. Frontier Press of Texas, 1953.
  Wyatt Earp: The Man & The Myth. Frontier Book Co., 1964.
  Wyatt Earp: The Untold Story. Frontier Book Co., 1963.

Bearss, Edwin C., and Arrell M. Gibson, *Fort Smith: Little Gibraltar on the Arkansas.* University of Oklahoma Press, 1969.

Bell, William Gardener, "Frontier Lawman." *American West,* Vol. 1, No. 3., Summer, 1964.

Billington, Ray E., ed., *People of the Plains and Mountains.* Greenwood Press, 1973.

Breakenridge, William M., *Helldorado.* The Rio Grande Press, Inc., 1970.

Breihan, Carl W.:
  The Complete and Authentic Life of Jesse James. Frederick Fell, Inc., 1953, rev. 1969.
  Great Gunfighters of the West. Naylor Co., 1962.

Buel, James W.:
  The Border Bandits. Historical Publishing Co., 1880.
  The Border Outlaws. Historical Publishing Co., 1882.

Burroughs, John Rolfe, *Guardian of the Grasslands.* Pioneer Printing and Stationery Co., 1971.

Butler, William J., *Fort Smith.* First Nat'l. Bank of Fort Smith, 1972.

Canton, Frank M., *Frontier Trails.* University of Oklahoma Press, 1966.

Castel, Albert, *William Clarke Quantrill: His Life and Times.* Frederick Fell, Inc., 1962.

Chrisman, Harry E., *Fifty Years on the Owl Hoot Trail: Jim Herron, the First Sheriff of No Man's Land, Oklahoma Territory.* Sage Books, 1972.

Clum, John P., *It All Happened in Tombstone.* Northland Press, 1965.

Crittenden, H. H., *The Crittenden Memoirs.* G. P. Putnam's Sons, 1936.

Croy, Homer, *Jesse James was my Neighbor.* Duell, Sloan and Pearce, 1949.

The Daily Nugget. Tombstone, Arizona, Oct. 29, 1881, to Dec. 2, 1881.

Dalton, Emmett, *When the Daltons Rode.* Doubleday, Doran & Company, Inc., 1931.

David, Robert B., *Malcolm Campbell, Sheriff.* Wyomingana, Inc., 1932.

Dimsdale, Thomas, *The Vigilantes of Montana.* University of Oklahoma Press, 1972.

Drago, Harry Sinclair, *Outlaws on Horseback*. Dodd, Mead & Co., 1964.

Dykstra, Robert R., *The Cattle Towns*. Alfred A. Knopf, Inc., 1968.

Elliott, David S., and Ed Bartholomew, *The Dalton Gang and the Coffeyville Raid*. Frontier Book Co., 1968.

Faulk, Odie B., *Tombstone: Myth and Reality*. Oxford University Press, 1972.

Fisher, Ovie C., and J. C. Dykes, *King Fisher: His Life and Times*. University of Oklahoma Press, 1966.

Fisher, Vardis, and Opal Laurel Holmes, *Gold Rushes and Mining Camps of the Early American West*. The Caxton Printers, Ltd., 1968.

Fred Barde Collection:
"Temple Houston Genius," Vol. 15, July to Nov. 29, 1905, Oklahoma Historical Society.
"Relics of Old Oklahoma," Vol. 8, Feb. 25 to Sept. 30, 1902, Oklahoma Historical Society.

Frink, Maurice, *Cow Country Cavalcade*. The Old West Publishing Co., 1954.

Fulton, Maurice G., *The Lincoln County War*. University of Arizona Press, 1968.

Gard, Wayne, *Frontier Justice*. University of Oklahoma Press, 1949.

Garrett, Pat F., *The Authentic Life of Billy the Kid*. University of Oklahoma Press, 1954.

Grisso, W. D., ed., *Tell Her To Go In Peace — Temple Houston*. Stagecoach Press, University of Oklahoma, 1963.

Hanes, Colonel Bailey C., *Bill Doolin, Outlaw O. T.* University of Oklahoma Press, 1968.

Hardin, John Wesley, *The Life of John Wesley Hardin as Written by Himself*. University of Oklahoma Press, 1961.

Harlow, Victor E., *Harlow's Oklahoma History*. Harlow Publishing Corporation, 1967.

Horan, James D.:
Desperate Men. Bonanza Books, 1969.
Desperate Women. Bonanza Books, 1952.
Pictorial History of the Wild West. Crown Publishers, Inc., 1954.

Horan, James D., and Howard Swiggett, *The Pinkerton Story*. G. P. Putnam's Sons, 1951.

Hunter, J. Marvin, and Noah H. Rose, *The Album of Gunfighters*. Hunter and Rose, 1951.

Jones, W. F., *Experiences of a Deputy U.S. Marshal in Indian Territory*. University of Oklahoma Press, 1937.

Keleher, William A., *The Violence in Lincoln County*. University of New Mexico Press, 1957.

Kennedy, Michael S., *Cowboys and Cattlemen*. Hastings House Publishers, 1964.

Koop, Waldo E., "Enter John Wesley Hardin, A Dim Trail to Abilene." *The Prairie Scout*, Vol. II, ed. by The Westerners. Ives Printing Co., 1974.

Larson, Taft Alfred, *History of Wyoming*. University of Nebraska Press, 1965.

Lavine, Sigmund A., *Allan Pinkerton*. Dodd, Mead & Co., 1963.

Lloyd, Everett, *Law West of the Pecos*. Naylor Company, 1967.

Love, Robertus, *The Rise and Fall of Jesse James*. G. P. Putnam's Sons, 1926.

Martin, Douglas D., *The Earps of Tombstone*. Tombstone Epitaph, 1959.

McReynolds, Edwin C., *Oklahoma: A History of The Sooner State*. University of Oklahoma Press, 1954.

Mercer, A. S., *The Banditti of the Plains*. University of Oklahoma Press, 1954.

Miller, Nyle H., and Joseph W. Snell, *Great Gunfighters of the Kansas Cowtowns. 1867-1886*. University of Nebraska Press, 1963.

Mullin, Robert N., "The Boyhood of Billy the Kid." *Southwestern Studies*, Vol. 5, No. 1, University of Texas, 1967.

Myers, John M., *The Last Chance: Tombstone's Early Years*. University of Nebraska Press, 1950.

Parsons, George W., *The Private Journal of George W. Parsons*. Tombstone Epitaph, 1972.

Penrose, Dr. Charles B.:
Correspondence and Memoirs, courtesy of the Western History Research Center, University of Wyoming.
The Rustler Business. Douglas Budget, 1959.

Prassel, Frank Richard, *The Western Peace Officer: A Legacy of Law and Order*. University of Oklahoma Press, 1972.

Rosa, Joseph G.:
The Gunfighter, Man or Myth? University of Oklahoma Press, 1969.
They Called Him Wild Bill. University of Oklahoma Press, 1964.

Schoenberger, Dale T., *The Gunfighters*. The Caxton Printers, Ltd., 1971.

Settle, William A., *Jesse James was His Name*. University of Missouri Press, 1966.

Shirley, Glenn:
Heck Thomas: Frontier Marshal. Chilton Company, 1962.
"Temple Houston, The Man with the Silver Tongue." *Real West,* Volume XIII, No. 85, September 1970.
The Law West of Fort Smith. University of Nebraska Press, 1968.
Shotgun for Hire. University of Oklahoma Press, 1970.
Six-Gun and Silver Star. University of New Mexico Press, 1955.

Siringo, Charles A.:
A Texas Cow Boy. M. Umbedenstock & Company, 1885.
History of Billy the Kid. Steck-Vaughn Company, 1967.
Riata & Spurs. Houghton Mifflin Company, 1927.

Smith, Helena Huntington, *The War on Powder River*. University of Nebraska Press, 1966.

Snell, Joseph, and Nyle H. Miller, *Why the West Was Wild*. Kansas State Historical Society, 1963.

Sonnichsen, C. L., *Roy Bean, Law West of the Pecos*. The Devin-Adair Company, 1943.

Steckmesser, Kent Ladd, *The Western Hero in History and Legend*. University of Oklahoma Press, 1965.

Streeter, Floyd B., *Ben Thompson: Man With A Gun*. Frederick Fell, Inc., 1957.

Stuart, Granville, *Forty Years on the Frontier,* ed. by Paul C. Phillips. The Arthur H. Clark Co., 1957.

"The True Story of Billy the Kid," LIFE Magazine, May 4, 1959.

Van Slyke, Lois, *Temple Houston*. Re-write 8/4/1939. Oklahoma Historical Society.

Wagoner, Jay J., *Arizona Territory*. University of Arizona Press, 1970.

Wellman, Paul I., *A Dynasty of Western Outlaws*. Bonanza Books, 1960.

Yost, Nellie S., *Medicine Lodge: The Story of a Kansas Frontier Town*. Swallow Press, Inc., 1970.

Young, Frederic R., *Dodge City*. Boot Hill Museum, Inc., 1972.

A

Abilene, Kans., law enforcement, 102, 103, 123, 176, 180
Alexander, William, 163
Allison, Clay, 39, 166, 170, 172-173, *174, 175*
Ammunition, 38, 40, *45*
Anderson, Bloody Bill, 56, 59, 62
Angus, W. E. (Red), 212, 216, 222
Apache Kid, *178*
Arkansas, Western District Court, 142, 145, 149-150, 152-153, 155, 157, 161, 163-164
Armstrong, John, 182, 201
Austin, Texas, lawmen, 113, 115, 118
Averell, Jim, 208, *212*

B

Bank robberies: first U.S., 55; sympathy for, 59, 61
Barber, Amos, 218
Bassett, Charles, 107
Bean, Roy, 142, *156*
Behan, John, 22, *24,* 25, 27, 30, 32, 33, 34, 106
Billy the Kid, 34, 110, 166, *168,* 169, 170, 181, 182, *183, 184-185,* 186, *187,* 188-190, *192-193;* letters, *189;* name, 182-183; wanted notice, 190
Bird Cage Theatre, 17, 23
Black Jack Bill, 37
Blake, Tulsa Jack, *226*
Bligh, D. G., 62, 80
Blue Duck, 155, *162*
Bonney, William H. *See* Billy the Kid
Boswell, Nathaniel Kimball, 101
Bothwell, Albert, 208
Bowman, Mace, *173*
Brady, William, 184, 186, 190
Brazelton, Bill, *231*
Bridges, Jack, 109
Brown, Arapahoe, 216
Brown, George, 110
Brown, Henry, 110-113, 114-115
Buck, Rufus, 155, *164;* poem, *165*
Bullion, Laura, *93*
Bush, Lew, 126

C

Cahill, Frank (Windy), 183
Calder, Billy, *138,* 139
Caldwell, Kans., lawmen, 109-113
Campbell, John, 101
Canton, Frank M., 208, 210, 214, *215*
Carr, T. J., *97*
Cassidy, Butch, 73, *90, 91, 92, 93,* 181
Cattle: brands, *210;* losses, 206
Cattle detectives, 199, 201, 204, 208-210, 212, 214, 215, 216, 218-219, *220-221, 222-223*
Cattle Kate, 208, *213*
Cattlemen's associations, 198, 199, 201, 204-206, 208-210
Centralia, Mo., raid on, 56
Chacon, Augustine, *179*
Chadwell, Bill, 75, 80
Champion, Nate, 212, *216-217,* 223
Cheeseman, Joe, *95*
Cherokee Bill, verdict, *160*
Cheyenne Club, 206, 208, 209, 223
Chisum, John, 183
Christie, Ned, 153, *157, 159, 230*
Civil War: guerrilla bands, 53, 56, 58-59, 60; and Indian Territory, 143; and loners, 166, 169; Order No. 11, Ewing's, 59, 60; and Pinkerton, 73
Clanton, Ike and Billy, 20; and O.K. Corral shoot-out, 15, 22, 25-27, 30, *32, 33*
Clanton, Phineas, 20
Clifton, Dynamite Dick, 116, 117
Cochise County, law enforcement, 25
Cockfight, *20-21*
Cody, Buffalo Bill, 46, 126
Coffeyville, Kans., bank robbery, 84
Colbert, Chunk, 123, *175*
Cold Chuck Johnny, 37
Collins, Shotgun, 37
Colt, Samuel, 40, 43
Colt's Patent Fire Arms Company of Hartford, 46; production of Peacemakers, 43
Cooper, Jack, petition, 209, *210*

Corydon, Iowa, bank robbery, 62-63
Courthouses, *136-137,* 141, 149
Courts, 137; district, 141, 142, 145; juries of, 141; local, 141, 156; verdict of, *160. See also* Judges; Law enforcement
Cowboys: black list, 208; and frontier towns, 20, 107, 109
Cravens, Ben, 116, *117*
Crimes: jurisdiction over, 141; by type, 107, 110-111
Cripple Creek Cole, *143*
Crittendon, Thomas, 82, 86

D

Dalton, Bob, Emmett and Gratton, 84, *85,* 142, 152, 158
Daniel, Edwin, 68
Dark Alley Jim, 37
De Billier, Frederic O., 206, 209, 219, 223
Deger, Larry, 119, 120, 122
Dodge City, Kans.: courts, 137, 140; cowboys in, 107, 109; and Frank Loving, 39; and Mastersons, 118, 119-120, 122, 124-125; and Luke Short, 35, 37
Dolan, J. J., 183-184, 188
Doolin, Bill, 158, 160-161, 215
Doolin gang, 158; dead members, *224-226, 229*
Dudley, Jim, 209-210, 212, 214
Dynamite Sam, 37

E

Earp, James, 16
Earp, Morgan, *16,* 17, 20; and O.K. Corral shoot-out, 15, 22, 25-27, 30, 33, 34
Earp, Virgil, *16,* 17, 20, 107; and O.K. Corral shoot-out, 15, 22, 25, 27, 32-33, 34; report, *26*
Earp, Wyatt, *16,* 17, 20, 24, 35, 37, 39, 107, 126, 134; and O.K. Corral shoot-out, 15, 22, 25, 27, 30, 33, 34; and Luke Short, 35, 37
Estes, Cole, *228*
Ewing, Thomas, 60; Order No. 11 of, 59, 60

F

Farnsworth, C. H., *98-99*
Fisher, John King, 166, *179*
Ford, Bob, *81,* 82, *83,* 86; report of James capture, 86
Ford, Charlie, 82
Fort Smith, Ark., 149; court, 145, 149-150, 152-153, 155, 157, 161, 163-164; executions, 148, 149, 161, 165
Foster, W. K., *98-99*
Foy, Eddie, quoted, 107, 122
Frémont, John C., 22

G

Gallatin, Mo., bank robbery, 62
Gambling, *131, 134;* equipment, *130-131;* and lawmen, 16-17, 101-102
Gangs, 52; Dalton, *84-85;* Doolin, 158, *224-226, 229;* James, *52-53,* 55-56, 61-62, *63, 64, 66, 67, 68, 69, 70-71, 72,* 73, 75, 78, 80, 82, 86-87, *88-89;* Wild Bunch, 73, *90-93*
Garrett, Buck, 223
Garrett, Pat, 189, 190, *191, 192,* 201; *The Authentic Life of Billy the Kid, 192-193*
Glick, George Washington, 37
Gosper, John, report, 25
Gunfighters: characteristics, 15, 34-35, 37-39, 166, 169, 198-199, 215; death portraits, *224-231;* pay, 201; training, 38. *See also* Lawmen; Loners; Mercenaries
Guthrie, Okla.: criminals shot in, *224-225;* lawmen, *104-105, 108-109;* mob, *202-203*

H

Hanging Judge. *See* Parker, Isaac Charles
Hansford, John, 139
Hardin, John Wesley, 166, 170, 175, *176, 179,* 180, 182; pardon, *177;* wife, 180, 182
Harrison, Benjamin, 219
Hartman, L. C., *97*
Helena, Mont., jail, *113*
Hesse, Fred, 206
Hickok, Wild Bill (James Butler), 37-38, 39, 102, 107, *123,* 176, 180
Hired guns. *See* Mercenaries

Holliday, Doc (John), 17, *27*, 107; and O.K. Corral shoot-out, 15, 22, 25, 27, 30, 32, 33, 34; and Luke Short, 35, 37

Horn, Tom, 201, 204, 206, *207*

Horner, Joe. *See* Canton, Frank

Houston, Temple, *144*

Howland, Bob, 198

Hutchinson, Billy and Lottie, 23

I

Indian Territory: encroachments on, 142-143, 145, 153, 157; establishment of, 142; justice in, 142, 143, 145, 149-150, 151, 152-153, 155, 157-158, 161, 163-164, 204-205

Indians: Five Civilized Tribes, 142-143, 157; Intercourse Act, 142

Irvine, William, 201, 206, 214, 223

J

Jackson, Charles, 139

Jails, *112, 113;* roster, *110-111*

James, Frank and Jesse, 34, 39, 46, *52, 54,* 56, *57,* 62, 68, *70-71,* 72, 80, *81, 82, 87, 88-89,* 142, 155; bank robberies, 55, 61-63, 75, 78, 80; bounty poster, *2, 4;* crimes, 56; end of career, 86-87; as guerrillas, 56, 58-59, 62; Kansas City Fair, 63; marriage and family, 72, 82, 86; sympathy for, 59, 61, 62, 63, 72; train robberies, 56, 63, 66-67, 72, 82

Johnson, Turkey Creek Jack, 39

Johnson County War, 197, 206, 208-210, 212, 214, 215, 216, 217, 218-219, 222-223; battle diagram, *218;* newspaper account, *222*

Jones, W. C., *108-109*

Judges, 137, 139-142, 145, 149-150, 152, 153, 155, 156, 157, 161, 163-164; characteristics, 140, 141, 142; district, 141; local, 141, 143

K

Kelley, James (Dog), 119-120, 122, 125

Kilpatrick, Ben, *93*

L

Ladd, Jack, 72

Law enforcement: at end of 19th Century, 225; judicial system, 137, 139-143, 145; 149-150, 151, 152-153, 155, 157, 161, 163-164; police system, 101-103, 106-107, 109-113, 115, 118-120, 122,124-125, 142, 145, 150, 152-153, 158, 160-161; unofficial, *36-37,* 101, 112, 139, 140, 170, 173, 194. *See also* Vigilantes

Lawmen, 101-103, 106-107, 109-113, 115, 118-120, 122, 124-125, 158, 160-161, 181, 223; badges, *100, 101,* 160; characteristics, 95, 102, 106; federal marshals, 103, 106, 201; graft, 106, 150, 152; in Indian Territory, 142, 145, 150, 152-153; pay, 201; rangers, 103; regulations, *152;* sheriffs, 103, 106; town marshals, 103, 106-107

Lawrence, Kans., raid on, 56, *58-59*

Lawyers, 141, 143, 144; and Judge Parker, 161, 163

Leadville, Colo., execution, *146-147*

LeRoy, Billy and Sam, *227*

Leslie, Buckskin Frank, *178*

Lexington, Mo., bank robbery, 61

Liberty, Mo., bank robbery, 55

Liddil, Dick, 82

Life and Times of Jesse and Frank James, 68, 69

Lincoln County War, 183-184, 186, 188

Loners, characteristics, 166, 169

Longbaugh, Harry. *See* Sundance Kid

Longley, Bill, 169, 170, *172;* quoted, 169, 170, 172

Loving, Cock-Eyed Frank, 39

Lull, Louis, 68

Lund, Alfred, 116, *117*

M

McCluskie, 38

McCarty, Bill, 90

McGregg, Buck, 116, *117*

McLaury, Tom and Frank, 20; and O.K. Corral shoot-out, 15, 22, 26, 27, 30, *32, 33*

McSween, Alexander, 183, 186

Madsen, Chris, 160

Maledon, George, 149, 155, *161*

Marshall, John, *96*

Mason, Joe, *97*

Masterson, Bat (Bartholomew), 35, 37, 107, 118-119, 120, *121,* 122, 124-125, 134, 144; expense check, *122;* quoted, 7, 38, 95, 106, 113, 115, 118, 124, 125; and Luke Short, 35, 37

Masterson, Ed, 118, 119, *120,* 122, 124-125; report of death, *124*

Masterson, Jim, 107, 118, 119, *120,* 125

Mather, Dave, 34-35

Maxwell, Pete, 190

Meagher, Mike, 110

Medicine Lodge, Kans., bank robbery, 111-112

Mercenaries, 198-199, 201, 204, 206, 208-210, 212, 214, 215, 216, 218-219, 222-223

Miller, Clell, 72, 78

Miller, Jim, *170-171*

Mimms, Zee, 72, 82

Moderators, 140

Montana Stock Growers Association, 204-205

Moonlight, Tom, 37

Moore, Bill, *178*

Morton, William, 184, 186

Mossman, Burt, quoted, 103

Murphy, Lawrence, 183-184

N

Newcomb, Bitter Creek, *224-225*

Newton, Kans., shoot-out, 38

Nix, Evett, 158, 160, 215

Northern Wyoming Farmers' and Stock Growers' Association, 208

Northfield, Minn., 76-77; bank robbery, 75, *78,* 80; townsmen, 78, *79*

O

O.K. Corral, shoot-out at, 15, 27, 30, 32-33; aftermath, 33-34; background, 16-17, 20, 22, 25-26; diagram, *30;* newspaper account, *31*

Oklahoma Guardsmen, 160

Oklahoma Territory, establishment, 157

Outlaws of the Border, 66-67

Overland Stage Line, 199

P

Parker, Robert Leroy. *See* Cassidy, Butch

Parker, Isaac Charles, 145, *148,* 149-150, 153, 155, 157, 158, 161, 163, 164, 215

Pence, Bud, 61

Penrose, Charles, 209; quoted, 209-210

Pierce, Charlie, *224-225*

Pinkerton, Allan, 63, 66, *73;* dynasty, 73

Pinkerton National Detective Agency, 63, 66, 67-68, 69, 72, 73, 75, 80, 93, 181, 182, 201

Pistols, 38, *40-49;* Barns, *49;* Colt, 38, *40, 41, 42, 43, 44, 46, 48, 49;* Deringer, 48, *49;* double-action, 46; pocket, 40, 48; Reid, *48;* Remington, *41, 46, 47, 48, 49;* single-action, 38, 40; Smith & Wesson, *45, 46, 47, 48;* Spies, *49;* Starr, *41*

Pitts, Charlie, 72, 75, 80

Pizanthia, Joe, 197

Place, Etta, *93*

Platt, George, 109-110

Posses, *116-117*

Prostitution, 22, 23

Pulaski, Texas, justice, 139-140

Q

Quantrill, William Clarke, 56, 58, 59

Quartzite, Ariz., duel, *166-167*

R

Ralston, Annie, 72, 82

Railroads: in Indian Territory, 143; police powers, 199

Ranchers, large vs. small, sheepherders and homesteaders, 199, 204, 206. *See also* Johnson County War

Ray, Nick, 212, 223

Reed, J. Warren, 161, 163, 164

Regulators, 140, 186

Richards, W. A., 201

Richardson, Levi, 39

Richmond, Mo., bank robbery, 61

Rifles, *50-51;* American Arms, *51;* Henry, *50-51;* Remington, *51;* Winchester, *50-51*
Ringo, John, 35
Ruffner, George, *102*
Russell, Charles M., paintings by, *6-13;* sketch by, *184-185*
Russellville, Ky., bank robbery, 61-62
Rustlers, cattle, 14, 15, 20; and vigilantes, 199, 201, 204-205, 206

S
Saloons, 15, *126-135*
Samuel, Zerelda, 56, 62, 67, 72, *75*
Schaefer, Jacob (The Wizard), 133
Selman, John, *179,* 182
Shelbyville, Texas, justice, 140-141
Shepherd, George, 61-62
Shinn, Lloyd, 120
Shirley, Myra Belle. *See* Starr, Belle
Short, Luke, 35, 37
Shotguns, 40, 50, *51*
Siringo, Charles Angelo, *181*
Six-Toed Pete, 37
Slaves: after emancipation, 170; held by Indians, 143
Smith, Bill, 111-112

Smith, Tom, 28, 210, 214, 223
Soldiers, and gunfights, *35*
Spence, Pete, 22, 34
Spicer, Wells, quoted, 17, 33-34
Stanley, Henry M., 38
Starr, Belle, 69, 155, *162;* grave, *163*
Starr, Henry, 52, 163, *178;* quoted, 163
Starr, Sam, 69, 155
Stilwell, Frank, 22, 34
Stinking Springs, N. Mex., 189
Stock inspectors, 199
Story, William, 145
Stranglers, 205
Stuart, Granville, 204-205
Sundance Kid, 73, *92, 93*
Sutton, Mike, 120

T
Teschemacher, Hubert, 206, 222
Texas: justice, 139-141, 142, 146; police, 170
Texas Kid, 212, 223
TA ranch, battle at, 214, 216, *218-219*
Thomas, Heck, *154,* 155, 158, 160-161
Thompson, Ben, 113, 115, *118,* 179
Thompson, Billy, *179*
Thompson, T., *97*

Three-Fingered Dave, 37
Tilghmann, Bill, 34, 160
Tolbert, Paden, *158-159*
Tombstone, Ariz., 16-17, 18-19, 20-21, 28-29; court, *136-137;* report on law enforcement, 25; theater, 23. *See also* O.K. Corral, shoot-out at
Towns, frontier, 15, 34; courts, 137; law enforcement, 101; saloons, 15, *126-135*
Tucker, G. R. 223
Tunstall, John, 183
Twain, Mark, quoted, 48, 141

U
Upson, Ushman, 192

V
Vigilantes, 101, 102, 139, 194, 197, *198, 199, 200,* 204-206; alliances with lawmen, 197-198; death toll, 194; motives, 197, 198, 206, 208; notice, *196,* 197. *See also* Mercenaries

W
Wallace, Lew, *188,* 189, 190
War on Powder River. *See* Johnson County War
Ward, E. F., painting by, *cover*
Watson, Ella, 208, *213*

Weapons, 38, *40-51;* handling, 38-39
Webb, Charles, 180
Wesley, John, 111-112
West, Dick, *229*
Wheeler, Ben, 111-113, *114-115*
Whicher, John W., 67
Wild Bunch, *90-93,* 181
Williamson, Robert M. (Three-Legged Willie), 140-141
Wister, Owen, 205, 206; quoted, 206
Wolcott, Frank, 206, 210, 214, 219, 222
Wyoming Stock Growers Association (W.S.G.A.), 208, 209, 210, 214, 222. *See also* Johnson County War

Y
Younger, Bob, 63, 69, 72, 75, *79,* 80, 84
Younger, Cole, 61, 62, *63,* 64, 69, 72, 75, 78, *79,* 80, 84, *89,* 155
Younger, Jim, *63,* 64, 68, 69, 72, *79,* 80, 84
Younger, John, 64, 68, 84
Yreka, Calif., execution, *194-195*

Z
Zogbaum, Rufus, sketch by, *199*